DISCARD

Street Lit

Representing the Urban Landscape

Edited by Keenan Norris

THE SCARECROW PRESS, INC.
Lanham • Toronto • Plymouth, UK
2014

Published by Scarecrow Press, Inc.
A wholly owned subsidiary of The Rowman & Littlefield Publishing Group, Inc.
4501 Forbes Boulevard, Suite 200, Lanham, Maryland 20706
www.rowman.com

10 Thornbury Road, Plymouth PL6 7PP, United Kingdom

British Library Cataloguing in Publication Information Available

Library of Congress Cataloging-in-Publication Data

Street lit : representing the urban landscape / edited by Keenan Norris ; foreword by Omar Tyree.
pages cm
Includes bibliographical references and index.
ISBN 978-0-8108-9262-0 (cloth : alk. paper) — ISBN 978-0-8108-9263-7 (ebook)
1. Cities and towns in literature. 2. City and town life in literature. 3. African Americans in literature. 4. American literature—20th century—History and criticism. 5. American literature—African American authors—History and criticism. 6. Street literature—United States—History and criticism. I. Norris, Keenan.
PS228.C54S88 2014
810.9'355—dc23
2013025234

Contents

Part III: Contemporary Street Lit, 1990s and 2000s

Foreword

Omar Tyree

When I began to write my second book, entitled *Flyy Girl*, more than twenty years ago in the Spring of 1989, I had just turned twenty years old and was still in my sophomore year at the University of Pittsburgh, studying pharmacy. I had no model to go on to write this new book; I just knew that I wanted to write it, based on a certain type of materialistic, Philadelphian, teenage girl that I had craved in my high school years, and still did. But I had no plans of writing *Flyy Girl* like the books I had read in my African American literature class. Most of those books, from Richard Wright, Alex Hailey, Jean Toomer, Zora Neale Hurston, and Toni Morrison, either were from the Harlem Renaissance era of the 1920s and 1930s or dealt with the institution of slavery.

Well, *Flyy Girl* was no old-school slavery book. I had read about slavery, and plenty of it. I had touched on the crippling institution, along with racism and a lack of education, in my first didactic title, *Colored, On White Campus* (now *College Boy* in my Urban Griot series). But with *Flyy Girl*, I wanted to tell a more naturalistic story about the neighborhoods of contemporary Philadelphia. So I wrote the book the way I wanted to, using my own voice in the narration, which was contemporary and urban, meaning it would sound like an inner-city Philadelphian, who was born in 1969, up North, and not during the slavery era of the South.

I was raised in the Philadelphian soul music era of Kenny Gamble and Leon Huff, including disco music, while hitting my teenage stride during the spawning era of Parliament funk, graffiti, rap music, break dancing, deejaying, and plenty of street vernacular, or what we called "slang." This fast-moving culture of music listening, sports playing, house partying, gold-chain wearing, designer clothes styling, fancy haircut teenagers, with our own style of American linguistics—later termed collectively as hip-hop—would become the natural model for my book. Even the title, *Flyy Girl*, was lifted from a very popular song by a rap group called The Boogie Boys in 1985, which happened to be the year of my sweet sixteen birthday. So I wrote the book in the natural swagger of my era, just like the so-called blaxpoitation movies of the 1970s. Those movies had the best dialogue, representing creative blackness.

At the time, I had the peculiar gift of being a very detail-oriented storyteller, who loved watching movies and memorizing entire scenes and lines, even mimicking the voices. I was the one dude in the crew whom you could count on to get all of the facts straight, and in chronological order, no less. I even added sound effects to heighten the excitement of my verbal tales. But these storytelling skills didn't become useful on paper until my college years, where my gift was discovered by African American course counselors. I was a bold, brave, and outspoken freshman with an uncanny ability to paint a perfect picture on paper that translated well vocally. From there, my skills took off, with the counselors asking me to write *The Diary of a Freshman* in a monthly student publication, which pretty much solidified my confidence and creative stature amongst my college peers, who became addicted to my writings.

Transferring from the University of Pittsburgh to Howard University in the fall of 1989, I left the field of pharmacy to become a journalism major, where I would learn to write newspaper articles and pick up on the powers of spin and marketing. While working for the black press of Washington, D.C., I learned how to make a story jump off the page, including coming up with attention-getting headlines. But by the time I was ready to edit and submit my first two book ideas for publication at black publishing houses, I quickly learned that Third World Press of Chicago, Red Sea Press of New Jersey, and Black Classics Press of Baltimore had no use for some twenty-two-year-old journalism major with a couple of contemporary novels. All of the mainstream white publishers turned me down too. So I did what the streets of hip-hop would do: I found a way of hustling up enough money from my friends and family, and I self-published in October 1992. I was twenty-three years old and had settled down in Hyattsville, Maryland, at the time.

Well, to be honest with you, even though I was a very aggressive salesman with *Colored, On White Campus*, a book about college, racism, and education, with a horrible yellow cover design—looking like something designed on an Etch-A-Sketch—I was only able to break even. But then I published *Flyy Girl* in April 1993, with a much stronger cover design; I traveled back home to Philadelphia just in time to catch a traveling Expo event, where I was on my way to becoming a book-writing legend. I made $1,500 that weekend and was practically forcing my books down people's throats for $13, $12, $10, $8, and even $5, depending on how many people were around us and how badly you wanted the book at a discount. The bottom line for me was moving the product, like a drug dealer would. So I

was willing to give away free samples to help sp.
And sure, I knew a few drug dealers. We all did in t.
the cultural times of the inner city, especially in Philly,

To make a long story short, my *Flyy Girl* book hit th
like a forest fire. These young, new school readers had n
book that used the exact words and events that we were stil.
the streets, on the news, in a movie, or on rap records. But I h
in a book, and from a girl's perspective. Why? Because I wa.   .ak
down exactly how a *Flyy Girl* thought, just like The Boogie Bo,   .ng had
done. So it made sense to write it that way. And the book blew folks *minds*!
They couldn't believe what they were reading!

"This shit is in a *book*! Really?"

The next thing I knew, I was selling multiple boxes of *Flyy Girl* books to
the stores and distributors up and down the East Coast, from Newport News,
Virginia, to Queens, New York. I was even stopped on the New Jersey
Turnpike on my way back to Maryland from New York, where a state troop-
er suspected me of distributing drugs instead of books. But he had nothing on
me. So I called my new book an "urban classic," understanding that I was the
first New Jack writer to do it. And I never used the word "street" because
"urban" sounded better. It was the new politically correct code word for
black, as in "urban radio." And with me being a college graduate from
Howard, who understood the term "spin," I wanted my books to sound a little
more upscale. An "urban classic" by Omar Tyree fit the bill.

By that time, in the early 1990s, I had found and read the street classics of
Iceberg Slim, Donald Goines, Chester Himes, and Claude Brown. Their stories were no longer as contemporary as *Flyy Girl* was. Nevertheless, I gave
these old-school authors a respectful shout out when I wrote and published
my third book, *Capital City*, in April 1994. I had respect for my elders and
had learned a few tricks of the trade from studying their work.

Now, if there was ever an official "street literature" book to jumpstart this
new era, *Capital City* was it. Writing about the violent drug culture in Washington, D.C., during the "Murder Capital" years of the early 1990s was as
hardcore as it gets. But I still called *Capital City* an "urban classic" and not
"street." I just didn't like that "street" word. I still considered myself an
academic, like an urban scientist. So I held strong to my own branding device
and continued to use "urban." My mission was to influence a nation of young
readers to think about getting *off* of the streets and not brag about it. That was
my whole purpose for writing these books, to express my acquired knowledge on the subjects, as my journalism degree and natural storyteller skills
had prepared me for.

Then a gender divide of marketing happened. With *Flyy Girl* and *Capital
City* both on the market, *Flyy Girl* continued to sell more books, at nearly
four to one. And it all had to do with women wanting to read their story as

men. Black males were still hard pressed to read, but black girls reading their asses off! They didn't like the harsh realities and the masculine violence of *Capital City*. They wanted to read the glitzier *Flyy Girl* talk of boyfriends, gear, sex, and family problems that they could readily relate to.

This was also the era of Terry McMillan and her popular relationship books. So the big publishers came knocking on my door, wanting *Flyy Girl* as a young women catcher, and nothing else. The mainstream publishers had seen the light, and the light was with black women readers and not the men. Well, as a young businessman looking to move on up, I understood the bottom line and signed a two-book deal with *Flyy Girl* as the first and a second book to be named. And here's where the history changed.

I had been selling *Flyy Girl* in softback at $12.95 in retail. That way, I could ask for $13 and pocket $6 to $8 after bookstore and distributor discounts. But when I signed up with Simon & Schuster in 1995, I wanted hardback money at $22 a book—where I would make $3 and change—with national distribution in every bookstore in America. And Simon & Schuster gave it to me. The big problem was, young girls were not paying $22 for a book, so I had to cater more to older women who could afford it, meaning my new stories would need to grow up and *fast*. So I wrote *A Do Right Man*, *Single Mom*, and *Sweet St. Louis* from 1997 to 1999, all classified as relationship books, like Terry, E. Lynn Harris, Eric Jerome Dickey, and Michael Baisden. But I was much younger than them, and I didn't really like the relationship direction. I couldn't use my hard, "urban" edge as much with those books. It wasn't really my style.

Meanwhile, *Flyy Girl* continued to sell to the younger readers in softback again at $14, from Scribner, a division of Simon & Schuster. The hardbacks never sold that well, but the softbacks were still selling, and the book had inspired a new crop of young writers on the way, including Teri Woods, Vickie Stringer, Nikki Turner, K'wan, and Shannon Holmes, who had all self-published after my example. And they had no problem with using the word "street." They were closer to it. I had done my time at Pitt and at Howard, where they had done their time in prison and on the hardcore streets, for *real*. But they were still self-published, and with Simon & Schuster's muscle behind me, they couldn't really compete with my national reach. By the end of the 1990s, I was selling more than one hundred thousand copies of every book I published, with *Flyy Girl* on its way to three hundred thousand.

Yes, I was making long and strong money, but I wasn't satisfied with my mission. I hadn't pushed my way into the writing and publishing game to become some relationship/romance writer. So even though I was making long cash, I wasn't feeling my movement. I then had a falling out with my literary agent about my creative direction. I wanted to return to the younger readers, who were still in love with *Flyy Girl*, but my agent wanted me to continue writing adult romance material. She even wanted me to leave Simon & Schuster to sign elsewhere for more money. But I wasn't feeling that move either. I had my own plan.

My plan was to remain with Simon & Schuster and write a sequel to *Flyy Girl*. The book was titled *For the Love of Money*, another Gamble & Huff hit from the OJays. And with a sequel to *Flyy Girl*, I knew that I would make some money. But I also wanted to teach a lesson about art and integrity. Money should never be the sole purpose for creating art. Art should always be inspirational in some way. Or at least that's how I saw it. So I set up my own meeting with Simon & Schuster, like Sean "Puff Daddy" Combs in the music industry—another Howard alum—and I outlined my whole game plan to market aggressively to the urban American youth, who were now ready for it, after my *Flyy Girl* book had fertilized the soil.

Ironically, during my success with *Flyy Girl* and the young urban market, Simon & Schuster had signed Sister Souljah to their PocketBooks division, and they were concerned about her new book, *The Coldest Winter Ever*, in hardback. They knew from my hardback experience that selling a $22 book to a young reader audience was economically risky. But I told them that aggressive marketing was the key and a much lower price tag at mass market. I had been trying to get Simon & Schuster to drop *Flyy Girl* from a trade paperback book at $14 to a smaller mass market book at $8 for *years*. But they wouldn't do it. *Flyy Girl* was already making them too much money at $14. No company wants to give up an additional $6 per unit for no reason. But for me, an $8 *Flyy Girl* book would have fertilized the soil even more. And I was painfully aware that thousands of *Flyy Girl* readers had been sharing books instead of buying their own. I could have sold a million books at $8 a pop. You feel me? Then I could have scored an early movie deal like Terry.

Anyway, Simon & Schuster was wide awake on my urban marketing plans with a *Flyy Girl* sequel, and they were more than willing to listen to me. So they signed me to a half-a-million-dollar contract for two more books, including the *Flyy Girl* sequel, *For the Love of Money*. Understanding that Sister Souljah was in the same marketplace and at the same publisher, I thought of reaching out to her to discuss a combined marketing plan. However, Sister Souljah had her own camp and her mission. She was already massively popular through her music connections and her political speeches around the country. She was a real firebrand, and I had all the respect in the world for her. She fought for the minds, souls, and culture of the people. However, I was never one for brownnosing, so I left her alone to do her thing as I did mine.

As the story unfolds, I began to market my sequel *For the Love of Money* a full year in advance through my website for a 15 August 2000 release date.

Simon & Schuster didn't even have a set date. But I told them that we needed one. So they went along with it.

I told them, "The young urban market is used to dates from the music and film industries. Everything comes out on a Tuesday or a Friday. So we *need* that."

Simon & Schuster had rarely done an exact date before. They didn't think it would make that much of a difference. But I knew that it would. So I printed up giveaway T-shirts with our book jacket design and the date of Tuesday, 15 August 2000. I included the promotion on key chains, fliers, and bookmarks, and I did it all with my own money. That's how much I believed in what I already knew. Advanced marketing works! Even Michael Jordan was selling his shoes with dates. And let me tell you, when 15 August 2000 finally hit, a wave of young readers, who were dying all summer long for the *Flyy Girl* sequel, snapped up *For the Love of Money* in hardback at $22, with more than fifty thousand copies sold in the first two weeks.

Prior to that, I had not sold more than thirty-five thousand copies in hardback *ever*! I had done the majority of my sells in softback. But once *For the Love of Money* hit, I became the first "urban contemporary writer" to land on the *New York Times* bestseller's list. The chain stores had to reorder boxes of books and hide them in their storage rooms just for me to do book signings that year, especially in Philly, New York, and D.C. Man, it was *great*! I had standing-room audiences that forced the stores to check their fire codes. I was also on my way to winning an NAACP Image Award for Outstanding Work in Fiction in early 2001. And I negotiated a bigger and longer contract with Simon & Schuster for a new, undisclosed amount.

Now pay close attention. This is where the story takes its dramatic turn. Although I had definitely come up on the streets of Philadelphia, from West Philly to Mt. Airy, I had become a spoiled college kid, who had never been locked up or gone to jail in my life—outside of a Maryland state warrant for a speeding ticket. Now, I'm not saying I was perfect, by any stretch of the imagination. I had done some dirt in the streets, just not enough to be sent away to jail for it. Ninety-seven percent of my cash was *honest* money. I had even been a barber in school. So by the time I had graduated from Howard, I began to promote education, hard work, and progress as my mission, and all of my books represented that; every single one of them packed a quality message. So in the *Flyy Girl* sequel, the infamous "Tracy Ellison" completes her undergraduate studies at Hampton, and then gets her master's in English, while continuing to write poetry.

Most of the young audience was fine with that part of the book, but with Tracy's love life, they actually expected a more "street" story with her return to Philadelphia, where she could link back up with her first real dude, Victor Hinson, who had become a Muslim—"Qadeer Muhammad"—and had gotten married to a Muslim woman upon his return from jail. Now granted, I'm from Philadelphia, and I know guys to this *day* who did the exact same thing. My city has a very large population of converted Muslims. Furthermore, I didn't feel comfortable in having a college girl come back home and marry a jailbird, who doesn't change his ways. It was the opposite of progress. But young female readers absolutely wanted it, and *badly*! Their story arc would have been more of a "street fantasy," so I didn't do it. As a result, even though *For the Love of Money* went on to sell eighty-five thousand copies in hardback and over a hundred thousand more in softback—making me a very wealthy man—I had worked my ass off with marketing, only to lose the audience. They didn't want a mission statement; they wanted their "street fantasy."

"Why didn't you let Tracy go back to Victor?" they demanded in count-less e-mails.

Like pop star Rihanna going back to Chris Brown, irrational love stories are *real*. So they wanted their urban *Romeo and Juliet*, but I refused to give it to them. This is where my logical goal to uplift lost the audience. They didn't care about what was logically right; they cared about what *felt* right. They wanted the burn of a hardcore love story, plain and simple. But I was now a grown man with a wife and kids of my own, and I didn't want to lead this young audience astray, even within a fictional book. That's when I began to experience the changing of the guard and the full transition from "urban" to "street."

Hard-biting e-mails came in from a group of new and hungry readers: "I just finished reading Sister Souljah's new book, *The Coldest Winter Ever*, and it was way more gangsta than your soft-ass *Flyy Girl*. I'm sorry, but Sister Souljah is my new favorite writer."

I BS you not! The praise for Sister Souljah's *Coldest Winter* started rolling in waves, and at the disdain of my *Flyy Girl* sequel. Not to say that folks were not finding and reading Sister Souljah's book on their own, because they were, especially after PocketBooks published *The Coldest Winter Ever* in mass market at $8, just like I had been begging Simon & Schuster/ Scribner to do with *Flyy Girl*. Sister Souljah had the same distribution mus-cle behind her that I had, and with a lower book price, and I had now pissed the audience off. It was a clear recipe for disaster.

Understanding the reality of marketing and fertilization, my crazy push of the *Flyy Girl* sequel, *For the Love of Money*, in the summer of 2000 served to boost the Sister Souljah wave even higher. That's marketing 101; when you push the people to the stores, like I did with my aggressive, urban strategy, they'll end up buying everything in the same category once they get there, particularly with *The Coldest Winter* at $8 and *FLOM* at $22. So *The Coldest Winter Ever* was now *scorching*!

But I didn't have time to complain about all of that. I was too busy mapping out my next mission of books, with *Just Say No! Leslie* and *Diary of a Groupie*. Each new book was ahead of its time, with a music industry addiction, a dramatic New Orleans poverty story—before Hurricane Katrina—and a celebrity opportunist before *Superhead* or Kim Kardashian. But it didn't matter. The door had been opened, and the damage had already been done. I was too fast forward and logical for my own good.

So when the new wave of Sister Souljah's support took off and continued to grow, once she failed to return with a follow-up book, Teri Woods's *True to the Game* began to sell like hotcakes; Vickie Stringer's *Let That Be the Reason*, Nikki Turner's *Wifey*, Shannon Holmes's *B-More Careful*, and K'wan's *Gangsta*, all with mostly female protagonists, filled the *Flyy Girl* and *The Coldest Winter Ever* void. And they didn't mind their work being called "street lit." It gave them more edge for an audience that now craved it. Nor did Sister Souljah step up to claim a genre preference. The branding game didn't matter to her. Books were books, and she was glad that our young people were reading them. We would all rather they read instead of getting into trouble, right?

However, since my "urban classics" had started it all, the mix of the two words "urban" and "street" continued to reverberate, where Sister Souljah suddenly began to receive the bulk of the credit. And I agree, the second and third wave of young urban readers came through with *The Coldest Winter*, but the first wave was *Flyy Girl* lovers. So when a hundred new "urban street lit" writers began to pop up overnight, the history of it all became confused. Sister Souljah was now the source, where Omar Tyree became an obscure side story. Ain't that a trip!

I bring this up because it's my job to share the facts. That's why I started writing books in the first place, to inform our people of who we are and why we do what we do. You publish to inform. So I can't allow my own story to slide out of history and go unpublished. I'm just telling it like it happened, with all of the facts included, since we're talking about "contemporary urban street lit." Like I stated earlier, Donald had done his thing for Holloway House two decades before me, and Chester Himes before him with his Harlem books. Sadly, many of these new "urban street lit" readers have never heard of Iceberg, Donald, or Chester.

More important, we now have far too many writers and readers who seem stuck on the same topics of yesterday. It's normal to relate to our recent history and the vile conditions that some of us continue to live in—even the horrific violence in present-day Chicago, the home-base city of President Barack Obama—but at some point, there needs to be a new vision for us to move forward as a creative, exploring, loving, and progressive people. So when Sister Souljah finally returned after nearly a decade with *Midnight*, and more recently with *Deeper Love*, I viewed her forward development of international stories and cultural consciousness and pumped my fist. "Right on, sister!"

Sister Souljah and I have had recent dialogue about the community ills, likes, dislikes, and needs. Nevertheless, as the readers moved away from forward-thinking ideas more than a dozen years ago, sadly I can only imagine what "urban street lit" lovers will think of any other progressive material. So the beat goes on to reclaim our creativity, where we can *dream* again of leaving the hood.

But one thing's for sure: new African American writers no longer have to go through what I endured to earn my stripes in this profession. My boys from Philly thought I was *crazy* back in 1988, when I first started talking about writing books. They laughed in my damn face.

"What you say, O, you gon' write a *book*? What, you think you Stephen King or somebody now, just because you up in college? Niggas don't write no books, man. You *crazy*! What dem college people got you on up there? Ha ha ha!"

At least the new writers don't have to hear that anymore. Now we *know* that black people write and read too. We just need to be able to diversify again. So enjoy it. This is a book about new and old black writers; that's a monumental subject in itself. Now let's see how much we can all learn from this.

Acknowledgments

The initial idea for this anthology was generated from my PhD research at the University of California, Riverside. My topic was the historical and current relationships between black American writers and the American publishing industry. It became clear to me that no such discussion was complete without thorough study of street literature. I was very lucky to have Erica Edwards as my dissertation committee chair. She was flexible enough in her approach to guiding the dissertation to see the crucial role that street lit would play in its completion, and she also has provided essential advice throughout the process of this anthology's completion. Likewise, Omar Tyree has provided a level of professional support that has provided this project with a unique momentum all its own.

In mid-2012, Scarecrow consulting editor Chris Nasso put forward the idea of a multiauthor anthology on the street lit topic, and I picked the idea up and ran with it. Thanks go to Nasso and to Scarecrow senior editor Stephen Ryan for shepherding this project along its way with Scarecrow.

I also would like to acknowledge the efforts of Susan Straight, E. J. Jones, Faith Adiele, Toby Miller, Regis Mann, and Jerry Ward Jr. on behalf of this work. I am grateful also to our gracious interview subjects David Bradley and Lynel Gardner, as well as to Vanessa Ta, who transcribed these as well as other unused interviews.

The contributing authors featured in this volume are, of course, its very bulwark. Without each of them, this vast undertaking would not have come to fruition. They are best acknowledged simply by reading what they have written.

Street Lit[erature] in America Past and Present

Keenan Norris

"Rainbow Life" by Tristan Acker

Even though I'm in the I.E.
I live that Rainbow life
Where you can't go wrong
And you can't go right
Go down to Granola Funk and smoke some shake at the stage
The anarchist kids said to wake up and rage
Then we chillin' with the freight kids
They tend to know where my part of the state is
Knowin' what's up, sayin' we puff tough
Trade tobacco leaf and weed for coffee beans in a cup
So here's another nerd ballad
We make word salads
and burn herb salads
while tryna make school and work balance
do our best to keep smiling
while preservin' our friends
Southwest Sierra desert dude we down there
Represent the California flag like brown bears
Get out of work, hit the parkin' lot
Get home load the vial and we spark some pot
BRAC shut down the March Air Force base
Now the kids do drugs so they can explore space
I'm not going to be acquiescin'
To your perception
that the government has me posted up and never stressin'
Yeah I'm a bureaucrat, you can be sure of that
But don't get it twisted by the FOXes that would blur the facts

It is my great pleasure, as editor of *Street Lit: Representing the Urban Land-scape*, to bring to the fore this groundbreaking collection of essays, inter-views, and other literature. This volume represents the most diverse and most thorough examination of the literary and commercial phenomenon that is contemporary street literature, popularly known as *street lit, urban literature*, or *hip-hop fiction*. Certainly, much ink has been devoted to the reemergence of this genre of American literature over the past decade or so. From the meditations of Gerald Early ("What Is African American Literature?" re-printed here) to the blog scholarship at racialicious.com and madame-noire.com, street lit has captured the attention of not only a wide readership but also a vast cadre of social commentators. There are the essential critical surveys provided by scholars Vanessa Irvin Morris (*Readers' Advisory Guide to Street Literature*) and Megan Honig (*Urban Grit*), as well as the columns by journalists Linton Weeks, Marc Reynolds, Broyard Bliss, and many others on the street lit phenomenon. The analysis by NPR contributor Karen Grigsby Bates on the literature of black and brown urban America has even taken the discussion from the page to the airwaves.

Those familiar with the broad sweep of African American literary history and with contemporary developments within African American literature in particular are well aware of the debate around street lit's validity as an artistic medium, a purveyor of values and ideology to black and other inner-city youth, and a cultural barometer of our times. In fact, I am hesitant to cast this volume solely in terms of its significance as a critique of trends within African American literature because street lit, while primarily produced by African American writers, is not exclusively an African American literary form. In the *Readers' Advisory Guide to Street Literature*, Morris reminds us that "literary fictions have been telling uncompromising stories of marginal-ized Americans for centuries. In the late nineteenth century, the genre mainly focused on the ghetto lives of European immigrants in New York City's inner-city slums" (Morris, 11).[1] Muckraking *New York Times* journalist Ja-cob Riis's seminal progressive work *How the Other Half Lives*, published initially through Scribner & Sons in 1890, details the inner-city Manhattan of his day in details just as gritty and raw as the narratives rendered up by modern-day street lit narrativists. *How the Other Half Lives* tells of superex-tensive immigrant slums and the vice, violence, deprivation, and depravity engaged in by the Irish, Italian, Jewish, and Chinese immigrants confined there.

With the historical diversity of American literature about inner-city situa-tions steadfastly in mind, the commentary featured in these pages is rendered by writers white as well as black, Latino as well as Asian, and international as well as American. The contributions to this volume by writers such as Debra Busman, Sterling Warner, and Juan Delgado underscore this point. Brazilian scholars Jaqueline Lima Santos (Ph.D. student, Universidade Estaduel de Campinas, São Paulo, and hip-hop archive research fellow, W. E. B. DuBois Institute, Harvard University) and Ana Lúcia Silva Souza (Federal University of Bahia) internationalize the scope of *Street Lit* and more importantly expand the definition and critical landscape of street lit by analyzing São Paolo's graffiti artworks. Reminding us that graffiti is one of hip-hop culture's four pillars, the scholars show how deeply linked hip-hop and street lit truly are. Indeed, street lit is not only a multiethnic phenomenon but also one that is hardly bound by national borders or conventional genre boundaries.

University of California, Berkeley, scholar Bonnie Rhee Andryeyev has contributed a fascinating piece, "Whose Mean Streets? Donald Goines, Iceberg Slim, and the Black Noir Aesthetic." The chapter draws the aesthetic lines of connection between the infamous 1960s-era street lit narrativists Donald Goines and Iceberg Slim and their white predecessors in the crime-dime novel literature of the 1920s, '30s, and '40s. Andryeyev's chapter reminds us that far from being conceptually bereft and art-free sociological narratives, when closely read, the best street lit texts have powerful aesthetic dimensions that deserve considerable critical attention for their kinship to the wider body of American crime fiction and literature about cities.

When defining street lit, it is helpful to conceptualize it in terms of what it has been, what it is, and what it might become. Street lit *was* the work of Riis and his fellow muckrakers in New York City and Chicago and America's other major cities at the turn of that century. In roughly the same period, street lit *was* also the work of the African American author Paul Lawrence Dunbar; *The Sport of the Gods*, published in 1902, chronicles the breakdown of a black family that, having migrated up from the South, finds only financial and personal ruin in New York City. By book's end, after having survived all manner of hardship, including the long incarceration of the head of household, the Hamiltons willingly move back to their old plantation home, though not quite into the enslavement that the genial racist Horace Talbot predicts for North-star-seeking Negroes at the novel's outset. We might even see Ann Petry's *Street* as a kind of street lit text. Published in 1945, Petry's novel begins in Harlem, New York City, with blacks born and raised on the rough, inner-city streets but, like Dunbar's novel, narrates an urban dystopia capped by the criminalization of a black male (the child Bub) and the protagonist Lutie Johnson's disgraced escape from the city.

A bit later on, street lit *was* also the work of white noir novelists of the 1920s, '30s, '40s, and '50s—most notably Raymond Chandler (taking as his setting the streets of Los Angeles) and Dashiell Hammett (a post-WWI San Francisco centering his stories). Using all the detective-gumshoe narrative devices of these writers, Chester Himes's Harlem books provide the bridge between noir and what we more commonly think of as street lit—a genre of post-WWII urban fiction authored by black novelists and usually centered

upon criminal activity. Moody, morally ambiguous, situationally homicidal
Harlem detectives Coffin Ed and Gravedigger Jones are Himes's answer to
Sam Spade and Philip Marlowe. Himes published *For Love of Imabelle* in
1957 and *The Real Cool Killers* and *The Crazy Kill* in '59. Himes had
published fully eight crime novels (*For Love of Imabelle, A Rage in Harlem,
The Real Cool Killers, The Crazy Kill, The Big Gold Dream, All Shot Up,
Run Man Run, The Heat's On*, and *Cotton Comes to Harlem*) before either
Iceberg Slim or Donald Goines had published their first novel. Iceberg Slim
(government name, Robert Beck) brings us fully into the category of what is
commonly understood to be street lit[erature] with the publication of his first
novels, *Pimp: The Story of My Life* and *Trick Baby: The Story of a White
Negro* in 1967. Goines's *Whoreson* then arrives on bookstore and prison
shelves in 1971.

   If that is what street lit *was*, street lit *is* a body of American literature
produced by post-1980s black and Latino writers and deriving its formal
structure, narrative technique, and themes from the determinist and naturalist
fiction of past epochs in African American and American literature. Specifically, the work of writers such as Omar Tyree (*Capital City* and *The Last
Street Novel*), Teri Woods (*True to the Game*), Sister Souljah (*The Coldest
Winter Ever*), Yxta Maya Murray (*Locas*), Cupcake Brown (*A Piece of
Cake*), and 50 Cent (*From Pieces to Weight*) is derived out of the narrative
techniques and, where present, the social concerns (this is the *was* of street
lit) of the muckrakers, noir writers, and early street lit narrativists, so that
writers as diverse as Dreiser, Crane, Norris, Hammett, Chandler, Petry,
Himes, Claude Brown, Robert Dean Pharr, Donald Goines, and Iceberg Slim
can be seen as its progenitors. The genre is also undeniably tied to hip-hop in
terms of its origins, raw content, and up-by-the-bootstraps entrepreneurship
in the production and distribution stages.

   What street lit might become necessitates a speculative foray perhaps best
left to the writers themselves. What I will say is that one can see, at the edges
of the genre, subtle challenges to the definition and demands of the traditional street lit narrative. Works such as *The Last Street Novel* and Kenji Jasper's
Seeking Salamanca Mitchell destabilize normative black and inner-city mas-
culinities in ways novel not only to the genre but also to popular culture in
general. These and other texts suggest exciting horizons that street lit might
yet explore, opening the literature's young and impressionable fandom upon
ways of seeing and being male that hip-hop, film, and the culture in general
rarely approach. Moreover, the muckraking element particularly at play in
the work of Sister Souljah, Cupcake Brown, Wahida Clark, and other female
street lit novelists around women's issues in deprived inner-city spaces not
only tends to echo Hurston's famous lament—that the black woman is "de
mule uh de world"[2]—but also can be read in conversation with the work of
Jody Miller (*Gettin Played*), Joan Morgan (*When Chickenheads Come Home*

to Roost), Nikki Jones, and numerous contemporary academics seriously concerned with the lives of marginalized and violated girls and women to illustrate the gender, race, and class-specific dangers faced by the Winters and Cupcakes in every American inner-city space. Perhaps it is best to say simply that street lit as a literary category will be what it becomes.

Street Lit can be read from many different perspectives: as the critical interrogation of a highly allusive literary aesthetic, as notes on the multiethnic experience in America's inner cities, and as the examination of a literature that derives much of its culture from Latin America and from Latinos in America. And, of course, our book can be read as a bravely, differently premised take on African American literature and the black experience from Harlem, New York, to Oakland, California. Indeed, for the reader who is coming to this critical study and to street lit, and perhaps even (shudder the thought) to African American literature, for the first time, it is crucial to understand the roots of the literary debate that in many ways has inspired not only myself but also many of the contributing writers to this volume to take up serious work on this subject. It is a debate central to the dialectical tension in University of Alabama doctoral candidate Kemeshia Randle's fantastic chapter "Gang Wars: The Academy versus the Streets," and it is the animating force in both Early's chapter and Omar Tyree's contribution to this volume.

THE CONTROVERSY AROUND STREET LIT

In a 3 October 2007 e-mail to publishing executives Carolyn Reidy (Simon & Schuster), Karen Hunter (Karen Hunter Publishing), and Louise Burke (Gallery Books), Terry McMillan excoriates not only the immediate recipients but "the other publishing houses" for their "relentless publication" of what McMillan characterizes as "exploitative, destructive, racist, egregious, sexist, base, tacky, poorly-written, unedited, degrading books."[3] The immediate reason for McMillan's e-mail was the publication of Karrine Steffans's memoir *Confessions of a Video Vixen*, wherein the former music video model recounted her unromantic affairs with Jay-Z, Ja Rule, Shaquille O'Neal, Kool G Rap, and others. McMillan, whose work, ironically, inspired much of the trend she so despises, promises that in concert with "a number of Black bookstores" and "other Black literary organizations" she will begin to make her disquiet at the publishing industry trend toward trash black literature known to the public. McMillan's missive even wonders at the fact that whereas literary luminaries Walter Mosley, Edwidge Danticat, and then-senator Barack Obama were not in the running for publishing house imprints, those writers who market tales of black super-squalor have been "allowed in the Big Publishing Houses['] Little Rooms enough to FINALLY get [their] own imprints."

In a similar vein, critically celebrated novelist Bernice McFadden's June 2010 *Washington Post* article "Black Writers in a Ghetto of the Publishing Industry's Making" recounts McFadden's interface with the publishing industry upon release of her debut novel, *Sugar*, in 2001. "The original cover depicted a beautiful black woman standing behind a screen door. *Sugar* was marketed solely to African American readers. This type of marginalization has come to be known among African American writers as 'seg-book-gation.' This practice is not only demeaning but also financially crippling." The marginalization of her work was not solely the result of her publisher's race-based stratagem but also the product of bookstores' separation of titles by black writers: "Walk through your local chain bookstore and you will not see sections tagged British Literature, White American Literature, Korean Literature, Pakistani Literature and so on. None of these ethnicities are singled out or objectified the way African American writers are," McFadden writes. She notes the deep internal divisions between different works by and about black Americans: "The work of many African American authors, myself included, has been lumped into one heap known as 'African American literature.' This suggests that our literature is singular and anomalous, not universal." This division and ghettoization, McFadden argues, allows for the crowding out of more intellectually and artistically ambitious novels in favor of street lit texts that "[reinforce] the stereotypical trademarks African Americans have fought hard to overcome" (McFadden, 1).

Viewed from the perspective of writers who consider their serious efforts impeded by the crass market strategies of street lit writers and promoters, McMillan and McFadden's conclusions are inevitable. In particular, the castigation of street lit and its publishing industry backers bears witness to the reincarnation of a history of white-over-black industry hierarchy, corporate manipulation, and cowardly black opportunism. McMillan and McFadden, figuring themselves as the serious and responsible bearers of the black literary flame, stand outside what they critique as a debacle in black letters. However, the problem here is that such an approach by the avowedly "serious" writer allows only two options, either to remain unsoiled and largely unrewarded for his or her efforts or to capitulate to what they perceive as an increasingly degrading market demand. Such capitulation seems to reenact the appellate position this introduction identifies. Against this history of capitulation and conditionally granted agency that characterizes much of black writers' interface with the publishing industry, beginning with the slave narratives, moving through the Harlem Renaissance, and on to the contentious battles between Richard Wright and Chester Himes and their respective editors both in the United States and abroad, street literature's impressive market position might actually provide a welcome alternative. Gerald Early makes precisely this case in "What Is African American Literature?"

> First . . . there is a young, mass, black reading audience of such size that a black author can write for it exclusively without giving a thought to being highbrow or literary or to crossing over for whites. Second, the taste of the masses is distinct from, and troubling to, the taste of the elite in large measure because the elite no longer control the direction and purpose of African American literature; it is now, more than ever, a market-driven literature, rather than an art form patronized and promoted by cultured whites and blacks as it had been in the past. The fact that blacks started two of the publishing houses for these books, Urban Books and Triple Crown, underscores the entrepreneurial, populist nature of this type of race literature: by black people for black people. Third, African American literature no longer has to be obsessed with the burden or expectation of political protest or special pleading for the humanity of the race or the worth of its history and culture as it had to in the past.

In this way of seeing things, the advent of a black pulp fiction is actually a positive development for it signifies the breadth of the black reading audience and the diversity of its tastes. The presence of serious black literature, in this view, is not in question. It exists and has existed. "Market-driven literature," pulp fiction in other words, is actually evidence of greater agency among the masses of black readers and black people who are no longer subject to the taste-making dictates of a publishing enterprise that has historically deemed the direct patronage and promotion of "cultured whites and blacks" as necessary to the publication, distribution, commercial success, and critical acclaim of black American literature. Now, the black reading public has a wider selection from which to choose and is naturally empowered by this choice. This set of choices, I would add, is more in line with general trends in the publishing industry across race and ethnicity. In Gideon Lewis-Kraus's 2009 *Harper's Magazine* article "The Last Book Party: Publishing Drinks to a Life after Death," agent Ira Silverberg laments that "our roots are in literary books. . . . They're not our day-to-day business; our day-to-day business is disgusting. You'll be hearing a lot about vampires this year. But here is where we can at least remember what we think differentiates us from widget salesmen." Silverberg is referring to the *Twilight* book series, which has sold in huge numbers to the same discerning teenage fandom that prefers whatever teen pop star has achieved international nova-star status as you read this to Cassandra Wilson. The article's setting is the 2008 Frankfurt Book Fair, the world's largest trade fair for books. Silverberg has stepped out of "the Hessischer Hof hotel to have a smoke with a beautiful woman of indeterminate European origin." Few scenes in all of world literature, let alone book-market journalism, so thoroughly bypass blackness. Surely one or two black writers, agents, or editors are to be found at the Frankfurt Book Fair; however, they receive only passing mention in Lewis-Kraus's article—Zadie Smith's blurbs draw notice, as does the fact that Lewis-Kraus's publisher uncle Bob Miller is marketing 50 Cent's business-advice manual *The 50th Law*. This near omission is of little consequence, however: The article illuminates tensions in mainstream book markets similar to those that prevail between different branches of the black literati. Silverberg's complaint is not that different from those who malign street literature. Vampire books are "disgusting" in his eyes, as, in the eyes of many, are the works of street lit narrativists (Lewis-Kraus, 41–51). Born in "literary books," the literature of black Americans has evolved, expanded, and diversified. Is it simply that this black pulp fiction is no more than vampires for the mass of black readers, particularly young black readers who now have books that fit their age-defined interests? And, as such, would it not be true that such a literature, however unsophisticated on its face, actually constitutes market sophistication insofar as no body of literature should be dependent for its vital existence solely on its elite product, its genius writers, its masterpiece poetry, novels, memoirs, and essays? I'd say yes.

A PREVIEW

Every chapter in this volume is deserving of note. I have already mentioned Bonnie Rhee Andryeyev's essay on street lit aesthetics and Kemeshia Randle's intervention into the conflict between the academy and the streets in the world of black letters. In "Street Literature: A Contextualization, Historiography, and Personal Narrative," Celena Diana Bumpus helpfully contextualizes the street lit genre, providing a historiography. This chapter explains how the literature has inspired the personas of hip-hop music and where the music has influenced the literature, and then goes beyond the arts to show the sociological context within which street lit has arisen and continues to evolve.

In "The Art of Storytellin'," my colleague, brother Khalid White, name checks Slick Rick's 1999 album in order not only to draw comparison between street lit and hip-hop but also to link black storytelling from the current street lit narrativists and rappers all the way back to the griot tradition born in Africa. Poet and professor Nikia Chaney asks us to look more closely at the language with which these modern urban griots tell their stories. "In Their Own Words: Street Lit, Code Meshing, and Linguistic Diversity" provides an analysis that is at once academic and also sensitive and sensuous in its examination of black speech on the pages of street lit novels and in American classrooms.

Alex White, another colleague and sister in literature and teaching, brings to the table a chapter entitled "Street Literature and Hip-hop's Ties to Slave Narratives and the Sex Slave Trade." The chapter takes as its reason for being the sexual slavery that too many young women on East Oakland's International Boulevard (formerly East 14th Street) have been forced into. It is a subject that has inspired one of street lit's most popular titles, Cupcake Brown's *Piece of Cake*. Brown's autobiography narrates the sexual abuse she suffered in foster homes, how she ran away, was pimped on the streets, and fell into gang life and a relentless drug addiction. Eventually, Brown is shot in a drive-by and starts to turn her life around, landing legitimate jobs and over the course of time kicking her drug habit. She makes her way up from sexual slavery, escaping her captors and her life on the streets to become a successful attorney. With the moral crime of sex slavery at its heart, Alex's chapter examines the ways in which both hip-hop and street lit have treated the issue of forced prostitution and the exploitation of underage and economically marginalized girls. The chapter is neither a glorification nor a condemnation of street lit or of hip-hop but rather a sober assessment of both.

Howard University scholar Dennis L. Winston contributes "(Re)Writing the 'Bad Nigger' Hero in Robert Beck's *Pimp*," which can be read in relation to this discussion of the sex slave trade on Bay Area streets. Robert Beck, whose pen name was Iceberg Slim, more famously than perhaps any other author, chronicled the life of black American pimps from their perspective. Winston's chapter not only confronts Iceberg Slim's novel *Pimp* as an encyclopedia of predatory pimp culture but also explains how the black outlaw pimp figure functions in Iceberg's work to destabilize an inherently corrupt and racist legal system and American status quo. Though deeply disturbing, the glorification of the archetypal pimp is not simply evidence of the pervasiveness of misogyny within African American and American culture (though it certainly is that); also, it is evidence of the need of dispossessed peoples for folkloric figures that transgress the legal and moral limitations of a society that has immobilized them as an underclass.

In "Hard Men of the Street," Cherie Ann Turpin examines the workings of black masculinity in Kenji Jasper's D.C.-based novels *Dark* and *Seeking Salamanca Mitchell*. These novels, Turpin's analysis suggests, presage the power of street lit to illumine the psychic lives of black men at the social margins, faced with not only economic but also ideological pressure to live up to a corrosive set of masculine ideals. Moreover, both the novels themselves and the work of Turpin, a professor at the University of the District of Columbia, remind us that even in 2013, in the wake of the reelection of our nation's first black president, in the nation's capital black men continue to confront a world of limited opportunities and often violent outcomes.

Texas Southern scholar Kimberly Fain contributes the chapter "Colson Whitehead's *Zone One*: Postapocalyptic Zombies Take Over Manhattan in the Age of Nostalgia, Despair, and Consumption." Her chapter is far and away the most extended and in-depth examination of PEN/Faulkner and Hurston/Wright award-winning author Colson Whitehead's underregarded 2011 novel *Zone One*, a novel that marks something of a departure from Whitehead's previous "literary" novels and as such has unfairly met with general critical disregard.

While a scholarly project in all regards, the form that *Street Lit* takes is genre bending, with short-form commentary, interviews, and poetry by Arisa White, Sterling Warner, Juan Delgado, and Juan's student Tristan Acker. Thus, in form as well as content, this volume is a unique literary endeavor. Omar Tyree told me, candidly, that book-length collections of critical essays can be like "drinking concentrated lemonade" and that strategies designed to leaven this effect for the more casual reader are good. I'm taking that advice. That's why *Street Lit* features my discussion with another PEN/Faulkner-winning novelist, David Bradley (*The Chaneysville Incident*). Bradley takes on an array of topics in this wide-ranging talk, from the ways in which sociology gets black urban America so very wrong to his inspiration to write for his debut novel, *South Street*, which is set in inner-city Philadelphia, and to his take on the archetypal tale upon which many a street lit narrative has been formed, the story of the life of Malcolm X. Bradley makes clear that his interest is not only in Alex Haley's widely read *Autobiography of Malcolm X* but also in the extraliterary narrative of Malcolm's life. With deep humor and generous insight, the acclaimed novelist delves the depths of street narrative, sociology, the influence of the black church, and the black urban experience in the past and present.

I also interviewed Lynel Gardner, whose personal story is both as sensational and as real as the most graphic stories street lit has to offer. Lynel's life journey began in East Palo Alto, California, where Lynel was raised by his loving grandparents. Lynel's grandfather was Sonny Liston, the heavyweight boxing champion cast as a monster by the popular media. Refuting this media portrayal, Lynel has written a book that dramatically redefines Sonny's life.

Lynel's upbringing was harsh; his parents were off leading difficult lives on the social margins. Lynel's father, upon whom Lynel's one-man show *Stories I Never Told My Father* is based, was a pimp. Rejecting the worst aspects of this street legacy, Lynel has forged his own, better path. He's found God and an artistic voice. Working in multiple artistic forms, he tells the story of his mission to raise consciousness and find a way forward for America's most deprived.

Our volume is, to date, the most comprehensive assessment of the street lit[erary] genre that exists. Enjoy. Consider.

NOTES

1. Morris's chapter "From Moll Flanders to *The Coldest Winter Ever*: A Historical Time-line of Street Lit," which is included in the *Advisory Guide*, makes this claim.

2. From *Their Eyes Were Watching God*: "Honey, de white man is de ruler of everything as fur as Ah been able tuh find out. Maybe it's some place off in de ocean where de black man is in power, but we don't know nothin' but we see. So de white man throw down de load and tell de nigger man tuh pick it up. He pick it up because he have to, but he don't tote it. He hand it to his womenfolks. De nigger woman is de mule uh de world so far as Ah can see" (Hurston, 11).

3. Terry McMillan, e-mail to Carolyn Reidy, Karen Hunter, and Louise Burke, 3 October 2007.

WORKS CITED

Hurston, Zora Neale. *Their Eyes Were Watching God*. 1937. New York: Harper Collins, 2006.

Lewis-Kraus, Gideon. "The Last Book Party: Publishing Drinks to a Life after Death." *Harper's Magazine*, March 2009.

McFadden, Bernice. "Black Writers in a Ghetto of the Publishing Industry's Making." *Washington Post*, 26 June 2010.

Morris, Vanessa Irvin. *The Readers' Advisory Guide to Street Literature*. Chicago: American Library Association, 2011.

Part I

Street Literature in America, Past and Present

What Is African American Literature?

Gerald Early

African American writer Nick Chiles famously castigated the publishing industry, young black women readers, and the current state of African American writing in his controversial 2006 *New York Times* opinion piece entitled "Their Eyes Were Reading Smut."[1] Although he was happy about mainstream bookstores like Borders devoting considerable shelf space to "African American Literature," he was more than a little nonplussed by what the store and the publishing industry considered "African American Literature" to be. "[All] that I could see was lurid book jackets displaying all forms of brown flesh, usually half-naked and in some erotic pose, often accompanied by guns and other symbols of criminal life," wrote Chiles. These novels have such titles as *Gutter*, *Crack Head*, *Forever a Hustler's Wife*, *A Hustler's Son*, *Amongst Thieves*, *Cut Throat*, *Hell Razor Honeys*, *Payback with Ya Life*, and the like. The well-known authors are K'wan, Ronald Quincy, Quentin Carter, Deja King (also known as Joy King), Teri Woods, Vickie Stringer, and Carl Weber. They occupy a genre called urban or hip-hop fiction, gritty, so-called realistic works about inner-city life, full of graphic sex, drugs and crime, "playas," thugs, dough boys (rich drug dealers), and graphic violence—lavish consumption juxtaposed to life in housing projects. In some instances, the works are nothing more than black crime novels told from the point of view of the criminal; in others, they are black romance novels with a hard-edged city setting. In all cases, they are a kind of pulp fiction; despite their claim of realism, they are actually about fantasy, as their readers are attempting to understand their reality while trying to escape it. Mostly young African Americans, primarily women—the gender that constitutes the greater portion of the fiction-reading American public—read these books, and the books are marketed exclusively for this clientele. Some of these novels sell

3

well enough to support a few authors without the need of a "day job," a rarity in the writing trade.

The existence of these books proffer three aspects of change for African American literature from what it was, say, thirty or forty years ago. First, despite problems with literacy and a dismal high school dropout rate among African Americans, there is a young, mass, black reading audience of such size that a black author can write for it exclusively without giving a thought to being highbrow or literary or to crossing over for whites. Second, the taste of the masses is distinct from, and troubling to, the taste of the elite in large measure because the elite no longer control the direction and purpose of African American literature; it is now, more than ever, a market-driven literature, rather than an art form patronized and promoted by cultured whites and blacks as it had been in the past. The fact that blacks started two of the publishing houses for these books, Urban Books and Triple Crown, underscores the entrepreneurial, populist nature of this type of race literature: by black people for black people. Third, African American literature no longer has to be obsessed with the burden or expectation of political protest or special pleading for the humanity of the race or the worth of its history and culture as it had to in the past. (This is not to suggest that African American literature has abandoned these concerns. They are most evident in African American children's and adolescent literature, which is frequently, as one might expect, highly didactic.) This is not to argue that the books that Chiles deplores have some neo-literary or extraliterary worth that compensates for them being trashy, poorly written novels. But these books do reveal some of the complicated roots of African American literature and of the construction of the African American audience.

"Blaxploitation" films of the early 1970s—such as Melvin Van Peebles's independent classic *Sweet Sweetback's Badass Song*; *Coffy, Foxy Brown* and *Sheba, Baby*, starring Pam Grier; *Hell Up in Harlem, Black Caesar, That Man Bolt*, and *The Legend of Nigger Charley*, starring Fred Williamson; *Superfly*; and the *Shaft* movies, starring Richard Roundtree—created the first young black audience for hard-boiled, urban black, seemingly realistic art centered on hustling, drugs, prostitution, and antiwhite politics (in which whites—particularly gangsters and policemen—are destroying the black community). The literary roots for this came from two streams in the 1960s. The highbrow, mainstream literary and leftist types endorsed such nonfiction black prison literature as *The Autobiography of Malcolm X*; Eldridge Cleaver's essay collection *Soul on Ice*; *Poems from Prison*, compiled by inmate and poet Etheridge Knight, which includes Knight's "Ideas of Ancestry," one of the most famous and highly regarded African American poems of the 1960s; and *Soledad Brother: The Prison Letters of George Jackson*. All of these books have become part of black literary canon and are frequently taught in various college literature, creative writing, and sociology classes.

On the pulp, populist fiction side in the late 1960s and early 1970s were the novels of former pimp Iceberg Slim and imprisoned drug addict Donald Goines—including *Trick Baby, Dopefiend, Street Players*, and *Black Gangster*. These novels are the direct antecedents of the books that Chiles found so dismaying in 2006. They occupied a small but compelling portion of the black literature output in the 1970s. Many saw them in a far more political light at that time; now these books dominate African American literature, or seem to. Then, as now, there is a strong belief among many blacks—poor, working-class, and bourgeois intellectuals—and many whites as well, that violent urban life represents "authentic" black experience and a true politically dynamic "resistance" culture.

Chiles probably would have preferred it if Borders and other bookstores did not label urban or hip-hop novels as "African American literature." It would be better for the public if such books were called "Afro-pop literature" or "black urban fiction" or "mass-market black fiction." Then, the category of "African American literature" could be reserved for those books and authors who are part of the canon: writers ranging from late nineteenth- and early twentieth-century novelist Charles Chesnutt, poet and novelist Paul Laurence Dunbar, and novelist and poet James Weldon Johnson; to 1920s and early 1930s Harlem Renaissance figures like poet and fiction writer Langston Hughes, novelist and poet Claude McKay, novelists Jessie Fauset and Nella Larsen, and poet and novelist Countee Cullen; to the great crossover figures of the 1940s through the 1960s, like novelist and essayist James Baldwin, novelist and short story writer Richard Wright, novelist and essayist Ralph Ellison, novelist Ann Petry, poet and novelist Gwendolyn Brooks, and novelist John A. Williams; to the black arts–era writers like poet and children's writer Nikki Giovanni, poet, playwright, and fiction writer Amiri Baraka, and poet Haki Madhubuti (Don L. Lee); and to post-1960s writers like novelists Toni Morrison, Alice Walker, Gloria Naylor, Walter Mosley, Colson Whitehead, Ernest Gaines, and Charles Johnson, poet and novelist Ishmael Reed, and poets Yusef Komunyakaa and Rita Dove. A few additional figures, like playwrights Lorraine Hansberry, Ed Bullins, Charles Fuller, and August Wilson, and some diasporic writers, like novelist and playwright Wole Soyinka, poet Derek Walcott, novelists Chinua Achebe, George Lamming, Jamaica Kincaid, Zadie Smith, Junot Díaz, and Edwidge Danticat, could be thrown in for good measure.

Chiles's concern about the supposed decline of African American literature reflects the elite's fear that the rise of hip-hop and the "urban" ethos generally represents a decline in urban black cultural life. The "urban nitty-gritty," as it were, seems like a virus that has undone black artistic standards and a black meritocracy. Now, there is only purely market-driven drivel aimed at the lowest, most uncultured taste. This is clearly a position of someone like novelist and culture critic Stanley Crouch. The sensitivity on this point is not by any means wholly or even mostly a matter of snobbery. It has taken a very long time for African American literature to reach a level of general respectability, where the general public thought it was worth reading and the literary establishment thought it was worth recognizing. Now, for many blacks, blacks themselves seem to be denigrating it by flooding the market with trash novels no better than Mickey Spillane. It is by no means surprising that blacks, a persecuted and historically degraded group, would feel that their cultural products are always suspect, precarious, and easily turned against them as caricature in the marketplace.

Another way to look at this is that urban literature has democratized and broadened the reach and content of African American literature. In some ways, urban lit may show the maturity, not the decline, of African American literature. After all, African American literature is the oldest of all self-consciously identified ethnic minority literatures in the United States, going back as far as 1774 to Phyllis Wheatley's first book of poems and to the slave narratives of the antebellum period that produced such classics as *The Narrative of the Life of Frederick Douglass* (1845) and Harriet Jacobs's *Incidents in the Life of a Slave Girl* (1861). African Americans have thought longer and harder about the importance of literature as a political and cultural tool than have other ethnic minorities in the United States. The Harlem Renaissance was a movement by blacks, helped by white patrons, to gain cultural access and respectability by producing a first-rate literature. The rise of urban lit does not repudiate the black literary past, but it does suggest other ways and means of producing black literature and other ends for it as well. Moreover, some urban lit authors are far from being hacks: Sister Souljah, a well-traveled political activist and novelist, is a more-than-capable writer and thinker, however provocative she may be. The same can be said of the lone novel of music writer Nelson George, *Urban Romance* (1993), clearly not a trash novel. Some of the books of Eric Jerome Dickey and K'wan are worth reading as well. A major figure who straddles black romance and urban lit is E. Lynn Harris, a popular writer whose books deal with relationships and other matters of importance for blacks, particularly black women, today.

When I approached Bantam Books two years ago to become general editor of two annual series—Best African American Essays and Best African American Fiction—I wanted to make sure that the books had crossover appeal to various segments of the black reading public, and so I chose Harris to be the guest editor of *Best African American Fiction of 2009*, the first volume in the series. I see these volumes as an opportunity not only to bring the best of African American letters to the general reading public—from younger writers like Z. Z. Packer and Amina Gautier to established voices like Samuel Delaney and Edward P. Jones—but also to forge a sort of marriage between various types of African American literature. I wanted to use E. Lynn Harris's reach to bring serious black literature to an audience that might not be aware of it or even desire it. It is far too early to say whether this attempt will succeed, but the mere attempt alone acknowledges a level of complexity in African American literature and a level of profound segmentation in its audience that shows that African American experience, however it is made into art, has a depth and outreach, a sort of universality, dare I say, that actually bodes well for the future of this and perhaps of all American ethnic minority literature.

NOTES

This chapter is reprinted from Gerald Early's "What Is African American Literature?" (distrib-uted by the Embassy of the United States of America, Brussels, Belgium, 10 February 2009).

1. The article's title is, clearly, a parodic paraphrase of the classic 1937 Zora Neale Hurs-ton novel *Their Eyes Were Watching God*, a feminist staple of the African American literature canon, considered by many literary scholars to be one of the great American novels of its era.

WORK CITED

Chiles, Nick. "Their Eyes Were Reading Smut." *New York Times*, 4 January 2006. www.nytimes.com/.

Gang Wars

The Academy versus the Streets

Kemeshia Randle

As an African American female pursing a PhD at a predominately white institution, the mantra of the street and the mantra of the academy have become synonymous: one must push through the coldest winter ever if the mission is "getting to happy"; the literature that is read in the streets and in the academy is not synonymous, however. Scholars are expected to abide by accepted standards in academia, that is, read, write, and discuss only canonized and therefore appropriate scholarly works. However, this limits the scope, content, and audiences of our scholarship. For this reason, some intellectuals resist and rebel against these guidelines and cater instead to the common people. These scholars desire to engage with, read about, and write for the communities of people they theorize about on a daily basis behind the confines of the ivory tower. Most notable amongst these rebellious thinkers is Harlem Renaissance author, folklorist, and anthropologist Zora Neale Hurston.

Alice Walker insists that Zora Neale Hurston belongs in the tradition of black women singers, rather than among the literati, because like the blues singers of her day, Hurston was both sensual and radical. Despite her position in the academy and her subsequent role as a representative of the race, she mapped her own paths and portrayed life as she saw fit. Essentially, she was not afraid to cross over the line into forbidden territory. When Hurston did cross the line, which was quite often, it was not the streets that threatened and eventually killed her; rather, the violent slaying came at the hands of her peers, the literary elite. Her most noted work, *Their Eyes Were Watching God* (1937), was immensely ridiculed during the time of its publication and later went out of print. Hurston's contemporaries criticized the work's "high-

9

ly charged language," insisting that it spoke too freely about insignificant, yet taboo issues, that is, female sexualities (Wright, 16). Several decades later, her works were revived, and Hurston became the revered author we now know, arguably a main staple in an African American literary canon.

This trend in the academy—of critiquing, defining, and therefore limiting certain works only to revive them later—does not seem to be shifting. Those who suffer are popular fiction writers like Hurston who resist and revolt against the academy's prescribed norms and boldly appropriate the inappropriate in their fiction. They, like Hurston, are oftentimes influenced by a genre of music, specifically hip-hop, and write with common people in mind, and their works are often criticized and castigated by literary scholars. However, I argue that it would be both a pity and a disservice to the field of literature/literary criticism to dismiss the works of popular fiction writers today, as Hurston's were dismissed in times past, only to go in search of them tomorrow. Street/popular fiction works, too, are valuable to both culture and the academy: they are indicative of the notion that there is no essential blackness, and they provide an intergenerational dynamic by which to bridge the gap between generations of scholarship, specifically that on black female sexualities. Some contemporary black women scholars recognize and appreciate the strength of this unity: bridging the gap between these two institutions can bring an end to decades of intellectual/class wars between the academy and the streets.

As a child growing up in a religious household under the guardianship of parents with strong Christian morals and beliefs, I was often denied the privilege of reveling in the street, both literally and figuratively. In my home, the streets were equivalent to BET (Black Entertainment Television) and certain films where viewer discretion was advised. Martin Lawrence and Will Smith's 1995 film *Bad Boys* comes to mind. I remember it being not the violence in the film that bothered my parents but rather the language used by the comedians that was not suitable for young ears. Conversely, the exposed bodies, not the lyrics, on the videos of rap and rhythm-and-blues artists incited a BET block on any television outside of the main family room. My siblings and I spent many nights attempting to figure out the code in order to enter the world that had been deemed indecent and inappropriate. We had watched videos before, so we knew the routine: guy in jewels and baggy clothes likes girl in heels and scanty clothes; there is some singing, some dancing, and maybe a little kissing and other forms of touching. At the end of the video, the couple either lives happily ever after together or separate and find someone else to live out their dreams with. But, after the block, I developed an intrigue for the videos; because I had been denied their luxury, they became a vital part of my existence. It was during this time in my life that I became a rebel. When my parents were not in the main family room, I would mute the television and indulge in a video or two. The lyrics were not of importance anyway; I was still allowed to listen to the same songs on the radio, so the words clearly were not the reason my siblings and I were denied access to what I now view a very vital part of my black and female culture. At such a young age, I did not watch the videos because I wanted desperately to see the displays of overt sexuality in the videos; rather, I watched because I was told that I could not. I had to know why the two people I love hated them. Now, as an adult, I pay more careful attention to lyrics, and I find great passion in music, but I also find myself continuously fighting for what others are fighting against. And, although I still do not agree with my parents' decision to limit my cultural experience, I understand why they did it. Aside from being presumably under the law of the institution of the church, I was young, impressionable, and unable to fully understand that expression of culture without being properly educated and trained.

A decade removed from my parents' household and authority, and having received proper education and degrees from several prestigious institutions of higher learning, I find myself again being denied access to a world of cultural expression because of its seeming improbability to advance cognition and its unsuitable depictions of violence and sexuality. The fields rebellious enough to indulge in such study are those fields that are almost always already considered the problem child of the academy: black studies, women studies, queer studies, and other fields devoted to the study of minority groups. While pursuing a doctorate in literature, a classic field and perhaps one of the academy's more favored sons, in the University of Alabama's Department of English, I have found myself having the urge to mute the television again, but I remember that I am a rebel, a rebel who now has a voice. More importantly, I am no longer that young, impressionable, and uninformed youth my parents thought I was. Still, I recognize that there are some battles I cannot fight alone. Some intellectuals are not as progressive as others, and to these intellectuals, crossing the line from the academy to the street is not quite fathomable. Elite scholars in the field of literature have an opinion about popular fiction very similar to that of author and journalist Nick Chiles's, expressed in his 2006 *New York Times* article titled "Their Eyes Were Reading Smut." Perhaps knowing but not fully understanding the significance of the title, Chiles relegates popular fiction authors and their works to the same banished corner that Hurston found herself in some seven plus decades ago. Chiles's recollection of his embarrassment and disgust as he walked through a Georgia bookstore only to find listed as African American literature a group of "oversexed" texts that seemed to have mated in the stockrooms to produce even more tasteless and inappropriate texts is quite reminiscent of Richard Wright's 1937 review of Hurston's *Their Eyes Were Watching God*, and Chiles's plea for more serious black writers is a direct echo of Alain Locke's review of the same work. Sexuality can be beautiful if maturely practiced, but it can be otherwise deeply incapacitating, and articulating this truth, whether through praxis or through literature, is undoubtedly serious and necessary.

A contemporary reading of Hurston's work, the archetype for African American women's literature, will perhaps disgust some and justify others, but it will no doubt demonstrate that there is a connection between the works we revere and the works we revile. Recognizing that *Their Eyes Were Watching God* is highly populated with sexual metaphor deemed inappropriate for its time, Donna Weir-Soley (2009) insists,

> *Their Eyes Were Watching God* revolutionized the depiction of black female sexuality in African American literature . . . in 1937, when she wrote her second novel, the damaging effects of nineteenth-century sexual ideology on black women's subjectivities and writings were fully entrenched. The black press cautioned writers to keep their submissions free of overt sexualities. (39)

Knowing that cautions like these existed and recognizing what white publishers would not print, Hurston created a character that would be considered a "bad bitch" according to modern definition and disguised her as a pretty, defenseless, mulatto girl led astray by an aging grandmother with a slave-like mentality, perhaps hoping not to avert those of the time who had an incessant obsession with race but knowing that the attentive, progressive reader would recognize, as she had, the importance and empowerment of female sexuality. Hurston's brief explanation of *Their Eyes* to librarian William Stanley Hoole is as follows:

> My next book is to be a novel about a woman who was from childhood hungry for life and the earth, but because she had beautiful hair, was always being skotched upon a flag-pole by men who loved her and forced to sit there. At forty she got her chance at mud. Mud, lush, and fecund with a buck Negro called Teacake. He took her down into the Everglades where people worked and sweated and loved and died violently, where no such thing as flag-poles for women existed. . . . This is the barest statement of the story. (Kaplan, 366–67)

Indeed, this is the barest statement of the story, only the top of the mud. Hurston's restricted 1937 terminology, "mud, lush, and fecund," can be easily translated contemporarily into musk, lust, and fucking. As vulgar as it may seem, this is a great deal of the novel, only Hurston could not articulate it in this manner. Perhaps it is best that she did not because reviewers like Wright who saw fit for women to be placed on flagpoles could not tolerate even the mud and the lush.

Janie has her sexual awakening at the age of sixteen, outside, amongst nature. Although diluted by the beauty and serenity of blooming trees and flowers, this is the epitome of overt sexuality. Hurston writes,

She was stretched on her back beneath the pear tree soaking in the alto chant of the visiting bees, the gold of the sun and the panting breath of the breeze when the inaudible voice of it all came to her. She saw a dust-bearing bee sink into the sanctum of a bloom; the thousand sister-calyxes arch to meet the love embrace and the ecstatic shiver of the tree from root to tiniest branch creaming in every blossom and frothing with delight. . . . She had been summoned to behold a revelation. Then Janie felt a pain remorseless sweet that left her limp and languid. (307)

The last line of this passage, in contemporary terms, expresses that Janie had come; more clearly, she experienced an orgasm. The trees and the bees are merely a distraction, a way to cover up the fact that a young black girl lies outside on the ground, for all to see; enjoys herself sexually; and lends no indication of shame. It is at this point that Janie recognizes the power of the erotic. Nanny, I am sure, had no idea that the next step after "mule" was "bitch." She was worried about "de men-folks white or black . . . makin' a spit cup outa" Janie's face, and as sure as Nanny rested in peace, Janie and her newly empowered sexual self went on to make spit cups out of men's faces (312). She recognizes her desires and wanders from place to place until she finds what she is looking for. Janie insists, and the narrator proclaims, "He don't even never mention nothin' pretty. . . . Ah wants things sweet wid mah marriage lak when you sit under a pear tree and think. . . . From now on until death she was going to have flower dust and springtime sprinkled over everything. A bee for her bloom" (314, 318). Janie wants things sweet with her marriage, and there is no doubt that she will have a bee for her bloom. There is no specificity for the bee, just a bee, as long as he can sprinkle springtime over everything. In essence, Janie "puts her looks, sexuality, intellect, and/or aggression to service" in order to meet her springtime needs, and according to Patricia Hill Collins (2005), that makes her a bad bitch (124).

One's simultaneous involvement in the academy and the street can allow one to both understand and appreciate this reading of Hurston's iconic work. Unfortunately, all scholars have not reached epiphany. African American scholars in particular cannot overcome our own judgmental stigma that every individual of the race is representative of the entire race. In a recent article entitled "Who Is Afraid of Black Sexuality?" (2012) published in the *Chronicle of Higher Education*, Stacy Patton acknowledges that black scholars for quite some time have been afraid of black sexuality. She insists, "Students and professors are sensitive, even squeamish, about portrayals of their communities" (6). Still, Patton acknowledges that some contemporary, more daring scholars have begun to show interests in black sexuality studies. They, like Hurston and I, acknowledge the fact that careers may depend on their abilities, or inabilities rather, to mute the television and secretly engage in the forbidden art forms in the privacies of their own homes. They realize that there is an importance in studying even the bad parts of black culture and hope that the rest of the world (read academy) will imitate their studies, engage in the culture, and put theory into practice. If apprehensive scholars first acknowledge why they are so thoroughly disgusted, repulsed, and embarrassed by the sight and mention of black bodies, they might in turn recognize the need for further critical discussion.

Scholar Jennifer Morgan examines the origin of and reaction to stereotypes of the black body in her work entitled "Some Could Suckle over Their Shoulder" (1997). Morgan acknowledges that the depictions of Africans in the early travel writings of Europeans during the sixteenth and seventeenth centuries shaped both the representations and the receptions of black bodies. As a result of the men's travel writings, would-be American settlers had a view of Africans, particularly African women, before they actually viewed African women. Morgan insists,

> The encounter had already taken place in parlors and reading rooms on English soil, assuring that colonists would arrive with battery and assumptions and predispositions about race, femininity, sexuality, and civilization. Confronted with an Africa they needed to exploit, European writers turned to black women as evidence of a cultural inferiority that ultimately became encoded in racial difference. Monstrous bodies became enmeshed with savage behavior as the icon of women's breasts became evidence of tangible barbarism. . . . By the mid-seventeenth century that which had initially marked African women as unfamiliar—their sexually and reproductively bound savagery—had become familiar. (191–92)

This familiarity, the depiction of the black female body as both desirous and shameful, is the reason for the carnal shame that African Americans possess today. Black people in general, but black women specifically, were/are overly concerned with upholding and adhering to a particular standard in an attempt to counteract these negative images and stereotypes, so we have developed our own stereotype, disguised it as a black womanhood, and often dismiss any writer who challenges this notion. Not surprisingly, however, we are the same women who are teaching and engaging *Their Eyes* as the epitome of feminism and reverencing Hurston as a literary foremother. This type of action is indicative of the notion that what is hated or seemingly irrelevant today is loved and reverenced tomorrow. I ask that we put an end to this cycle, that we (critics) accept difference and change, read and (re)examine works for what they could be as opposed to what we would like them to be, and acknowledge that our past does not have to be our future but ultimately recognize that blacks can have a healthy and active sexuality, if only the concept is engaged and redefined.

In an attempt to spur the field and redefine these parameters, hip-hop feminist Gwendolyn Pough, in her work *Check It While I Wreck It* (2004), acknowledges and laments that in spite of commercial success and the creation of billion-dollar markets by black women writers such as Terry McMillan, there is "no substantial body of critical work" on popular fiction, and this is due in part to the displays of black female sexualities in these works (70). Because of this disregard, many are unaware of the depth (particularly in relation to black female sexualities) of works such as Sapphire's *Push* (1997), Sister Souljah's *Coldest Winter Ever* (1999), or Terry McMillan's latest work, *Getting to Happy* (2011). Written during the 1990s, when the display of female sexuality in rap videos was on the rise, Sapphire's *Push* is the tale of Precious Jones, an illiterate, black, inner-city, teenage girl who is made to perform sexual favors for both her mother and her father. Precious bears two of her father's children and contracts his deadly disease. In the midst of these encounters, she finds solace in films and music videos that display only in her imagination. Even in her imaginary world, however, she cannot deny how powerful her own sexuality is. The novel's language, in the words of Wright, is highly charged, but, in fact, one of the most gruesomely violent and highly charged scenes of the novel is also the most pivotal. In the voice of Precious, Sapphire writes,

> I can't talk about Daddy now. My clit swell up I think Daddy. Daddy sick me, *disgust* me, but still he sex me up. I nawshus in my stomach but hot tight in my twat and I think I want it back, the smell of the bedroom, the hurt—he slap my face till it sting and my ears sing separate songs from each other, call me names, pump my pussy in out in out in out awww I come. . . . Orgasm in me, his body shaking, grab me. . . . You LOVE it! Say you love it. I wanna say I DON'T. I wanna say I'm a chile. But my pussy popping like grease in frying pan. (111)

Audre Lorde (1984) declares that the erotic is dangerous and that female sexuality is energizing; Precious Jones is proof. She cannot fathom why an act that she loathes can cause her to feel so strongly inwardly that she might in fact "want it back" or desire it. She admits, "I HATE myself when I feel good" (58). But the energizing feeling, "awww," is too powerful to resist. Another fact to note is that while Precious is noticeably illiterate, and certain sections of the novel are almost incomprehensible as a result, each passage depicting a sexual encounter with one of her parents, even before she is taught the barest rules of language, is quite often more intelligible than other passages in the novel. Perhaps Sapphire is suggesting that the power of sexuality is always inherently clear. And through its depiction of sexuality, the novel acknowledges abnormalities in black culture and begs for a more critical discussion of it.

As if engaging in the conversation, Sister Souljah, in *The Coldest Winter Ever*, depicts the life of a sexual orator, Winter Santiaga, teenage daughter of a prominent Brooklyn drug lord. Winter grows up too soon and is convinced that along with innate street savvy, her body and sexuality are a surefire way to getting what she wants. After her father is incarcerated, she uses her sexuality to provide a somewhat feasible lifestyle for herself and her family. Though, later in the novel, Winter, too, finds herself incarcerated, physically and sexually. The same girl who vividly describes her birth as the day she came "busting out of [her] momma's big coochie," the same girl who proudly proclaims that "[men] didn't have to look no particular way to eat [her] pussy," is the girl who in the height of the novel has very few words for her feelings during a sexual encounter with a controlling boyfriend (1, 23). Sister Souljah writes, "He pulled my head up and said, 'A nigga wants pussy. This is my pussy, right?' he questioned. I answered with a nod. 'A little blood aint gonna hurt this big dick.' He was all up in me. How can I describe the feeling? It wasn't pleasure. It wasn't pain. It was nothing, like a dick plunging into an ocean. But still, I conjured up some moans for him" (406). Winter had just undergone an abortion (hence the comparison of her vagina to an ocean) and was beginning to rethink the choices she had made in life, but after growing up thinking that the only way to appease a man was to give "him some pussy just to keep him in line," there was little else she knew to do other than conjure up moans (26). Black feminist Rebecca Walker, in her essay "Lusting for Freedom," insists, "The question is not whether young women are going to have sex. . . . The question is rather, what do young women need to make a dynamic bridge between sex and sexuality, between the isolated act and the powerful element that, when honed, can be an important tool for self-actualization?" (23). By the time Winter began to make this connection, at only seventeen years of age, her life had been consumed and influenced by a sexuality powerful enough to destroy. Her mother had only told her about the material things she could obtain from using her sexual wiles, and her father had only warned her to avoid men who lusted after her beauty. Essentially, neither engaged her in critical conversation, similar to how scholars, particularly black scholars, are avoiding the same conversations.

Since scholars in the academy are not discussing the topic critically, Terry McMillan creates intellectual female characters to do just that. *Getting to Happy*, noted as the sequel to *Waiting to Exhale* (1992), is on the surface an examination of the growth of the lives of the four women from the previous novel—Bernadine, Gloria, Robin, and Savannah—after a fifteen-year time period. The growth that they experience, however, oftentimes comes after having intellectual conversations with teenage girls not unlike Precious and Winter, who inform their parents that times have changed, and it is now okay to express and engage in conversation regarding their own individual sexualities. Sparrow, a fifteen-year-old, tells her mother, Robin, that she and her friends, Bernadine, Gloria, and Savannah, have not yet gotten to happy because they "live so much by the book" (24). After assuring Robin that "times have changed," Sparrow then encourages her mother that, like her, she should probably consider dating outside of the race if dating black men has not given her the satisfaction she had hoped (26). Sparrow's reasoning for dating white boys is because "a lot of the black guys at school aren't attracted to girls like [her]"; she states, "I'm my own person. I don't fit the mold" (27). In response to Sparrow's teaching, Robin declares, "She's the daughter. I'm the mother. What makes her think her opinions or her little teenage insights are worth their weights in gold? I know she means well. And there's a chance she may be right. But you shouldn't let your kids know when they know more than you" (25). In terms of the development of scholarship on black female sexualities, contemporary scholars are not concerned about whether they know more than the scholars that came before them but are more concerned with bridging the gap between the two worlds, quite similar to how McMillan's characters find themselves connected by the novel's end.

Perhaps McMillan herself would not be all too pleased with me situating her in conversation with the abovementioned authors, or street fiction authors in general. In 2007, McMillan was noted for having written a scathing e-mail to street lit publishers, detailing how they were "harming black consumers by publishing 'exploitative, destructive, racist, egregious, sexist, base, tacky, poorly-written, unedited, degrading books'" (Alexander). Conceivably, she recognized that she was in essence threatening her own literary being and as a result later retracted some of her words. Regardless of her reasoning, however, the fact remains that she, like the abovementioned authors, are regulated to a very minute space in literature. Elite scholars, like Chiles, would much rather they recognize their place, stay there, and not confuse their work with the likes of authentic or serious African American literature.

Noting the connection between the two schools of thought—academic and street—however, Gwendolyn Pough states, "In a sense, the women of the Hip Hop generation are building a home for themselves on ground that was cleared by the Black women thinkers, writers and activists of the late 1800s and the early to mid-1900s and broken by those of the 1970s." Pough continues, "The head start made by earlier black women has made claiming a space from which to speak somewhat easier; however, Black women today are still plagued with some of the same issues. For example, the issues of sexual stereotypes" (73). Indeed, literary foremothers' attempts at carving out a space and mapping out the field of black female sexuality from the late nineteenth century to the present is precisely why contemporary writers such as Sapphire, Sister Souljah, and Terry McMillan can write more personal tales about uncomfortable and controversial topics such as black female sexualities. I am not concerned with the debate of whether the works of popular fiction writers are worthy of being called African American literature; my concern is that the dismissal of these works results in a lack of critical conversation on critical topics. Also, it forces future generations to embark upon a journey similar to Alice Walker's decades ago, in search of a work that speaks to their individual black female experiences. A careful study and analysis of contemporary black women's popular fiction can not only bridge the gap between generations of scholarship by adding depth and diversity to the current body of criticism on black female sexuality but also possibly end a long fought war between the academy and the streets. Let the rivalries cease.

WORKS CITED

Alexander, Amy. "Terry McMillan vs. Ghetto Lit." *Nation*, 29 October 2007. www.thenation.com/.

Chiles, Nick. "Their Eyes Were Reading Smut." *New York Times*, 4 January 2006. www.nytimes.com/.

Collins, Patricia Hill. *Black Sexual Politics: African Americans, Gender, and the New Racism*. New York: Routledge, 2005.

Hurston, Zora Neale. *Their Eyes Were Watching God*. 1937. New York: Harper Collins, 2006.

Kaplan, Karla, ed. *Zora Neale Hurston: A Life in Letters*. New York: Doubleday, 2002.

Locke, Alain. Review of *Their Eyes Were Watching God*. 1937. In *Zora Neale Hurston: Critical Perspectives Past and Present*, edited by Henry Louis Gates Jr. and Kwame Anthony Appiah, 16–23. New York: Amistad, 1993.

Lorde, Audre. *Sister Outsider: Essays and Speeches*. New York: Crossing Press, 1984.

McMillan, Terry. *Getting to Happy*. New York: Viking, 2011.

Morgan, Jennifer. "Some Could Suckle over Their Shoulder: Male Travelers, Female Bodies, and the Gendering of Racial Ideology, 1500–1770." *William and Mary Quarterly*, 3rd ser., 54, no. 1 (1997): 167–92.

Patton, Stacy. "Who Is Afraid of Black Sexuality?" *Chronicle of Higher Education, Chronicle Review*, 3 December 2012. http://chronicle.com/.

Pough, Gwendolyn. *Check It While I Wreck It: Black Womanhood, Hip Hop Culture, and the Public Sphere*. Boston: Northeastern University Press, 2004.

Sapphire. *Push*. New York: Vintage, 1997.

Souljah, Sister. *The Coldest Winter Ever*. 1999. New York: Pocket Star Books, 2006.

Walker, Alice. *In Search of Our Mothers' Gardens*. Orlando: Harcourt, 1983.

Walker, Rebecca. "Lusting for Freedom." In *Listen Up: Voices from the Next Feminist Generation*, edited by Barbara Findlen, 19–24. Seattle: Seal Press, 2001.

Weir-Soley, Donna Aza. *Eroticism, Spirituality and Resistance in Black Women's Writings*. Gainesville: University Press of Florida, 2009.

Wright, Richard. "Between Laughter and Tears." *New Masses*, 5 October 1937. Repr. in *Zora Neale Hurston: Critical Perspectives Past and Present*, edited by Henry Louis Gates Jr. and Kwame Anthony Appiah, 16–17. New York: Amistad Press, 1993.

Part II

Early Street Lit, 1950s–1970s

Whose Mean Streets?

Donald Goines, Iceberg Slim, and the Black Noir Aesthetic

Bonnie Rhee Andryeyev

The streets were dark with something more than night.
—Raymond Chandler, *The Simple Art of Murder*

It is knowledge itself that is dangerous in the noir world of American race relations.
—Paula Rabinowitz, *Black and White and Noir: America's Pulp Modernism*

You will not find Donald Goines's *Whoreson* (1972) or Iceberg Slim's *Pimp: The Story of My Life* (1969) on any conventional list of noir texts.[1] True, there are no telltale signs of noir in these novels; there are no private eyes, no femme fatales, and the mystery is not tied up in the plot. However, reading these black pulp novels alongside hard-boiled fiction provides a way to read America's urban past in a particular historical and political context. Critical examination of the racial politics in noir texts and films begins by identifying the curious absence of racial minorities in the urban settings the genre is known for. During the noir period (1920–1960), America was fast becoming an urban nation, and the effects of the Great Migrations (1910–1930, 1940–1970) drastically changed the racial demographics of cities in the United States. While the anxiety in literary and cinematic noir is often perceived as a crisis in relation to new gendered identities, we should also consider the role of race as a significant yet often overlooked source of anxiety, considering that the changing racial makeup of the American city posed an imminent threat to the whiteness of noir's landscape.

Since noir has been characterized as a largely urban genre, it is significant that on the whole, noir texts and films did not register the true racial makeup of the cities they portrayed. Scholars such as Liam Kennedy, Megan Abbott, Benigno Trigo, and Kelly Oliver, however, have argued that noir anxiety is more insidiously about the new racialized boundaries in metropolitan America. As such, we can read the way noir registered these gendered and racial anxieties by producing new metropolitan conceptions of white masculinity based on an insidious appropriation of minority identity and ways of being to help maintain the white, working-class male's right to urban space and culture. The white noir hero's transgression of social, racial, and class boundaries characterize a kind of figurative passing. Classic noir authors, I contend, often utilize the passing trope as a means to refashion whiteness in confrontation with the miscegenated identity of the new American metropolis. In the hard-boiled world, not only is race symbolized through liminal identities and implications of inner-city and underworld realities, but also racialized urban spaces are rendered as places that disguise the visibility of the white noir hero, a powerful revision in response to the anxiety of urban white identity being swallowed up by the "dark city."[2]

During the end of the classic noir period in film and literature, black pulp writers of the late 1960s and '70s such as Iceberg Slim (also known as Robert Beck) and Donald Goines, writing post-white flight, presented narratives that not only exposed the city as no longer white but also characterized ghetto knowledge as an urban epistemology inaccessible to whites. As such, black pulp fiction or street literature has often been marketed to attend to (and critique) the white desire to voyeuristically inhabit the racialized ghetto. As Miles White claims, the black ghetto was (and remains) a surrealistic playground of racial fantasy for whites (28). Hailed by the *Village Voice* as "the voice of the ghetto itself,"[3] the novels of Goines (and Slim) symbolize an important historical moment within a particular racialized noir genealogy that considers the racialization of the American city a significant contextual key to unlocking the power and class dynamics at work in the genre. Central to an alternative genealogy that considers unusually paired authors like Dashiell Hammett and Iceberg Slim is the paradigmatic gesture that works to disentangle notions of racial and urban epistemology through noir's pulp politics and nationalist agenda to claim the city as the primary locus of cultural production.

To identify Goines and Slim as noir writers exposes new dimensions to the cultural production of black street literature. Representing a black pulp aesthetic that effectively challenges the realism of white noir, these authors work to destabilize the relationship between whiteness and urban authority present in hard-boiled writing. In his work *The Simple Art of Murder*, Raymond Chandler famously proclaimed the American indigenization of crime fiction through its realistic determination to pair criminality with the underclass. Written like a noir manifesto, Chandler claims that Dashiell Hammett was the purveyor of a new subgenre of detective fiction that defined the gritty lives of those most affected by the "mean streets" of the American metropolis: "[Hammett] wrote at first (and almost to the end) for people with a sharp, aggressive attitude to life. They were not afraid of the seamy side of things; they lived there. Violence did not dismay them; it was right down their street. Hammett gave murder back to the kind of people that commit it for reasons" (14). This quote reveals the way Chandler's work constructs the noir mystique through a purposeful romanticization of the disenfranchised experiences of the urban lower classes; however, neither Hammett nor Chandler's fiction fully live up to his definitions. Furthermore, with the exception of noir's representations of ethnic enclaves like Chinatown, hard-boiled fiction works hard to avoid the urban racial politics (white flight, urban decay, blockbusting, and segregation) that were prevalent during the height of the noir period. If we read noir as a genre that established its seductive power through narrativizing a kind of urban realism that does not include the African American urban experience, we can see how the ghettoes of Goines and Slim revise the so-called mean streets of hard-boiled fiction. Depicting the gritty realism of the ghetto as a hyperreal environment where consistent surveillance produces new black subjectivities based on racial masquerade, performance, and parody, these authors expose the white noir city as nothing but a clever, yet one-dimensional mise-en-scène.

The noir genealogy that Paula Rabinowitz utilizes in *Black and White and Noir* includes writers like Richard Wright and Ralph Ellison, which foreground the significance of the historical criminalization of the black male during the mid-twentieth century. Her definitions of the traditional noir protagonist as a symbolic entity allude that it is the American black experience that is the true symbolic reference of the noir aesthetic: "Guilt, knowledge, desire, deceit, vengeance, a past weighing heavily on the present, and a lone man, an outsider, who . . . is 'crammed with guilty knowledge'—provides a frame for understanding African-American experience" (91). The frame she provides is particularly useful in reading the protagonists of Goines and Slim as quintessential noir writers who narrativize their "guilty knowledge" while producing a new affective experience for the noir reader. If traditional noir always left us with wanting to know more, the noir of Goines and Slim transfers their guilty knowledge to us, leaving us with the epistemological dilemma of knowing too much.

Following in the footsteps of Chester Himes, contemporary black noir challenges the "hardness" in the hard-boiled "urban real" by offering up hyperreal and hyperracialized images of the modern city. As such, Goines and Slim's graphic urban narratives expose the noir city as a contested site for racial and masculine possession over urban space through a particularly racialized knowledge and identification. Moreover, we can see how the noir city provided a blueprint for Goines and Slim's ghetto settings. Their novels read like noirish manifestoes that reveal paths to power and urban survival through any means necessary while simultaneously performing an intimate racialized knowledge of the American ghetto.

Working in the noir tradition, Goines and Slim epitomize the fundamental description of noir writers as urban truth tellers. As Sean McCann points out, hard-boiled writers were formally "against the 'bunk' of oversophistication," and in contrast, "they promised to deliver the stark truths of contemporary society—'ugly, vicious, sordid, and cruel' . . . they linked this antiliterary sensibility to a complaint against social corruption. Revealing unpleasant reality was not just pulp sensationalism, the fiction's writers and editors implied; it was part of a moral struggle against dishonesty" (39). In *The Naked Soul of Iceberg Slim* (1986), Robert Beck writes, "I want to say at the outset that I have become ill, insane as an inmate of a torture chamber behind America's fake façade of justice and democracy" (17). While Slim and Goines are rarely considered in the noir canon, they perfectly illustrate several basic tenets of noir, including Woody Haut's notion that "contemporary noir fiction, often vicarious and voyeuristic, can be read as quasi-anthropological texts, or as narratives evoking prurient interests; descriptions of what America has become, or chapters in a survivalist's handbook" (3).[4] Indeed, the ghetto conditions of Slim and Goines's worlds reveal the racial stakes of urban survival. They exploit and refashion many of the basic tenets of noir, including the way noir necessitates crime as an urban way of life, a theme firmly established in the works of writers like Hammett and Chandler.

Black noir not only indicts American society for the criminal living conditions of the ghetto but also reveals the new urban identities generated by such conditions. Similar to the dynamic in traditional noir, the ghetto heroes of Slim and Goines collapse the boundary between hero and criminal. In black noir, the living conditions of the ghetto are revealed as criminal, and as a response, the protagonists of Slim and Goines learn how to utilize criminal infrastructure as a kind of ghetto empowerment. Their works reflect the notion that crime can be an equalizer to combat social inequality. As Jon Thompson argues of hard-boiled fiction,

> Crime is in one sense democratic and entrepreneurial: it has the potential of making those excluded by class society financially and politically as powerful as those who have benefited from class division. Moreover, [the hard-boiled genre's] antibourgeois social vision also grants criminals a kind of integrity: they may be criminals, but they don't pretend to adhere to ethical standards they can't maintain. They thus lack the hypocrisy found in legitimate society, which condemns criminals and yet sanctions and participates in illegal activities. (145)[5]

We can see how crime in the black noir of Goines and Slim especially fulfills Thompson's definition of criminality in the hard-boiled world. For Goines and Slim, crime is an urban sensibility, a mode of survival, and an alternative means to power. In these works, significant revisions to the hard-boiled world have been made from the transition of white to black—noir might not be dead, but the detective figure is no longer the supreme urban authority. In his place, utilizing the same masculinist practices of telling it "straight" in order to lay claim to urban space and culture, Goines and Slim's protagonists include urban outlaw figures such as the pimp, the con man, and the drug lord. Illustrating Stephen Soitos's claim that "black authors opted from the beginning to create nonstandard detectives" (31), Goines and Slim utilize these iconic stereotypes of the urban underworld to reveal the ways in which the detective is an outdated symbol of the mean streets.

Noir is not simply a matter of utilizing the city as a setting or the protagonist as a hard-boiled male; what is crucial to the noir aesthetic is the possessive nature of the relationship between the protagonist and the city. Following in the footsteps of Chester Himes, the first writer to write of the gritty world of noir through a racial lens, Goines and Slim were the frontrunners of a new black noir aesthetic that represented the city as the preeminent site for racialized cultural production. Just as the unknowable city became more knowable to the readers of noir through the noir protagonist, the protagonists of Goines and Slim reveal ghetto epistemology through the figures of the pimp, the con man, and the drug lord. Throughout their works, Goines and Slim utilize these popular urban icons as truth tellers of the black ghetto whose characters actively perform an intimate knowledge of the city that is problematized by the cultural framing of the black ghetto and its inhabitants as voyeuristic subjects. As Liam Kennedy argues,

> The framing of the postindustrial ghetto as the space of the black underclass has given rise to stock images of people positioned in the mise-en-scène of urban wasteland streets, concrete playgrounds, project housing and derelict building. The ghetto appears as a carceral space, confining its inhabitants as both visible and exotic, subjected to the distanced gaze of the viewer. (93)

If part of the pleasure of white noir is based on the viewer or reader's voyeuristic experience of the city through the white noir hero, in black noir, our voyeuristic gaze is troubled by the black noir protagonist's awareness as a racialized subject under constant surveillance. In response to this, Slim and Goines's characters utilize masking and performance as modes of resistance that work to problematize the voyeuristic gaze on the urban black subject.

If we consider the noir aesthetic as an establishment of a nuanced combination of masculinist performance, racial appropriation, and urban epistemology, we can see how the figure of the pimp is a revised embodiment of all these things, exoticized and mythologized as a product of the meanest streets. Although Iceberg Slim is credited with writing the first pimp narrative, Donald Goines is largely considered the best-selling author of "black experience" novels published by Holloway House in Los Angeles during the late 1960s and beyond. Goines first attempted to write Westerns (a genre that John Cawelti and Paul Skenazy argue is a precursor to the hard-boiled novel), but after reading Iceberg Slim's autobiography, *Pimp: The Story of My Life*, Goines became inspired to give up Westerns and write his own versions of ghetto life.[6] While Goines's themes touch on many aspects of ghetto culture, his characterization of pimping in his second novel, *Whoreson*, share many similarities with Slim's first autobiographical novel as well as Slim's later novel *Trick Baby* (1967). Both Goines and Slim's pimp narratives of "the life" read like noirish confessions, revealing the racialized psychology produced by American ghettoes and the way these protagonists confront oppression and poverty through their utilization of alternative methods to gain capital and power.

The cover of the Holloway House edition of *Pimp* includes the following summary of the novel, whose rhetoric reveals the kind of voyeuristic impulse that fuels much of the noir aesthetic:

> Iceberg Slim is the name he used in the black ghetto. His real name is Robert Beck and he was a pimp. This is his story, told without bitterness and with no pretense at moralizing—the smells, the sounds, the fears, the petty triumphs in the world of the pimp. No other book comes anywhere near this one in its description of the raw, brutal reality of the jungle that lurks beneath the surface of every city. Nobody but a pimp could tell this story, and none ever has . . . until Iceberg Slim. He was young, ambitious, and blessed with a superior IQ. He spent twenty-five years of his life in Hell. Other pimps died in prison, or in insane asylums, or were shot down in the street. But Iceberg Slim escaped death and the drug habit to live in the square world and to write—about his people and his life.

The contents of the back cover blurb indulges in the voyeuristic nature of the reader and the mythology of the world of the pimp and street life, in addition to representing the pimp as a short-lived character whose fate is, almost always, an early death. The dynamics between the reader and noir storyteller is also mirrored in this introduction. The focus here is on the reader's voyeuristic impulse and his or her dependence on Slim as an urban authority and ghetto tour guide. Nicholas Christopher's description of the noir protagonist as an urban insider who takes us into the depths of the city reveals the similar aesthetic at work in Slim's narrative: "Here we have a tour guide to the labyrinth like no other, for the hero has actually traveled to the labyrinth's terrible center, where every street is a one-way street, and 'died' to tell about

it" (12). Slim also plays into the voyeuristic expectations of the noir reader in
his preface:

> In this book I will take you the reader with me into the secret inner world of
> the pimp. I will lay bare my life and thoughts as a pimp. The account of my
> brutality and cunning as a pimp will fill many of you with revulsion, however
> if one intelligent valuable young man or woman can be saved from the de-
> structive slime then the displeasure I have given will have been outweighed by
> that individual's use of his potential in a socially constructive manner.

As he states here, Slim uses his authority to try to persuade the reader from
living through the same experiences; however, the affective power of this
novel (according to gangsta rappers and real-life pimps) proved that it did
just the opposite. Slim narrativized a profession and lifestyle that would be
endlessly mimicked and appropriated in order to front the seductive symbol
of the pimp that effectively combined urbanness with blackness in a powerful and metaphorical way.[7] While Slim's preface sets up the novel as a
potential "warning," it has been marketed and widely received as both a
"style manual" and an inspirational guide for future pimps. Black urban
writers, real-life pimps, and gangsta rappers have collectively marked Slim
as an icon of black popular culture and an urban truth-telling messiah. As
Milton van Sickle states, "To many, Slim has become a folk hero and his
followers dream of emulating him. They are thrilled with the excitement of
the street, and feel strong enough to weather its deadly dangers" (11). In her
article "Pimp Notes on Autonomy," Beth Coleman explains the power of the
pimp figure in the popular imagination: "Pimps, with the help of popular
culture, have made a fetish of their business. A business which is, of course,
based upon the appropriation of a person for commodity" (70). This fetishization of the pimp persona is as much about a performance of race as it is
about a performance of urban knowledge and power that the pimp possesses.
Moreover, the commodification of the pimp figure is based on his urban
survival skills and his embodiment of the energy of the streets as a racialized
symbol of urbanity. It is no mistake that in the novels of Goines and Slim, the
pimps often name themselves after cities or introduce themselves by stating
which city they hail from.

Throughout *Whoreson* and *Pimp*, Goines and Slim stress the importance
of the story and the setting of a pimp's becoming. They both reveal how they
got into "the game," presented as a kind of ghetto bildungsroman that explains how the aspiring pimp inherits, by oral tradition, the necessary street
knowledge to begin a life of pimping. Whoreson proclaims that his "real"
street education begins at the age of twelve by his mother Jessie and her
friend Fast Black. Similarly, Slim has several different pedagogues and role
models in the novel ("Sweet" and "Party Time" to name a few), and as we
come to learn through both characters, the pimp's education is based on his

knowledge of reading urban spaces, the mastery of language, utilizing psychology as oppression, and performing the pimp persona (even before he has the goods).

In terms of setting, Slim and Whoreson operate in several different cities to avoid the law; as such, their urban knowledge is similar to the noir hero's ability to read the physiognomy of the streets. As Slim and Whoreson demonstrate, a pimp can arrive in any city and figure out within a few days which area he will work out of, which pimps are the most powerful, and which prostitutes are the most worthy for the taking.[8] After fleeing from the law in Detroit, Whoreson proclaims, "Here I was, in a strange town, with a pregnant whore to support, and yet I didn't have any doubts about living. Because if the sun came up, by the time it went down, I'd have figured out a way to get fresh money" (116). Above all, the pimp is a street hustler whose knowledge of illegitimate means of accessing capital allows him to exploit urban economy to the fullest. In a chapter entitled "The Player's World" in *Black Players*, Richard and Christina Milner allegorize the city as adhering to what Coleman calls a "pimp economy":

> Sociologists and pimp philosophers agree: it's like a gigantic game in which individual players may enter, leave, or change sides, but the game goes on, the structure persists, the pattern remains, and the cash flows back and forth as a symbol of the exchanges which are constantly taking place. Money flows from lawbreaker to law enforcer, from illegitimate business to legitimate business and back again. Each has its place and its function in the city's ecosystem; each plays its part in the overall pattern of interrelationships. It is farcical to pretend that only the "legitimate" recipients of money constitute the economy of a city. (6)

According to the Milners, the pimp, then, is a kind of urban philosopher, "able to move within a social milieu yet can see above and beyond it" (7); in short, pimps epitomize the ethics of the city.

As Goines and Slim reveal, the pimp expresses his urban knowledge through the use of a highly stylized speech and slang. Much like the hard-boiled utilization of dysphemisms and slang, the pimp's vocabulary works to represent a particularly urban cool that is both a performance and an act of belonging within the pimp community. While Whoreson was literally born in the streets, Slim begins his story as a young boy, and his initial attraction to pimping is represented as a means of escaping "small town" mentality: in his first encounter with a pimp, he says, "he was spouting clichés but to a small town boy he came off witty as hell" (35). Slim reveals that pimping is based on masculinized language games and homosocial education; indeed, as Slim points out, the first seduction is between the male urban neophyte and the pimp. This seduction is further extended by pimp appropriation in popular culture since Slim's novel has been known to inspire not only future pimps but also gangsta rappers and other black writers of urban fiction (mostly all male).[9] Acquiring language is the primary means of asserting and performing power; as Jessie tells Whoreson, "You got to learn how to sell conversation, baby" (40). As Eithne Quinn states, "The mythic pimp . . . is able to convert subcultural capital into economic capital. A feed-back loop emerges: the pimp logic is *in order to get something you need to look like you've already got something*" (125). Pimping, then, begins as a linguistic performance that relies on signifying street experience that one does not yet have. In more ways than one, Slim's autobiography and Goines's novel enact a kind of "spieling" between author and reader that becomes a commodity spectacle. In an effort to "educate" its readers, Holloway House decided to publish a glossary as a reading companion to the novel.[10] Within this urban dictionary, Slim translates both familiar/common words in the context of the streets and "new" words.[11] These stylized forms of urban speech articulate the trickery and mastery of language that the pimp both embodies and performs. Moreover, the dictionary allows readers from the "square" world to mimic the language of the pimp and learn a new ghetto lexicon in the place of actual experience.

Mastering language in the ghetto is not only a means to power but also an act of racialization. In Coleman's words, "The pimp is the boss because he masters the art of black representation" (72). Indeed, scholars have already linked the pimp to the trickster figure, which links the performativity of the pimp as linguistic play. Utilizing a particularly ghetto form of wit and guile, the language a pimp uses is constantly signifying his extreme urbanness, hipness, and most importantly, "blackness." In a discussion on the shared foundations of popularized black urban icons, the pimp and the gangsta rapper, Quinn explains the importance of signifying as a primary link:

> The term signifying . . . means encoded and highly rhetorical black vernacular speech: in short, clever word-play. Geneva Smitherman summarizes the characteristic features of signifying: exaggerated language (unusual words); mimicry; proverbial statement and aphoristic phrasing; punning and plays on words; spontaneity and improvisation; image-making and metaphor; braggadocio; indirection (circumlocution and suggestiveness); and total semantics. Signifying operates in black urban language use and, as one of its dominant contemporary cultural manifestations, in rap music. (120)

In sum, Quinn characterizes the pimp as one who "wreaks havoc on the signified"; in utilizing a strategic essentialism that privileges ghetto subjectivity, the pimp paradoxically problematizes blackness as a knowable signifier through performance and parody. Within Slim's narrative, pimps often exchange slang words for common words and engage in signifying speech acts so that an outsider (police, in particular) cannot comprehend the conversation. In Goines's novel, alternative speech acts are also exposed as survivalist methods of bypassing constant surveillance. While in prison, Whoreson describes the way inmates create new ways of communication that remain undetectable: "We had to remain silent at all times during this outing, but the men and young boys quickly learned how to talk without their lips moving" (181).

Moreover, pimp signification reveals that language and identity are inextricably linked: "In black vernacular, signifying is a sign that words cannot be trusted, that even the most literal utterance allows room for interpretation, that language is both carnival and minefield" (Leland, 172). [12] Through the dynamics between language and knowledge, we can see how the trickster speech acts of Slim and Whoreson become a metaphor for racial epistemology through a pimp poetics: As Slim says, "You gotta always be a puzzle, a mystery to them. . . . Tell them something new and confusing every day" (197). The linguistic play that highlights the invisibility or hypervisibility of the pimp brings about the problems of essentialism and racial authenticity in deconstructing the process of racialization. The pimp's utilization of performative speech acts symbolize the way language is a powerful urban commodity and a way to expose authenticity as farce; as Whoreson confesses early on, "artifice became my bible" (29). If the economy of power in noir relies on racial metaphors and racially signified urban experiences, we can see how the pimp figure is unveiled as a kind of postmodern noir protagonist.

The pimp's performance, however, does not happen without consequence. In order to "become" the pimp, these narratives expose a sacrifice of identity that can be seen through a refusal of self; Slim calls the emotional void that a pimp must inhabit the "icy front," while Whoreson calls his performances the product of "trickology." In essence, pimp performativity must, in a sense, murder the self in order to assert an identity based on fantasies and fetishizations of blackness. Both Whoreson and Slim reveal how much power they possess through mere performance; in this way, *Pimp* and *Whoreson* offer up a new noir paradigm that shows the artificiality of the relationship between epistemology and urban power. In the ghettoes of Goines and Slim, real knowledge is not power; performing knowledge is power. Like the city itself, the pimp as trope and type is interpreted by appearance more than substance. As Quinn argues, "The dandified spectacle foregrounds the importance of impression management: naming . . . reputation . . . and recognition. When the Milners describe the subcultural pimp as an 'aristocrat' who is admired and recognized, they point to the acute purchase placed on reputation, appearance, and leisure" (122). [13]

If, as Sweet says in *Pimp*, "the pimp is really a whore who has reversed the game on whores," we can see the way in which pimping is fundamentally based on power reversals of male and female, self and other (275). Moreover, the pimp figure is uncovered as one who accesses power because of his ability to perform both sides of the self and other binary in multiple modes:

black/white, male/female, top/bottom, and master/slave. In the context of noir, the exploitation of playing both sides of the binary reflects the way in which urban epistemology is fundamentally based on a pimp's shape-shifting ability. Moreover, the ultimate pimping tool of manipulation is an ability to invent and narrativize a particularly black urban psychology that is enacted by the pimp as a study and practice of street power. The pimp as urban psychologist adds yet another dimension to the noir aesthetic; part of the allure and power of the pimp's unknowable yet highly commodified identity is derived from an appropriation of those same characteristics of the city.

To say that these novels offer up their own versions of the "urban real" is a gross understatement; the worlds of Slim and Goines so often mirror the grotesque and fantastic quality of Chester Himes's Harlem that they, too, read more like allegories of race and the city. The real affect of the narrative warrants another term that speaks to the fine line between real and surreal in these works; indeed, "hyperreal" seems to be the word that best describes the way the "real" worlds of Goines and Slim almost teeter over the edge. For most of the novel, Whoreson claims to love the Detroit slum he comes from, but while in jail, he has an epiphany about his relationship to the ghetto he calls home: "As I now see it, it is not the eccentricity of a single individual but the sickness of the times themselves, the neurosis of our generation. Not because we are worthless individuals, either, rather because we are the products of the slums. Faced with poverty on one side, ignorance on the other, we exploit those who are nearest to us" (187). This reflects the way Slim, too, frequently describes the city as a destructive and decaying force that is particularly reminiscent of early noir: "They didn't know I had started to rot from street poisoning" (*Pimp*, 41). Resonating with the noir protagonist's relationship to the city à la Hammett and Personville/Poisonville,[14] turning native to the primitive culture of "the city" or "the streets" is a repeated theme in Slim's narrative: "My mental 'eyes' had been stabbed blind by the street" (42). Man versus the city is a universal theme that noir made immortal through stylization; but, while the white male noir protagonist is often characterized as either the last man standing or one who experiences a slow death throughout the narrative, the pimp figure is one whose triumph exists in the moment just before facing an inevitable doom. As Paul Schrader comments on the nature of environment in noir, "There is nothing the protagonist can do; the city will outlast and negate even his best efforts" (57). The narratives of Slim and Goines give this pessimistic description of the noir universe new meaning.

As the novels of Goines and Slim reveal, the pimp is a necessary revision of the hard-boiled protagonist in the context of the racialized ghetto; trumping the mean streets of early noir, the "urban real" of the ghetto is brutal to the point of disbelief, and the narrative is framed by the exceptional survival of Slim and Goines's Whoreson as figures who miraculously lived to tell their tales. The subtext of this aspect of the noir narrative, of course, is laden with the clichéd myth that the city's underworld is a dangerous and violent place where you would be lucky to come out alive. Both Slim and Whoreson experience near death several times, and Slim's name, "Iceberg," comes from his "cool" behavior during a shooting incident where a bullet grazes his hat and he does not so much as flinch. While audacious bravery and coolness brand the pimp as a king of the streets, both confess that they are completely out of their element in the square world. In a voyeuristic reversal, Slim's epilogue reveals the ex-pimp's attempt at assimilation: "This square world is a strange place for me. For the last five years I have tried hard, so hard, to solve its riddles, to fit in" (311). For Whoreson, too, the square suburbs were another world: "No broken-down houses staring you in the face. Everything neat and clean, the streets unlettered with tricks accosting every woman that walked past" (259). While this dynamic is not fully developed in the narrative itself, it is a significant part of the reception and framing of the novels. Slim and Goines's characterization of the square world as an alien space has various implications for epistemological understanding of urban and race politics in American culture. In these works, the square world, not the underworld, is described as the unreal. Positioning themselves as aliens, Slim and Goines ensure that the black ghetto would be consistently characterized as the "urban real" in future popular discourse. [15]

If the noir narrative exploits the unknowable character of the city and the reader's voyeuristic impulse in engaging in the danger of city life, these works push this relationship to the extreme. As Mark McCord writes, "No one had ever read anything like it before. There was a growing audience that couldn't relate to books about the civil rights movement or slavery; they wanted to read stories about life in the ghetto as only one of their own could tell." McCord implies that most of the initial readers of *Pimp* were blacks living in the hood, and several scholars have been careful to state that Goines was a best-selling black author among blacks. However, it is not entirely clear as to how these novels were perceived by audiences outside the black ghetto, for whom the glossary of urban slang in *Pimp* was partly intended. According to editors of Holloway House, *Pimp* was the first "black experience" novel that paved the way for writers like Donald Goines, Odie Hawkins, and Joe Nazel to record their experiences of the harsh, gritty life on the streets. [16] Even so, these works are typically dismissed, even though the black pulp aesthetic they collectively produced made a strong impression on black urban writers and the future lyricists of the booming industry of gangsta rap and global hip-hop culture, which has received much more critical and scholarly attention. [17]

As Greg Goode points out, the influence of Iceberg Slim and Donald Goines's literature on black urban culture has been considerable. In his lifetime, Robert Beck sold over six million books, while Donald Goines sold over five million; together, they created the genre of the "black experience" novels. Their stories were the first of its kind, and their protagonists gave rise to the validity and importance of narrativizing the black urban experience and the harsh reality of ghetto life. While one of the pitfalls of racialized fiction is that it tends to be relegated to the genre of autobiography as a means of literary condescension and race essentialism, critics and scholars seem overly eager to brand these novels as autobiographical experiences rather than what they are: iconic ghetto manifestoes. The work of Goines and Slim depicts alternate representations of urban power dynamics, creating two worlds at war: the square world and the players' world. While the marketing of these novels has been based on their so-called realistic depiction of the ghetto, to read their works as such is somewhat reductive. Utilizing the noir aesthetic to stylistically depict the confrontations between mainstream and alternative urban cultures, Goines and Slim reclaimed pulp fiction as a subversive means to increase the cultural capital of the ghetto both literally and figuratively, without subscribing to the laws of the square world. The antihero of this world that represents the rejection of the square world and an apotheosis of ghetto power, of course, is the pimp figure. As Coleman explains, "The magic trick of pimping is to make something from nothing. He is a student of power, a classic trickster. The pimp sees an impossible situation, then finds a way to maximize it" (72).

Like Liam Kennedy's summary of *Sweet Sweetback's Baadasssss Song* (directed by Melvin Van Peebles, 1971), Slim and Goines offer up the "pimp-hero as the product of an oppressed yet self-validating ghetto community" (93). While scholars rightly problematize the proliferation of "negative" images of black male identity in popular culture, it is a significant gesture to understand how the pimp figure offers up more than gross misogyny and capitalism. Isaac Julien articulates the importance of exploring the "transgressive" as a site of possibility: "The project of producing positive images is an impossible one. Though it may have the best intentions of redressing imbalances in the field of representation, it is bound to fail as it will never be able to address questions of ambivalence or transgression" (261). In line with Julien's argument, my critical examination of the cultural potency of the pimp figure is a means of exploring the possibilities and the meaning produced by the fantasy and fetishization of black urban masculinity in popular culture.

Scholars such as Coleman, White, and Quinn have argued that the pimp fetish reflects a cultural fantasy that reveals a national obsession with the black outlaw figure. As such, we can see a trajectory of this obsession by noting that the pimp figure fathered the persona of the gangsta rapper and its many offspring in urban culture that uses an overtly sexual and masculinist black narrative as a means to power. Within this paradigm, of course, lies a double bind; on one hand, it seems that the historical criminalization of black identity is reclaimed by pimp poetics as a backlash against traditional trajectories of upward mobility. On the other hand, Coleman exposes the mimicry of white-black power relations in the heroism of the pimp/criminal:

> In the Americas, due to the devilry of slave culture, he was made manifest. The black pimp produces such glee in his audience precisely because he cross-wires the machine. For him to be the master is a local revolution unto itself; for him to trade in a localized zone of human labor is the twist of the screw to the point of giddiness. The irony is that if he does his job well, in order to become a free agent, he must reproduce a peculiarly limited mode of bondage. For, of course, the commodity of pimping is sex. It is a commodity rendered *lifestyle* by the pimp, formatted across much the same blueprint as the plantation system. One might say pimps are simply repeating a scene of mastery dear to the history of Western culture. Fast-food slavery for a commodities market. (73)

While Coleman outlines how the slave economy produced the American pimp, she also recognizes the possibilities for recuperating the pimp as a metaphor for race and identity politics. The pimp is a powerful yet contradictory combination of primitivism and modernity; utilizing primitivist behavior in his sexual and criminal politics while exaggerating a wealthy "aristocratic" front, the black pimp seems to be a parody of the city itself.

Much like the white noir hero, who is celebrated in spite of his criminality and misogyny, the pimp figure is the apotheosis of ghetto culture and capital. Pimp poetics and politics is hard-boiled cynicism at its peak, highlighting and reenacting a criminal identity, even with the knowledge that the inevitable will come: incarceration (social death) or death. The courage behind the short-lived glory of an outlaw becomes a metaphorical bravery for living in an endlessly cynical world on one's own terms. As such, the pimp persona goes over the top; he becomes "the dandified spectacle" of the ghetto, an absurd joke on capitalism with a grotesque display of wealth walking on the poorest streets of the city.[18] Performing the pimp means to broadcast a kind of urban cool that is affiliated with a "hard" outlaw mentality—one that is recognizable by ways of walking, talking, dressing, and acting. The allure of the pimp figure, as Quinn argues, is based on the way in which it models an entrepreneurial pursuit that exists outside normative discourses of power: "The pimp constitutes an icon of upward mobility for black working-class males, spectacularly refusing, through their heightened style politics, the subservient type-casting that has historically been imposed by the dominant social order" (124). But another dimension of the lasting power behind the figure of the pimp is his elusiveness; as Coleman argues, through endless repetition, mimicry, and appropriation, "the pimp perfects that peculiarly black American skill to hide in plain sight. One's life becomes quite literary on account of that trait. You are a purloined letter, the missing phallus and missing link, activating the troubleness of a sign" (80). The pimp identity utilizes an aesthetic of omission and a racial allegory of identity where the performance masks any genuine attempt at real representation. In other words, the pimp reveals that identity, for blacks, is always inextricably linked to performance. The appropriation of the pimp in popular culture, then, also reveals that the act of racial mimicry, in this case, is a kind of postmodern simulacrum that produces multiple copies that refer to an original source that does not exist. The figure of the pimp is, as Coleman seems to suggest, a kind of racialized hero because of his ability to create moments of transformation in which he embodies a performance of blackness so thoroughly that "he is a parody of propriety, a levered mechanism, an electronic Negro. The essential overvaluation of the object, the black fetish, is his trump card" (79).[19]

In proposing a specific kind of outlaw masculinity that reminds us of noirish tendencies, Goines and Slim's versions of the "urban real" in noir revealed the parody and performance of racial epistemology in urban culture. The "urban real" for Goines and Slim is a point of departure and a political stance: while white noir writers appropriated racialized forms of masculinity in order to lay claim to urban space, black noir writers like Goines and Slim questioned the very notion of "blackness" in relation to the urban. In his chapter "What Is This 'Black' in Black Popular Culture?" Stuart Hall reminds us,

> Popular culture, commodified and stereotyped as it often is, is not at all, as we sometimes think of it, the arena where we find who we really are, the truth of our experience. It is an arena that is *profoundly* mythic. It is theater of popular desires, a theater of popular fantasies. It is where we discover and play with the identifications of ourselves, where we are imagined, where we are represented, not only to the audiences out there who do not get the message, but to ourselves for the first time. (32)

While Goines and Slim offer up different versions of noir narratives that reveal the stakes of racial epistemology in relation to urban identity, they also expose the "profoundly mythic" nature of noir itself; whereas white noir works have been able to move beyond the category of pulp and enjoy critical acclaim as well as scholarly attention, Goines and Slim have reclaimed the category of pulp as a response to the historical silencing, dismissal, and suppression of black urban realities.

Various neo-noir revivals throughout the twentieth and twenty-first centuries have proven that the genre's seduction is not, and might never be, complete. Until noir is able to fully expunge its racial anxieties, or at the very least directly address them, the pleasure and the pain of noir will be forever entangled within a never-ending cycle that represses the race politics that lie within the buried heart of the genre. The dynamic in noir that symbolizes a pimp poetics is further articulated by Coleman, in her assertion that "for the history of black people in America to have had profound impact yet to remain profoundly invisible fits again into a pimp economy. It is an economy of pleasure based on an economy of pain" (77). While part of the pleasure of the noir text is based on the utilization of racial metaphors that never fully rise to the surface, black pulp writers like Goines and Slim revise the noir tradition to effectively alter the nature of that pleasure by repossessing the "dark cities" of noir as theirs to define.

NOTES

1. In his canon of contemporary crime fiction that he calls "neon noir," Woody Haut mentions the noirish achievements of black urban writers like Donald Goines, Iceberg Slim, Vernon Smith, and Clarence Cooper Jr.: "Though they stand slightly outside the scope of this study, each writes about the life—that is, the world of crime, including hustling, pimping, dope dealing and surviving on the streets of urban America" (212).

2. In addition to the many texts and films that allude to the "dark city," critical noir surveys similarly appropriate this romanticization of racial ideology and the noir city but do not significantly deal with the racial politics of noir. Some of these critical works include Eddie Muller's *Dark City* (1998), John Naremore's *More Than Night* (1998), and Nicholas Christopher's *Somewhere in the Night* (1997).

3. On the back cover of the 2007 edition of *Whoreson* is an excerpt of Michael Covino's review in the *Village Voice*: "All those [other black] writers, no matter how well they dealt with black experience, appealed largely to an educated, middle-class, largely white readership. They brought news of one place to the residents of another. Goines's novels, on the other hand, are written from ground zero. They are almost unbearable. It is not the educated voice of a writer who has, so to speak, risen above his background. It is the voice of the ghetto itself."

4. Haut briefly mentions Iceberg Slim and Donald Goines, but like most critics, he mostly focuses on analyzing the work of Chester Himes as a primary example of African American noir. His definitions, however, are useful in establishing links between what he calls "neon noir" (contemporary crime fiction) and black noir.

5. Here, Thompson is referring specifically to the work of Dashiell Hammett, but I contend that this statement is true of most hard-boiled fiction.

6. Goines's *Whoreson* is considered to be a homage to Slim's *Trick Baby* (1967).

7. In the last decade or so, pimping has garnered attention from critics and popular culture. The NPR show *This American Life* featured a segment called "Pimp Anthropology" on 16 April 1999, featuring a short discussion on Iceberg Slim. See also *Pimpology: The 48 Laws of the Game* (Pimpin' Ken and Karen Hunter 2007), *The Pimp's Bible: The Sweet Science of Sin* (Alfred Bilbo Gholson 2001), *Gentlemen of Leisure: A Year in the Life of a Pimp* (Susan T. Hall and Bob Adelman 2006), and *Pimp* (directed by Robert Cavanah, 2010).

8. In order to escape police surveillance and risk being taken back to jail, Slim moves from city to city and hustles on the streets of Chicago, Cleveland, and Detroit.

9. Miles White (2011) links hardcore rap music to pimp narratives through their employment of the vernacular of the urban street and reveals that this urban vernacular has tremendous emotive power because of its apparent authenticity and legitimacy. White also reveals that the language of pimp narratives is no longer exclusive to the culture of pimps, hustlers, ex-convicts, and street poets who have helped to perpetuate them.

10. According to Mark McCord, Slim's book of slang was a constant reference source in black literature.

11. An example of a common word that acquires a new meaning in Slim's glossary is "bite: price" (313). Examples of "new" words used in pimp culture are "flat-backer: a whore who gets paid for straight sexual intercourse" and "slum hustler: a phony jewelry salesman" (315–16).

12. John Leland cites definitions from the novelist John Edgar Wideman and refers to the seminal work of Henry Louis Gates Jr., *The Signifying Monkey: A Theory of Afro-American Literary Criticism* (1988).

13. Social anthropologists Richard and Christina Milner published a study of urban pimp culture in 1972 entitled *Black Players: The Secret World of Black Pimps*. They interviewed many of the top pimps in the Bay Area, and their book includes an interview with Iceberg Slim, whom they refer to as a legendary pimp because of his recognition among the pimp community.

14. In *Red Harvest* (1929), Hammett's Continental Op attributes his "blood-simple" ways to assimilating to the city: "It's this damned town. Poisonville is right. It's poisoned me" (104).

15. The dynamic of suburban (artificial culture) versus urban (real culture) follows a similar logic of Raymond Williams's notions of country versus city and is a repeated theme that gets played out in popular culture. The term "urban real" is a concept I argue is crucial to the noir aesthetic. I theorize this concept in depth throughout my dissertation "Hearts of Darkness: Race and Urban Epistemology in American Noir" (PhD diss., University of California, Santa Cruz, 2012).

16. Holloway House Publishing put out an advertisement for black writers; the first of the "black experience" writers would be Robert Beck, but Donald Goines would soon follow in his footsteps as well as other writers that would later be labeled as generic contemporaries.

17. Among the many rappers that are indebted to Slim's legacy are Ice-T, who credited Iceberg Slim for his stage name; Jay-Z, who sometimes refers to himself as Iceberg Slim; and Dave Chappelle, who jokingly refers to himself as Iceberg Slim (and refers to his audience as his whores).

18. In a television interview, Iceberg Slim mentioned that in his day, pimps would carry exotic animals like cheetahs, bears, and tigers as pets on leashes.

19. Coleman interestingly uses Marlene Dietrich as an example of an overvaluation of the object that reveals the emergence of yet another link between noir and pimp culture since Dietrich is known as an iconic femme fatale who was a precursor to the femme fatales of noir.

WORKS CITED

Abbott, Megan E. *The Street Was Mine: White Masculinity in Hardboiled Fiction and Film Noir*. New York: Palgrave Macmillan, 2002.

Avila, Eric. *Popular Culture in the Age of White Flight: Fear and Fantasy in Suburban Los Angeles*. Berkeley: University of California Press, 2004.

Chandler, Raymond. *The Simple Art of Murder*. New York: Vintage, 1988.

Christopher, Nicholas. *Somewhere in the Night: Film Noir and the American City*. New York: Free Press, 1997.

Coleman, Beth. "Pimp Notes on Autonomy." In *Everything but the Burden: What White People Are Taking from Black Culture*, edited by Greg Tate, 68–80. New York: Broadway Books, 2003.

Dent, Gina, ed. *Black Popular Culture*. Seattle: Bay Press, 1992.

Diawara, Manthia. "Noir by Noirs: Toward a New Realism in Black Cinema." In *Shades of Noir*, edited by Joan Copjec, 261–78. New York: Verso, 1993.

Flory, Dan. *Philosophy, Black Film, Film Noir*. University Park: Pennsylvania State University Press, 2008.

Gates, Henry Louis, Jr. *The Signifying Monkey: A Theory of Afro-American Literary Criticism*. New York: Oxford University Press, 1988.

Gholson, Alfred Bilbo. *The Pimp's Bible: The Sweet Science of Sin*. 2nd ed. Chicago: Research Associates School Times Publications, 2001.

Goines, Donald. *Dopefiend: The Story of a Black Junkie*. Los Angeles: Holloway House, 1971.

———. *Whoreson*. Los Angeles: Holloway House, 1972.

Goode, Greg. "From Dopefiend to Kenyatta's Last Hit: The Angry Black Crime Novels of Donald Goines." *MELUS* 11, no. 3 (Autumn 1984): 41–48.

Hall, Stuart. "What Is This 'Black' in Black Popular Culture?" In *Black Popular Culture*, edited by Gina Dent, 21–33. Seattle: Bay Press, 1992.

Hall, Susan T., and Bob Adelman. *Gentlemen of Leisure: A Year in the Life of a Pimp*. New York: PowerHouse Books, 2006.

Hammett, Dashiell. *Red Harvest*. New York: Knopf, 1929.

Haut, Woody. *Neon Noir: Contemporary American Crime Fiction*. London: Serpent's Tail, 1999.

Julien, Isaac. "Black Is, Black Ain't: Notes on De-essentializing Black Identities." In *Black Popular Culture*, edited by Gina Dent, 255–63. Seattle: Bay Press, 1992.

Kennedy, Liam. *Race and Urban Space in Contemporary American Culture*. Edinburgh: Edinburgh University Press, 2000.

Leland, John. *Hip: The History*. New York: HarperCollins, 2004.

Lott, Eric. "The Whiteness of Film Noir." *American Literary History* 9, no. 3 (1997): 542–56.

McCann, Sean. *Gumshoe America: Hard-Boiled Crime Fiction and the Rise and Fall of New Deal Liberalism*. Durham, NC: Duke University Press, 2000.

McCord, Mark. "The Next Hustle." *Wax Poetics*, no. 38 (December 2009). http://hiphopandpolitics.wordpress.com/.

Milner, Richard, and Christina Milner. *Black Players: The Secret World of Black Pimps*. Boston: Little, Brown, 1972.

Muller, Eddie. Dark City: *The Lost World of Film Noir*. New York: St. Martin's Griffin, 1998.

Naremore, James. *More Than Night: Film Noir in Its Contexts*. 1998. Berkeley: University of California Press, 2008.

Oliver, Kelly, and Benigno Trigo. *Noir Anxiety*. Minneapolis: University of Minnesota Press, 2003.

Phillips, Gary. "The Cool, the Square and the Tough: The Archetypes of Black Male Characters in Mystery and Crime Novels." *Black Scholar* 28, no. 1 (Spring 1998): 27–32.

Pimp. Directed by Robert Cavanah. Coppola Productions et al., 2010.

Pimpin' Ken and Karen Hunter. *Pimpology: The 48 Laws of the Game*. New York: Simon Spotlight Entertainment, 2007.

Quinn, Eithne. "'Who's the Mack?': The Performativity and Politics of the Pimp Figure in Gangsta Rap." *Living in America: Recent and Contemporary Perspectives*, special issue of *Journal of American Studies* 34, no. 1 (April 2000): 115–36.

Rabinowitz, Paula. *Black and White and Noir: America's Pulp Modernism*. New York: Columbia University Press, 2002.

Schrader, Paul. "Notes on Film Noir." 1972. In *Film Noir Reader*, edited by Alain Silver and James Ursini, 53–64. New York: Limelight Editions, 1996.

Slim, Iceberg (Robert Beck). *The Naked Soul of Iceberg Slim*. Los Angeles: Holloway House, 1986.

———. *Pimp: The Story of My Life*. Los Angeles: Holloway House, 1969.

Soitos, Stephen F. *The Blues Detective: A Study of African American Detective Fiction*. Amherst: University of Massachusetts Press, 1996.

Tate, Greg, ed. *Everything but the Burden: What White People Are Taking from Black Culture*. New York: Broadway Books, 2003.

Thompson, Jon. *Fiction, Crime, and Empire: Clues to Modernity and Postmodernism*. Urbana: University of Illinois Press, 1993.

van Sickle, Milton. "Introduction." In *The Naked Soul of Iceberg Slim*, by Iceberg Slim. Los Angeles: Holloway House, 1986.

White, Miles. *From Jim Crow to Jay-Z: Race, Rap, and the Performance of Masculinity*. Urbana: University of Illinois, 2011.

(Re)Writing the "Bad Nigger" Hero in Robert Beck's *Pimp*

Dennis L. Winston

Pimp: The Story of My Life (1967) is Robert Beck's semiautobiographical novel loosely based on his experiences as Iceberg Slim, a pimp who often struggled and sometimes thrived in Chicago's violent underworld. *Pimp* reflects Beck's life in the Chicago slums after the Great Depression. Throughout the novel, Beck describes himself and other poor black people in his community as "street niggers and strugglers" living in a criminal society. *Pimp* draws on the gritty realism of life for men who are constantly negotiating the murky politics of what Beck refers to as "the life" on the streets of Chicago and in the city's dangerous underworld. Beck weaves a relatively autobiographical tale that dramatizes the cultural performances in and around Chicago's South Side neighborhoods. Ultimately, the triumphant highs and dramatic lows, which highlight the psychological and cultural chaos for black men looking for wealth in the ghetto, structure the novel. "The streets," particularly the "bad nigger's" improvised negotiations of South Side Chicago, becomes the driving metaphor and structural design of *Pimp*. Robert Beck's birth name is Robert Lee Maupin, and he was given the nickname "Iceberg Slim" several years into his tenure as a pimp. Beck's well-known pimp moniker is mythologized in his first novel. It is said that he obtained the nickname by sitting unmoved at a bar finishing his drink while a violent shootout raged about. This "Wild West bar fight" cliché is further dramatized when Beck recalls how his hat was struck from his head by one of the bar brawler's bullets. Indeed, a more likely explanation for the name "Iceberg Slim" is its reference to Beck's ice-cold ruthlessness as a pimp and his slender physique. Because *Pimp* has the distinction of being a "semiautobiographical novel," I separate my reading of Beck as a writer from his illustration of himself as Iceberg Slim.

While contemporary readings of the term "the life" frequently refer to gay culture, Beck is signaling the experiences of individuals negotiating a culture of criminality. "(Re)Writing the 'Bad Nigger' Hero in Robert Beck's *Pimp*" offers a reassessment of Beck's illustrations of violent criminals in this cult classic, street lit novel. While much of the scholarship surrounding Beck's first novel focuses on elements of misogyny, homophobia, and nihilism in the life and actions of his black male characters, particularly his protagonist Iceberg Slim, this chapter affirms these examples of nihilistic behavior as politically viable and integral to the pursuit of self-empowerment among black men struggling in poor urban communities across the United States. By defining violent and criminal practices as not only tragic but also heroic, particularly when examined through the lens of poverty, "street culture," and criminal life, I show how *Pimp* provides a perspective on racial and class politics that speaks to the disillusionment many young black men faced in the late 1960s and continue to confront today.

For Beck's characters, the images they see in "the streets" reflect their imperfect, human selves. Thus, I read radical acts of resistance, such as Iceberg Slim's decision to become a pimp and to pursue a life of crime in Chicago's underworld, as the "bad nigger" hero's quest for stability not only in the disjointed urban ghetto but also in a mainstream society governed by racial and class discrimination. Beck's characters exist in a politically marginalized, racially exploitative, and culturally vile environment, which thus makes success within "the streets" a radical social phenomenon and emancipatory act. That is to say, if someone is capable of achieving some semblance of the American Dream, particularly in the spaces where dreams are routinely and systematically deferred, that individual is capable of becoming a symbol of self-determination and self-empowerment for an otherwise dispirited black community.

At the center of this chapter is my reading of the literary and cultural trope of the "bad nigger" that emphasizes the relationship between black masculinity and the threat or actuality of death. Borrowing from Abdul JanMohamed's theory of "death-bound-subjectivity," I reveal how black male characters in *Pimp* either pursue death or function as "agents of death" as a radical challenge to the racial and class system that marginalizes them and threatens to destroy them. Furthermore, I show how Beck ties his black male characters' sense of "authenticity" to their embrace of "social" or actual death. Thus, the death-bound-subject, framed by "street politics" and "authentic" blackness, becomes a site of potential "revolution" and the constitution of new racial and class identities.

Beck's novel reveals an important characteristic of the "bad nigger" hero: the threat or actuality of death, or what JanMohamed calls "death-bound-subjectivity," impacts decision making, particularly among young and poor urban black men. In his book *The Death-Bound-Subject: Richard Wright's Archaeology of Death* (2005), JanMohamed focuses his attention on the political role of death as well as the threat of death in the lives of characters living in the Jim Crow South illustrated in works by Richard Wright. With the help of Orlando Patterson's theory of "social death" outlined in his book *Slavery and Social Death* (1982), along with Wright's novels and autobiography, JanMohamed defines the death-bound-subject as a black person living in the Jim Crow era who is formed, from infancy on, "by the imminent and ubiquitous threat of death" (2). His reading of death in Wright's work examines the political value of life and death for blacks relegated to the margins of Jim Crow society. JanMohamed historicizes "social death" in terms of Jim Crow society's reliance on the threat, and JanMohamed offers a reframing of Patterson's antebellum concept of "social death," which is to say that the slave is socially dead—a purgatorial figure deprived of community and honor. See Patterson's *Slavery and Social Death* (1982) for more elaboration. The actuality of death through lynching and other forms of terror ensured African Americans' position as second-class citizens, and maintained their powerless existence.

While JanMohamed's definition of the death-bound-subject focuses on the threat of death imposed by white authoritarianism during the Jim Crow era, my reading of *Pimp* offers an expansion of the death-bound-subject's theoretical frame. Beck's illustration of the "bad nigger" is that of a tragic hero who, because of his decision to "make it" on the streets of Chicago, carries with him the danger of the loss of life. Thus, his decision to join the underworld is a profound act of rebellion insofar as it enacts a heroic challenge to the racial and social-class systems that marginalize him and threaten to destroy him. Iceberg Slim's authenticity in both the black community and the further marginalized underworld is integral in demystifying mainstream black and white masculine identity as citizen, hero, and leader. In other words, Iceberg Slim's authenticity is tied to his embrace of "social death." Furthermore, Beck does not only illustrate the threat of death in the life of a "bad nigger" imposed by white people in power. He also discusses the threat of death imposed upon poor black people by other black people in similar socioeconomic circumstances, thereby reproducing patriarchal acts rooted in white supremacy and authoritarianism. Indeed, Beck's unique take on death-bound-subjectivity expands and multiplies JanMohamed's discourse on the "circuits of death."

Much like Wright's works, *Pimp* offers a number of examples of black people's death-bound-subjectivity rooted in the Jim Crow South. Partly through a series of deliberate decisions, but partly through sharp intuitive choices, Beck develops a concept of the "bad nigger" as a death-bound-subject whose psycho-political construct is penetrated by an unpredictable threat imposed by politically and socially powerful whites. JanMohamed's argument that death-bound-subjectivity is rooted in the Jim Crow South is most evident in Beck's illustration of the Wisconsin Green Bay reformatory, a facility that, while situated in the Midwest, operates much like the Old South. In fact, Beck suggests that the threat of death imposed by whites in the Jim Crow South is foundational to the U.S. justice system at large. For instance, at his sentencing for pandering—the first of five convictions over a twenty-year period—Iceberg Slim talks about being "led to the slaughter" by Williams, his "Deep South Nigger" lawyer who appeared to be so "shook up by the stern face and voice of the white hawk-faced judge that he forgot to ask for leniency." Slim goes on: "That awful fear the white folks put into him down South was still painfully alive in him" (26). Here Beck not only ties death-bound-subjectivity to a fear of death at the hands of powerful whites but also situates the origin of this subjectivity in the same Jim Crow South Wright frequently illustrates in his work. For Beck, the history of Jim Crow society's overwhelming reliance on the threat of death to control African Americans in the Southern states constitutes Williams's fear of the white judge. The reader soon learns that Slim also relies on and manipulates that very same history in order to survive his first of many prison sentences.

Upon Iceberg Slim's arrival at the Wisconsin Green Bay reformatory, Beck metaphorically connects the facility to white supremacy and the threat of death. He begins by describing the structure as "three casket-gray cell houses [which] stood like mute mourners beneath the bleak sunless sky" (28). When ushered before the warden, a "silver-maned, profane, huge, white-bull," Iceberg Slim is told that the two results for "fucking up" is either a period in a stripped cell *buried* "twenty feet below ground" or "out that North gate in a box." Slim recalls that "the only thing [he] said before [he] eased out of there was, 'Yes Sir, Boss Man,' and [he] was grinning like a Mississippi rape suspect turned loose by the mob" (32). In this not-so-subtle allusion to lynching, Iceberg Slim's death-bound-subjectivity produced by the Wisconsin Green Bay reformatory, an institution framed by a history of white authoritarianism in the Jim Crow South, is similar in certain fundamental ways to antebellum society. Relying on Patterson's theory of "social death" among slaves, JanMohamed notes that "the slave was effectively controlled by the fact that he lived under a conditionally commuted death sentence" (5). Indeed, Beck likens Iceberg Slim's experience in prison to slavery, particularly the fundamental relationship between powerlessness and the threat of death.

Perhaps Beck's illustration of the tragic conflict between Iceberg Slim's Wisconsin Green Bay reformatory cellmate Oscar, a "rock-ribbed square" who was sentenced to a year at the reformatory for having a forbidden relationship with a young white girl, and "the dummy," a mute Alabamian prison guard with a dangerous lead-loaded cane and a deep hatred for blacks, is the most dramatic example of what JanMohamed describes as death's pervasive unpredictability in the lives of black people. On their first night in the reformatory, Iceberg Slim and Oscar are told that "the dummy" is the cruelest of all the prison guards, having killed two white cons and four blacks. They are also told that the mute prison guard lost his voice after his wife, the mother of his young daughter, frustrated by his verbal and physical abuse, committed infanticide and suicide.

In this illustration of Iceberg Slim's first prison stint, Beck uses "silence" in an extended metaphor to emphasize the unpredictable threat of death. Instead of allowing "the dummy" to speak, Beck gives him a cane with which he purposefully directs the prisoners under his guard. Beck writes that Slim's time in the reformatory was a "rough battle of wits" that centered on "staying out of sight and trouble with the dummy." He goes on to say, "[The dummy] walked on the balls of his feet and could read a con's mind. . . . He didn't pass out an instruction leaflet running down the lingo of that cane. If you misunderstood what *it* said, the dummy would crack the leaded shaft of it against your skull" (32, my emphasis). At the reformatory, the young black inmates' death-bound-subjectivity is conditioned by "the dummy's" silent threat. Even more so, the young cons must learn to listen to and understand the cane, which is more "vocal" than "the dummy." Through the process of learning the unfamiliar language of "silence," Beck's illustration of death-bound-subjectivity constitutes JanMohamed's concept of death's ability to psychologically "unbind" and "rebind." In other words, the threat of death "unbinds" or disjoins the life of the subject from his own set of beliefs and values, from his understanding of himself and the world around him. The threat of death then "rebinds" or fixes the individual "around his fear of death" (JanMohamed, 25).

The process of "unbinding" and "rebinding" conditioned by the mute guard's silent threats of death, however, went unheard, as it were, by Oscar. While Oscar was certainly "unbound" by "the dummy's" wrath, he sought to "rebind" himself to his Christian faith instead of his fear of white authority. Iceberg Slim attempts to help Oscar understand that, in order to live in the reformatory—a physical manifestation of the Jim Crow South—he must exist under and manipulate the historic fear of death at the hands of powerful whites. Slim tells Oscar, "It's driving the dummy off his rocker to see you reading that Bible. Pal, why in the Hell don't you stop reading it for your own good?" Oscar replies, "I appreciate your advice, but . . . Jesus will protect me" (33). Unable to convince his friend that only a fear of death could protect them from actual death, it is simply a matter of time before "the dummy put one over on Jesus and busted Oscar" (35).

While mopping the flag of the reformatory, a cell-house runner brings Iceberg Slim two wieners from a pal in the kitchen. Slim gives one to Oscar, who gingerly puts it in his shirt pocket, and hurriedly eats the other himself out of fear of being found with contraband food. Later, Slim recalls Oscar nibbling slowly on his wiener in a supply closet "like he was at the Last Supper" (34). Suddenly, "the dummy" appears. Before Oscar can protect himself, the prison guard cuts a slice of bloody flesh from the side of the young boy's head with his cane and leaves him to die on the flag.

Beck's graphic illustration of the "thread of flesh dangling like an awful earring near the tip of [Oscar's] ear lobe" (34) eerily foreshadows Hortense Spillers's use of the term "flesh" to define the absolute powerlessness of slaves in her article "Mama's Baby, Papa's Maybe." In her analysis of the terror endured by the captive slave who exists at the "frontiers of survival," Spillers insists on this telling distinction:

> I would make a distinction in this case between "body" and "flesh" and impose
> that distinction as the central one between captive and liberated subject-posi-
> tions. In that sense, before the "body" there is "flesh," that zero degree of
> social conceptualization that does not escape concealment under the brush of
> discourse, or the reflexes of iconography. (260)

JanMohamed makes a similar point in his discussion of Wright's works in which the critic emphasizes Spillers's metaphorical use of the terms "body" and "flesh" to define the utter abjectness of the subject-position occupied by the death-bound-subject. In an extension of Spillers's formulation, JanMo-hamed introduces the term "meat" as a way to define "the zone inhabited by the death-bound-subject . . . that between flesh and meat" (10).

While Iceberg Slim's insistence on "rebinding" to the "the dummy's" threat of death reinforces his "captive subject-position," Oscar's transforma-tion from "body" to "flesh" under the weight of the mute guard's lead cane demonstrates an ironic anti-Hegelian view of the master-slave struggle. Os-car's refusal to "take it" or live under the constant threat of death can be read as an active pursuit of death rather than the continued conditions of inhuman-ity on which the reformatory depends. The threat of white terrorism plays a pivotal role in structuring black life throughout Beck's novel, and characters are keenly aware of the power white authority has over their lives. Because their lives are constantly threatened by death and because the characters continually struggle with the racist use of violence, their lives are highly traumatic and frequently catastrophic. However, Beck's novel reveals a more dynamic observation of the "bad nigger" as a death-bound-subject, which speaks to the revolutionary, albeit problematic, nature of violence, particular-ly among poor and young black men. On the one hand, the "bad nigger" functions in the traditional role of the death-bound-subject outlined by Jan-Mohamed; that is, the "bad nigger's" death-bound-subjectivity is indeed rooted in the threat and actuality of death wielded by Jim Crow society and, specifically, white men who reinforce institutions of racial inequality. On the other hand, Beck reveals how his "bad nigger" characters actively participate in the terrorization of other poor black people, particularly black women, and act as coercive agents of white patriarchal ideals. Furthermore, Beck suggests that the "bad nigger's" embrace of social death, then, becomes a form of authenticity. That is to say, while structuralized racism through various circuits of Jim Crow terror continue to ensure a degree of disempowerment for black characters in *Pimp*, the threat of death inflicted upon black people by other poor black people opens up a more comprehensive and complex reading of the political implications embedded in nihilistic behavior among poor black men, particularly when seen through the lens of JanMohamed's "familial/communal circuits of death."

JanMohamed says "familial circuits of death" are a "direct or indirect product of Jim Crow society's deployment of death as a mode of coercion" (140). Death-bound-subjects, like all other forms of subjectivity, have a tendency to preserve their status based on the logic that they are conditioned to reproduce the relations of production that produced them in the first place. "In certain specific ways," JanMohamed says, "there is a direct connection; for instance, one can argue that in her use of violence to discipline [an adolescent Richard Wright] for fighting white boys, his mother, Ella, functions as a coercive agent of the white racist society" (140). However, JanMohamed insists that given the limited autobiographical and biographical evidence for Wright, it would be "impossible" to speculate beyond "indirect and partial" connections between familial and social Jim Crow circuits of death in the formation of Wright's own death-bound-subjectivity.

Nevertheless, JanMohamed deduces from Wright's works that the author is formed as a death-bound-subject first within the family circuit and then later within Jim Crow society's "apparatus for producing black boys." *Pimp*, however, complicates the relationship between "familial circuits of death" and Jim Crow circuits of death. Through a close reading of Iceberg Slim, I contend that although the "bad nigger" is formed as a traditional death-bound-subject, particularly within the judicial and prison systems, a re-creation of Jim Crow society, he is not produced as a traditional death-bound-subject within the family circuit, or in Iceberg Slim's case, the community circuit. (I make the distinction between "family" and "community" because Beck's "bad niggers" are aligned with the underworld community or "the streets" more so than the black family or community at large.) Instead, Iceberg Slim functions as a coercive agent of death, inflicting terror upon poor black people, particularly upon black women's "bodies," with the intent not to (re)empower white masculinity but to empower the black male subject apart from Jim Crow society.

In his explanation of Wright's relationship to familial/communal circuits and Jim Crow circuits of death, JanMohamed argues that because both circuits insist on producing Wright as a death-bound-subject, he is never in a position to seek refuge from one circuit in the domain of the other; he is doubly produced as a death-bound-subject by the synergistic action of both circuits (142). Furthermore, JanMohamed defines his theory of "familial circuits of death" as a "product of Jim Crow society's deployment of death as a mode of coercion" (140). In other words, JanMohamed's theory of "familial circuits of death" functions within the context of a black community at odds with Jim Crow society. However, *Pimp* forces the question, How do "communal circuits of death" function within a culture that is outside the mainstream black community, which is produced by Jim Crow circuits of death? That is to say, Wright is unable to seek refuge from Jim Crow society in the mainstream black community because it is produced by that very same racist power structure. Beck's "bad niggers," however, exist in the underworld, a subcommunity (or better yet, a countercommunity) that resists mainstream white values and morals, as well as the mainstream black cultures it produces. Therefore, the underworld is capable of functioning as a refuge for Iceberg Slim and other "bad niggers" wishing to re-create themselves not as traditional death-bound-subjects but under new postmodern subjectivities as agents of death.

The most vivid and yet fundamentally problematic example of the "bad nigger" as a producer of death-bound-subjectivities is perhaps found in Beck's illustration of Iceberg Slim's relationship to black women. Iceberg Slim's position as an agent of death is overwrought with vile, grotesque misogyny. Just as powerful whites living in the Jim Crow South used dramatic acts of terror such as whippings, mutilations, and lynching to ensure the powerlessness of African Americans, Beck's "bad niggers" threaten to, and often do, inflict physical harm on black women who refuse to submit to their physical, social, mental, economic, absolute power. Thus, Beck's black men ironically reenact patriarchal elements of the master-slave dialectic as a way to assert the kinds of power relationships that are nearly impossible for them in mainstream society. Furthermore, because Iceberg Slim "enjoyed" certain kinds of freedom that his "stable" of women did not, and because, in spite of this relative freedom, he *felt* as if he were disempowered, he constitutes the perfect "witness" to death-bound-subjectivity, someone who is simultaneously within and outside the experience of death-bound-subjectivity.

Iceberg Slim's first experience as an agent of death and, more specifically, as a producer of death-bound-subjectivities takes shape in the relationship between himself and Phyllis, the first prostitute who agrees to work for him. Shortly after leaving his job as a grocery store clerk in Milwaukee to "make it" as a pimp among thieves in Chicago's underworld, Iceberg Slim quickly learns the rules to "pimping." Slim finds a valuable mentor in a seasoned "boss pimp" named Sweet Jones. In an exchange likely similar to the conversations between slave owners frustrated with the insurrection of "bad nigger" slaves, Jones and Slim hash out a plan to "break [his] whore" Phyllis (Beck,

166). In effect, Jones tells Iceberg Slim the most important thing a pimp must do is to create death-bound-subjects out of the women he controls. According to Jones, the only pimps with respect are the ones who can administer enough brutal force upon a woman's "flesh" that she submits to him her "body": "You gotta have strict rules for a whore. She's gotta respect you to hump her heart out in the streets. . . . Put your foot in her ass hard. If that don't work, take a wire coat hanger and twist it into a whip" (166).

Today, the "business of pimping" continues to thrive in the U.S. underworld. Many instances of prostitution can be found in American gangs. Some of the tactics used to punish women illustrated in *Pimp* have generated colloquial terms such as "pimp stick" or "pimp cane," which refers to a wirehanger whip similar to the one used to beat Phyllis. Another tactic now referred to as "trunk" or "trunking" means locking a "difficult" prostitute in a small space. In chapter 15 of *Pimp*, Sweet Jones "trunks" two young women in a small hallway bathroom. For more on "pimping," see Mickey Royal's *Pimp Game: Instructional Guide* (1998).

Before he administers Jones's cruel advice, Slim begins the process of "unbinding," saying to Phyllis, "Bitch, I already passed the death sentence on you. It's good you had your last meal. I'm gonna send your dead ass to your daughter, Gay. Take off that gown and lie on your belly, bitch" (168). After having whipped Phyllis to the point that the white bed sheets "looked like a red zebra had lain down and his stripes faded on it," she "rebinds" to a fear of death and says to Iceberg Slim, "I don't need any more whipping. I give, Daddy. You're the boss. I was a dumb bitch. It looks like you got a whore now" (170). Ironically touched by Phyllis's words, or perhaps by his metamorphosis from a death-bound-subject to an agent of death, Iceberg Slim says, "I felt a tear roll down my cheeks. Maybe I was crying in joy that I broke her spirit" (170–71). Unlike JanMohamed's theory of "communal circuits of death," which suggests that black people function as coercive agents of death in order to reproduce subjectivities already produced under Jim Crow society, Iceberg Slim becomes a coercive agent of death to produce new subjectivities: an individual who is "unbound" by the threat of death and who then "rebinds," not to white supremacy but to a powerful black masculinity. Although the "bad nigger" produces a death-bound-subject that mimics American slavery and Jim Crow society's creation of disempowered black people, it is in affirmation of black male subjectivity, a kind of "underworld" subjectivity where white men have no power over black men, or at the very least, white men must compete with black men for power.

To exist in this manner is what Beck sees as the "authentic" representation of respectability, blackness, and manhood. While the dominant ideology among mainstream black and white civil rights activists in the 1960s argued for an escape from racial isolation and for sociocultural assimilation, Beck writes that, as Iceberg Slim, he reveled in the fact that his mind was "straight-jacked into the pimp game," which signified his allegiance to the underworld black community: "Back in the joint I had dreamed almost nightly [of the streets]. . . . They were fantastic. I would see myself gigantic and powerful like God Almighty. My clothes would glow. My underwear would be rainbow-hued petting my skin. My shoes would be dazzling silver. The toes were as sharp as daggers. Beautiful whores with piteous eyes groveled at my feet" (55). The tone of the passage is that of a "bad nigger" superbly, robustly laughing and satisfied with the city not only because it is a familiar space but also because the images he sees complement his social, cultural, and personal character. Iceberg Slim's ability to see himself "gigantic and powerful like God Almighty" within an oppressive system of race and class discrimination demystifies the concept of an all-powerful white masculinity framed by mainstream values and beliefs. While these descriptions are born from his observance and celebration of "the life," they also are tied to his own self-indulgent masculine subjectivity. Beck's illustration of the "bad nigger" hero is deeply invested in paying homage to the culture and people from the inside, a culture and people who speak for the "truly disadvantaged."

The term stems from William Julius Wilson's *Truly Disadvantaged: The Inner City, the Underclass, and Public Policy* (1993). In his book *A Hope in the Unseen: An American Odyssey from the Inner City to the Ivy League* (1998), Ron Suskind argues that the ghetto, despite its squalor and violence, held a certain kind of glamour and romance; it is the "imprimatur of coolness." In other words, "coolness" is defined by and within the black urban ghetto. Bruce Jackson highlights the complex ideals surrounding the coolness of ghetto culture where crime and violence signify black manhood in his introduction to *Get Your Ass in the Water and Swim Like Me: African American Narrative Poetry from the Oral Tradition* (2004). Jackson recalls an interview between Susan Fawcett and her student Joe. When asked, "What are the subjects of most of the toasts you heard?" Joe said,

> People who are in the fast life or underground, you know. Or it be somebody that's super strength, you know . . . doing something as far as pimping or hustling or shooting up some people, being a gangster or something. Or it's about some other kind of dealing, all dealing in an illegal thing. Usually if he's not a pimp he's a hustler, if he's not a hustler, it might be a jive bartender, or it just might be a guy that think he bad, that throw his weight around. . . . Usually at the time I heard them, when I was young, that was like an insight on being big personally. Say, "Yeah I like that. Wow, he was bad!" . . . Seemed like everybody would like to be whoever that guy was. (Jackson, 9)

Fawcett's interviewee poignantly illustrates the paradoxical relationship between the "bad nigger" and mainstream black communities—that is, the "bad nigger" hero is admired and feared, race conscious and nihilistic.

The publication of *Pimp* inaugurates and establishes Beck's notion of "bad nigger" authenticity. And like the young man in the passage above who admires the "super strength" of pimps, hustlers, and jive bartenders, Beck's designation of the "bad nigger" as a hero in poor communities empowers black people who function within the culture of the ghetto—a culture that often turns to violence and crime as a way to resist systematic oppression as well as to find strength and liberation. Beck presents poor urban communities, or "the streets," as cultural capital and a place for the gathering of "the realest" and toughest black men. The lure of "the streets" for Beck's characters is the "push and pull": the push to remove themselves from the state of powerlessness embodied by the urban ghetto and the pull to build within the ghetto—a space that is outside or on the edge of mainstream society—a community whose culture is defined by physical and psychological survival. Removing oneself from the state of powerlessness while seeking to establish a new nonslave self constitutes the "bad nigger's realness," which is based on finding, expressing, and performing the "idea" of a true self—a self that is not oppressed.

Thus, Beck's detailed and gritty semiautobiography allows for an exploration of the threat of death and, more specifically, violence as a tool for self-empowerment in a way Wright's work, in many ways, does not do. As JanMohamed explains, "*Black Boy* seems unable or unwilling to connect, in a conscious, exegetic manner, the productive relations between the two circuits [familial and Jim Crow], preferring instead to present the familial circuit as a diegetic explosion of death acted out and the Jim Crow circuit via a carefully considered exegetic analysis" (140). Beck's decision to depict "bad niggers" as they appear in everyday life is critical in *Pimp*'s ability to establish new and radical black realities as well as to offer alternative forms of liberation and self-empowerment.

Beck illustrates "bad nigger" authenticity as the ability to overcome adversities within the urban ghetto while maintaining a resilient and uncompromising connection to poor black people and the impoverished communities from which they come. In *Pimp*, Beck constructs a specific identity based on the "code of the streets" in an effort to project and protect the "bad nigger's" true self at all cost. In the following scene in which Iceberg Slim defends his manhood, Slim's reliance on "bad nigger" authenticity forces him to symbolically devise the kinds of adaptations necessary for his survival—adaptations to otherwise adverse economic and social environments. Iceberg Slim says, "Look Preston, I got lots of heart. I'm not a pussy. I been to the joint twice. I did tough bits, but I didn't fall apart . . . I won't give up no matter what happens. If I go stone blind, I'm still going to pimp. If my props [legs] get cut off I'll wheel myself on a wagon looking for a whore. I'm going to pimp or die. I'm not going to be a flunky in this white man's world" (78).

The eighteen-year-old Iceberg Slim (then known as Young Blood) tries to convince Pretty Preston, an old "washed-up ex-pimp," that he has what it takes to become a "boss pimp" on Chicago's "fast track." The linguistic performance of Chicago's underworld condensed in the pledge "pimp or die"—the "bad nigger's" take on John Stark's famous quotation—is typical of Iceberg Slim's recognition of the inner city as always already a "bad nigger" space while simultaneously framing it in his own image. The phrases "I got lots of heart" and "I'm not a pussy" are also typical of the linguistic self-aggrandizement and deception of black male sensibility, and it points to how allegiance to self-making, to black authenticity, is the "bad nigger's" most urgent priority: "I'm not going to be a flunky in this white man's world." The passage also signals the popular image of the pimp as authentically black and masculine. In fact, the phrase "pimp or die," which signifies fearlessness, determination, and perseverance, is a contemporary pop-cultural term frequently used by gangsta rap artists such as Father MC, Mack 10, and Jay-Z to signal black male authenticity.

In 1803, the famous American Revolutionary War soldier General John Stark wrote the toast, "Live free or die. Death is not the worst of evils." In the song "Soon You'll Understand," from *The Dynasty: Roc La Familia*, Jay-Z says, "Take your time when you liking a guy / Cause if he sense that your feelings [are] too intense, it's pimp or die." This is certainly a reference to the instability of romantic love in black communities. In a significant way, this line evokes Cornel West's argument in *Race Matters* (1993) that "lovelessness" is a fundamental threat to black communities. The "bad nigger" hero is, essentially, Beck's cultural and literary legacy. Gangsta rappers in particular have been influenced, either explicitly or implicitly, by Beck's notion of authenticity, "coolness," and death, which make up the most important features of the contemporary "bad nigger" trope. Gangsta rappers routinely mimic and reperform Beck's illustrations of the "bad nigger" hero—be it in the reincarnation of a misogynistic criminal-artist, a revolutionary "ghetto superstar," or a hybridized version of both—as a counternarrative to mainstream masculinity. Perhaps Beck's most powerful contribution to popular African American literary culture is that he reminds us the glamour of "the streets" is neither heroic nor romantic. His novels are important because he does not sensationalize "street life" nor does he leave his reader believing in untarnished heroism. Without diminishing the courage of his characters, he shows us the other side of "the game," projecting the struggle between magnificently violent men in total control and the despair of ghetto brutality. To be sure, street lit writers love to complicate images of black manhood. They illustrate their heroes' fearlessness partly through their violent opposition cultivated in "the streets."

As the implication goes, the tendency for violence emerges from frustration with social and economic injustices. But, through the brutality of Iceberg

Slim, Robert Beck emerges and reminds us that "the life" is not romantic, and violent behavior is more complicated than simply a display of displaced rage. Urban fiction, whether street lit, rap, hip-hop novels, or yardie fiction, forces its audience to become voyeurs in the display of gruesome brutality. However, the glory is not in the gilded treasures of the streets but in the heroes' ability to transcend that ruthlessness and redeem themselves as bringers of new, more productive forms of resistance.

WORKS CITED

Beck, Robert. *Pimp: The Story of My Life*. Los Angeles: Holloway House, 1967.

Carter, Shawn (Jay-Z). *The Dynasty: Roc La Familia*. Roc-a-Fella, 2000, compact disc.

Jackson, Bruce. *Get Your Ass in the Water and Swim Like Me: African American Narrative Poetry from the Oral Tradition*. New York: Routledge, 2004.

JanMohamed, Abdul. *The Death-Bound-Subject: Richard Wright's Archeology of Death*. Durham, NC: Duke University Press, 2005.

Patterson, Orlando. *Slavery and Social Death: A Comparative Study*. Boston: Harvard University Press, 1982.

Royal, Mickey. *The Pimp Game: Instructional Guide*. Los Angeles: Sharif, 1998.

Spillers, Hortense J. "Mama's Baby, Papa's Maybe: An American Grammar Book." In *African American Literary Theory: A Reader*, edited by Winston Napier, 257–79. New York: New York University Press, 2000.

Suskind, Ron. *A Hope in the Unseen: An American Odyssey from the Inner City to the Ivy League*. New York: Broadway Books, 1998.

West, Cornel. *Race Matters*. Boston: Beacon, 1993.

Wilson, William Julius. *The Truly Disadvantaged: The Inner City, the Underclass, and Public Policy*. Chicago: University of Chicago Press, 1993.

A Conversation with David Bradley

On Philadelphia Negroes, Pseudosociology, South
Street, *and the Life Narrative of Malcolm X*

Keenan Norris

David Bradley is the author of *The Chaneysville Incident* (winner of the
PEN/Faulkner Award) and *South Street*. He has published literary (as opposed to scholarly) essays on Jean Toomer, Richard Wright, Herman Melville, William Melvin Kelley, and Alice Walker, and has published articles in
Esquire, *Redbook*, the *New Yorker*, the *New York Times Magazine*, the *Philadelphia Inquirer Magazine*, the *Los Angeles Times*, the *Village Voice*, and
other periodicals. His awards and honors also include a National Endowment
for the Arts Literature Fellowship for creative nonfiction (1991), a Guggenheim Fellowship for fiction (1989), and an Academy Award from the
American Academy and Institute of Arts and Letters (1982). I interviewed
David in his San Diego home in August 2012.

KN: What was the reaction from family and those you were close to when
it came to the subject matter in *South Street*? It's a novel we might call
"street lit" if it were published today.

DB: Oh yes. My daddy was a preacher, my granddaddy was a preacher,
my great granddaddy was a preacher, my great uncle was a preacher, and
I wrote *South Street*. And it caused some consternation. The portrait of
the church was not appreciated by some. There was a street church, and
we were African Methodists. It was a big church, hierarchy and crap. . . .
My father bought five copies—supposedly to give to some of the bish-
ops—and he read the book, and he didn't like it. Never talked about it,

never said anything. He was proud, he was proud, but we just don't have to bring that up.

KN: At the time, if I had told you the definition of street lit, would you have called your book that?

DB: I wouldn't have had a problem with that. I was pissed off at sociology when I went to college—I went to college in 1968—and you know that was the year when social science was going to save the world, studying the fuck out of everything, but there was also this thing called the Moynihan Report, and you know, it was one of my section leaders in the sociology course and the guy, I feel sorry for him now. He was a white guy and he didn't know shit. And all he knows is what he's supposed to know. All he knows is what he's taught in going to class, what the lecturer says. The theory was that the ghetto had dehumanized black people. Well, I didn't know anything about the ghetto. I was a kid from the country. There were five thousand people in my town, and we lived in the suburbs. So all I knew was that I came out of the dormitory, I looked out my dormitory window, and I saw more traffic lights in a straight line than there were in my entire town. I had to drive around four traffic corners to see four traffic lights. And I walked down to the University of Pennsylvania. I walked down Spruce Street and crossed a bridge and looked up, and it wasn't Spruce Street anymore. I said, "What the hell is this?" Well that was South Street. And okay, there are black people there. Well, unlike most of my cohort at the university, I wasn't white so I wasn't afraid of black people. I didn't assume they were going to kill me. I thought they might just let me walk through. And I came back to sociology class, and I said, "Well, maybe they're dehumanized, but they don't seem to know it." All I saw was the same kind of stuff that went on in my hometown, maybe a little larger, maybe the people who were doing it were all black as opposed to some black and some white, but there was the same storefront church; everything was the same. I mean, I went to the bar—I had never gone to a bar in my hometown—I go and sit down. They didn't card me or anything, and I ordered gin because I didn't know what else to order. People talked to me, and people asked me questions. After a while, I'd go to the same place and people would tease me. Everybody would call me young blood, that whole sort of thing. Everybody called me brother. And I go back over to the university and tell the guy these people are just living their lives like anyone else. He said, "No, they're dehumanized." I said, "Well, why don't you come with me? Come on down. I'll show you." I mean, I didn't think it was a good idea, and he said no. He was probably right, but I'm thinking, "You're a social scientist, man. You're supposed to go look." And then I discovered *The Philadelphia*

Negro, which was written about that area. That was the southern border of the area that Du Bois studied. Du Bois went into everybody's house. He freaked people out; he went into their houses, just talked to them. Have you ever read it?

KN: Yeah.

DB: He has that wonderful passage where he talks about barriers to actually getting information, how people don't trust you. He sort of knocked social science into a cocked hat. But you can imagine not trusting Du Bois; I don't know if anybody trusted Du Bois. The guy talked with a British accent. Can you just imagine that?

KN: He would've been a mystery.

DB: Yeah. There was another anthropologist in Philadelphia. He actually had a house in that area, and the house had an enclosed porch. And he made a deal with the local guys that he would leave a couple jugs of wine and a tape recorder out on the porch and if they were willing to come up and make toasts basically and let him record them, collect their stuff, then they could drink the wine. Well, that worked out fine, he thought. But I heard the story this way: there's a guy up there who lets you drink wine if you make stuff up for him. But there it was in the library, and this guy had done all this collecting, and it was all authentic street stuff. So I just started thinking about these people, and there were stories down there that I would hear. That's where I got the idea of this person who had these intellectual pretentions and fighting his way there and encountering people and what he would come up against. That was the whole idea, but it was because I was pissed off at sociology.

KN: Ralph Ellison said that when he went to college and heard the great sociologist of his time, [Robert] Park, say that "the negro is the lady of the races," that this inspired him to write and to give what he felt was a truer-to-life story.

DB: Ellison at least went to a black school [Tuskegee University]. But Park was real big with Booker T. [Washington]. You know, he wrote one of Booker T.'s supposed autobiographies, *Up from Slavery*. He was the actual author. But then he went on the Chicago School thing and all that crazy shit. I didn't last long as a social scientist; I read too much. Instead of reading the textbook, I'd go, "I want to read the rest of this," so I'd go and I would read the original documents, and they didn't say what everybody said they'd say. You know, I started working on something new about redlining in Philadelphia. Redlining came from the assumption that mixed neighborhoods were unstable, a social science concept. A guy with this theory happened to go to work for the Federal Housing Administration so nobody could get home loans. They could only get them at a higher rate or whatnot and so forth. . . . And that produced the cityscape that we know. Okay, we have this idea that the ghetto happened. No. The ghetto was made. And when you realize this, while it's easy to say the banking industry, the real estate guys, all this stuff was in fact based on sociology; it was based on supposed intellectual stuff. Then it gets really scary.

KN: Did you know sociologists who read *South Street*? How'd they take it?

DB: I didn't associate with those sociologists. *South Street* came out in '75, and I was not in academia at the time. I know a couple of guys read it, but most of those guys aren't going to read something like *South Street*. And it didn't turn out to be sociology; it wasn't as heavy as I thought it was going to be. I know there was one guy who wouldn't return my phone call. When I did get into academia, it was about two years, three years later. There were some very strange interactions, not so much with the sociology department but with Africana studies or whatever they would call it. This was Temple, where they were into Afrocentrism and everything. We had some interesting conversations.

KN: I think, for me, part of what's interesting about street lit is that these books that take on the—to use an umbrella term—"black urban underclass" is that they kind of undercut a lot of different assumptions and theories from a lot of different angles.

DB: Yeah, well, *Native Son* followed the theory, you know. *Native Son* used Robert Park—that whole Chicago School thing—and the Communists, of course, who taught that people are going to be controlled by their circumstances, when in fact the history of black people is that of a people who refuse to be controlled by their circumstances. Niggers are so beautiful. They come up with all the most amazing ways to slip and slide around shit they're not supposed to do. People get mad at me when I use that word, but to me it means a kind of political invention. And not direct confrontation, because that'll get you killed, but you know, you left this loophole so I'm just going to slide through. And it just amazes me the more I read history. Oh man, somebody got away with that? You know? Didn't get away with it for very long and not too many of them did, but there was somebody getting away with it. That's probably what I learned on South Street—people just finding a way to live under conditions that you or I might not. And I think a lot of black people since have thrown up their hands and said, "You can't win." These people had redefined winning, and you know they were going to win because they were going to redefine it until they won. They actually redefined the game.

KN: Yeah, slip the yoke and change the joke. Change the laws and all that. So that leads to my next question: if this were Shannon Holmes's writing or if this were Donald Goines's writing, I think the main character in *South Street* would probably be [the gangster] Leroy. Why'd you focus more on characters like [the janitor] Rayburn and [the wino] Jake?

DB: Well, because Leroy was part of the scene, but you know the ghetto is not defined by crime. The cops define the ghetto in terms of crime; the media defines the ghetto in terms of crime because it leads and it bleeds. But you know, let's face it, 92 percent of the time, people are just coming home, doing their job, you know, getting off the bus, going up the street, going to their houses, you know, making love, having fights, whatever the hell they're doing. It's just life. And you know, even Leroy was afraid. He wasn't a monster. I knew some criminals, but they were like middle criminals. They had to answer to people—this was Philadelphia. The boss was down the street in South Philly. And if you didn't do what he said, you ended up with your head blown off. That's where that whole thing went down. I used to take my girlfriend—I had this Italian girlfriend (how I ended up with an Italian girlfriend is another story; she was clearly rebelling against something)—anyway, she liked this restaurant. It was nice and cheap, but the guy who owned it, I later found, I mean he, there was something about it. He sat in the corner. He never came out. He was back in the back there, but he liked us. For some reason he liked us. We always got extra stuff. It was a sticky little place. It was never crowded. So I said, "What is the story with that guy?" Well, you know, like most city places when it doesn't look like they're doing much business that they're supposed to be doing, they're probably doing some business they shouldn't be doing. I didn't go in the back. I'm just a piano player. Well, you know we were welcome there. It was '68; an interracial couple in Philadelphia was not——

KN: Typical.

DB: You'd get looks and stuff like that. This was downtown. . . . In Philadelphia the mob is always with us. There's crime and street crime and then real crime and then big people's crime, which is how they manipulate the real estate and everything else. Du Bois said it was the most corrupt city in America, and he wasn't far off. Chicago's corruption is pervasive. Philadelphia lives on corruption. It's just, which corrupt guys are you dealing with now? It's a way of life. It's sort of like parts of the third world. People get bribed all the time; it's not a big deal. But anyway, that was sort of part of my education because I didn't know cities and I was learning on South Street. . . . There are these little deals that people would make, and you realize that this is a community, this is a culture, and somebody who comes with expectations and a theory, well, you could prove damn near any theory you want, but that doesn't say anything about the way it goes. And people go along with it. You say something. Oh, okay, sure, whatever you want, but that wasn't how it worked. It worked like every other community. People worked out the rules, and there were lines. There were lines of propriety and lines you didn't cross, and even amongst individuals, there were things that, you know, you could call somebody all kinds of things, but there was that one thing you couldn't call them.

KN: One thing that stuck out to me about the novel was, at the bar, they're talking to each other, and you can tell because of the way they're snappin' on each other that these people have known each other a long time.

DB: Well, they're old. Big Betsy ain't no young whore. She's an old whore.

KN: At first I didn't see why everybody's so repulsed by Big Betsy, but then as the story went on, I wasn't feeling Betsy either.

DB: Betsy, you know, she was an old lady. You don't think about old whores. First of all, because a lot of them don't get a chance to be old, and then a lot of them look old when they're still young, but there are some women who stay in the life and make their way. I think she was getting social security . . . she was getting some kind of thing.

KN: One other thing that struck me, the prostitutes and all the folks who are in one way or another being eaten up by the city—this is still just 1970 or so. This is still before a lot of the great plagues that have hit the inner city: mass incarceration, crack cocaine——

DB: Philadelphia has a long history of segregation, of de facto stuff, of school segregation. And Philadelphia didn't really have a ghetto until the late '40s. It had its little pockets. The whole South Street area was black because the upper-class, white urban area was just north of it, and these people walked over there to be domestics. When Du Bois was there, almost all of the blacks there were domestics. . . . And Philadelphia had little pockets of black people, sometimes only six to eight blocks. The ghetto thing happened after the redlining and after white flight. When the factories moved out, that area became dilapidated. That's when North Philly became a ghetto, and West Philly was a different story because there was actually a fight, the university was there—University of Pennsylvania. So there was a force to keep it from being seen as a ghetto. It had a lot to do with streetcar lines and all kinds of shit. One of the weirdest stories about Philadelphia is, in the middle of World War II the transit company had to respond to Roosevelt and trained some black guys to run streetcars. Eight of them, they picked eight guys. They were training to run these street cars, which formerly were owned by the Italian and the Irish. The union shut down the transportation system in one of the biggest war production areas. . . . That's the way Philadelphia is. We'll step on our own dicks. We'd rather lose the war than have a nigger run a street car. That's what it came down to. And a lot of people were shocked because it really showed that this solidarity thing on the home front wasn't real. This was like '43 or '44. A lot of people woke up after that.

KN: I noticed when I read *Philadelphia Negro* that Philadelphia wasn't all that segregated. It was segregated, but it wasn't residentially segregated the way we think of it.

DB: It wasn't this big expanse of people with no jobs. People were there because they had jobs. The South Street ghetto was maybe Fourth Street to Twenty-sixth. Actually, it wasn't even that far. Then there was another little pocket up on the other side of what's called Benjamin Franklin Parkway. It was so small that they tore the whole damn thing down. The only thing left is a church. People still come to that church. The block of the houses where the black people live, which is right next to Eastern Correctional Penitentiary, they just tore it down. Bill Cosby talks about Diamond Street and all that; that's North Philly up near Temple University. That became an industrial zone, which itself became ghettoized. Public housing, that sort of crap. Cosby's writing about it from a vantage point and time when it was still a fairly middle-class neighborhood.

KN: It was transitioning; it was changing.

DB: Yeah. The North Philly ghetto really was the ghetto. They had riots, and they had all the usual stuff, but that was again created by redlining and the industrial transition stuff, but that was later, long after Du Bois.

KN: One thing that I really picked up from *South Street* was that it seemed like this kind of timeless book. If age didn't reap its harvest, Betsy and all them would still be there.

DB: They're still there now.

KN: Crackin' on each other right now.

DB: They are doing that. They're not the same people, but there were a number of them [like that] in Philadelphia. I just keep using Philadelphia because that's really the only city I know. I lived in New York for a little bit, but that was different. New York is so fucking weird because it grew in a whole different way. At a certain point, somebody suddenly arbitrarily decided, "We're going to move all the niggers north of this big park." Anyway there was a street in Philly, Columbia Avenue, they call it Cecil B. Moore now, but it was the main street, and when I first started teaching at Temple in '77, there were still businesses, you know the old Jewish tailors, that sort of thing. There was a street in West Philly, Fifty-second Street, this main street, this little black community street with businesses and everything else. But the thing that didn't happen for black people in Philadelphia was food. It was really hard to find a grocery store, or a grocery store that had anything you wanted to buy. It was maddening. You live there, you want to get good food, you want a tomato, man. You can't find a fucking tomato. And then they wonder why black people are fat. Of course, if somebody had a car, you could ride a mile across the line into Delaware County, and there would be a great big Pathmark store with all kinds of fresh stuff, and cheaper. It's worse than all the guns and drugs because everybody's unhealthy. I'll be healthy if you give me a grocery store instead of a McDonald's. I'll go to the grocery store. But if I just got off the bus, man. If I've been waiting on this bus, I'm going to grab what's close. My kids want it. They watch the TV. Give me a Whole Foods—cut the price down a little bit.

KN: Trader Joe's how about.

DB: It makes me furious to hear politicians and people who supposedly know what they're talking about talking about free will. People do take the easy road. You can't be always expecting people to take the hard road. Ain't nobody super human, but you know, give them a real choice. You can't say, "Here's your Marlboro lights; why are you smoking?" The ghetto sits there, people sit there, and they are the way they are because that's what they're offered. They are satisfied with their education because that's what they're offered. You can't assume that people want something different from what you want. You have to assume that people, left to themselves, want exactly what you want. Why don't they have it? Because you won't give it to them. Or you won't create the situation where they can get it.

KN: Let's transition to another topic. I'm reading Manning Marable's book on Malcolm. Marable writes in his preface that Malcolm fascinates him because Malcolm more than anyone else represents inner-city black attitudes toward race, economics, law, and politics during the mid-twentieth century. Malcolm has been lionized as a symbol of powerful black manhood, thus Marable's assertion that Malcolm participated in homosexual liaisons in order to finance his drug habit before he went to prison stirred up a furor. Are there novels that have helped to nuance our understanding of black men, and have there been movements that have done the opposite?

DB: Black people are the most homophobic people in the world. They've got too much church, even the ones who don't believe in God have too much church in them. To me, that's one of the issues that tests whether we really want liberation or if we just want it for ourselves. It was easy when I was coming along, man, we just wanted to get up. We didn't have to worry about nobody else. Now all the sudden, you get up and there are some other people saying, "Well, hey, you know, we want equal treatment here too, and we've been oppressed." I've been writing about Malcolm since '83. I actually had a piece of the *Malcolm X* movie at one point. It was this incredible conflict with Jewish Hollywood people who really didn't want to accept that Malcolm was anti-Semitic, and my mistake with them—it wasn't a mistake; it was a mistake if I want to be good—was saying there were reasons for it because if you look at what he was seeing, if you look at the experience of a black man in the 1950s, just gotten out of jail, he's working, he's on parole, his life is controlled by his employer. You know, you can see why there might be a little resentment. People knew what happened in the ghetto. People moved but kept their businesses. I'm not saying Jews are exploiting motherfuckers or anything like that. I'm saying it's harder to run a ghetto business is what I'm saying, and if you happen to be the one who owns it, then a lot of shit comes down on you. That's all I'm saying. But you can understand why viewing those things in that way, articulating it back to the populous that lives in that neighborhood, would enable you to have authority and power. Malcolm saved my life. You know the passage in the autobiography, "Do you know what they call a black man with a PhD? They call him nigger." I'm eighteen years old. I'm in a high-class Ivy League school. I'm thinking that education is the key to everything about who I'm supposed to be, right? And I'm convinced that all these educated people around me do not look at me like the ignorant farmers in my hometown did, and I read that and I was more shocked than anybody in Malcolm's audience could be. I said, "Holy shit, I'm here by myself in a library in a private study lounge. You mean, this ain't the answer to all that?" I started looking. I didn't want to believe that. I said, "That's not true, that's not true." But Malcolm was honest about his compromises, about his mistakes in a way that you have to sort of read through; you have to read through the narrative, because the narrative—not the autobiography, the narrative—of Malcolm puts things in an order that makes it look like he always knew what he was doing. You read the autobiography; it's very clear that he didn't know what he was doing. [Alex] Haley moved things around to make it look like he knew what he was doing, but Malcolm was finding his way. People said, Malcolm did this, Malcolm didn't do that, Malcolm didn't do the other thing. I don't know that Malcolm was gay or that I really care. I would not be surprised at anything he did. . . . When you look at the kind of evolution and thought that Malcolm went through, it was clear that he kept changing his mind, not so much rewriting his narrative but rewriting his thought. But politics does not allow for someone to evolve. There are people who swear up and down that the day that Martin Luther King got shot through the head he believed as much in nonviolence as the day he started out and I don't think that's true. . . . I think that Malcolm was a street man in the sense that he was not afraid of those in the streets in the way that a lot of so-called leaders, the entire NAACP, were. He wasn't afraid of them; he wasn't afraid of drug addicts. Unlike Saint Paul and like Jesus, he did not look down on whores. He looked down on whores if they kept on being whores, but everybody can be there once. There's a remarkable part in the autobiography where he remembers something he said to a white girl. He gave a talk at Harvard, and this white girl flies all the way to Harvard and shows up at this little restaurant and asks, "What can I do?" And he says, "Nothing." He later comes back and says, you know, "I wish I could undo that." You find me a politician, you find me one. . . . To me, the autobiography is in a long line of American autobiographies starting with [Benjamin] Franklin, and Franklin very frankly says, "I'm going to leave out the stuff that wouldn't be good to tell the kids."

KN: And Franklin, we know about.

DB: These were not confessions. That was Augustine; that was a different tradition. This was intended to inspire and direct and also make money because Malcolm didn't have any. Because the Nation [of Islam] had taken everything, so there was that and then there was also Haley. When I wrote the script, I still like the idea of it; they didn't like it but that's okay . . . was that the real story of the autobiography was how somebody like Alex Haley, who was middle class as all-get-out, didn't like Malcolm, didn't understand Malcolm, didn't really want to be around Malcolm but wanted the story. Gotta work for *Reader's Digest*, man, and suddenly he's confronted by Malcolm. And he'd get it wrong. Malcolm wasn't telling the truth. He would put out these napkins. Malcolm would scribble things on them. When Malcolm wasn't looking, he'd grab the napkins, but he came to understand what Malcolm was about and the truth that he was telling. . . . It wasn't supposed to be confessional. It was supposed to tell a story; it told a great story. I mean, Jesus did some shit too, I'm pretty sure. I don't think that he and Mary Magdalene were just friends. . . . Malcolm told enough. Yes, he combined some characters, no shit. Let me tell you what the movies wanted me to combine, and they did combine. They combined Shorty and a couple other people. That's what you do when you popularize a story. And some people weren't too happy with Malcolm—Oprah would've been pissed at Malcolm. Let's put it that way. But he's an amazing figure to me. And I keep writing about him every once in a while because my own ideas change about him, more information comes out. You know, this guy's been dead for a long time, and people still got information coming out. Some of the things he said. . . .

KN: It strikes me, and this is somewhat of a different topic, that before we went on record, you were talking about Betsy and Jake, and with Jake you said, "I don't know where Jake lives." I remember being an MFA student and professors telling me, "You want to know not only what you write about your characters but all this other stuff." Right? And with Malcolm you said, "There's a lot of stuff we don't know." You're okay with not knowing.

DB: About Malcolm?

KN: Well, what I'm getting is that when it comes to narrative and the things that are left out, you're comfortable——

DB: I make a distinction between fiction and nonfiction. First of all, when I first started going down to South Street, I wasn't writing a book. I don't know what the hell I was writing. Somebody had to say to me, "Oh, hey, that's a great story." "Really? Okay." I remember what it was, it was: the first section that went on paper was the story about Rayburn. The story about him going up to the bank and cleaning the bank and dreaming, because I had been sitting next to a guy who cleaned a bank. It had a big glass tower, and he'd clean the top floor; he was very proud that he cleaned the top floor. He cleaned the president's office. And I'm sitting there thinking, "What the hell. But the man's got pride in what he does." I'm eighteen, nineteen years old, you know. This is the kind of crap that's bouncing around in my head. One side's the middle class, and the other side was . . . well, let's really examine this. Maybe that's what he does and I wrote about that and somebody thought, "That's a good story." So, I said, "Okay, they were all good stories." And for me, that's all it was; it was to take off from these people and their circumstances. . . . There was this bartender; his business was tending bar. I don't know if he made a profit. I thought he was a social worker in terms of how he interacted with people and everything else. He told me one time, he said, "You know what, if you're going to be a bartender, you gotta learn how to get along with people." Get along with drunk people! One of the strangest things about that bar was there was the *line*. Remember how I was talking about lines before? There was the line when he cut you off. It was different for everybody, and it didn't have to do with behavior. Somebody could be sitting there very quietly and he'd say, "That's it for you." And for the most part, people accepted that; people didn't question it. And I'd seen stuff like that in church. I'd seen how people, no matter what they stand up in testimony and say, some knew the truth about them. But this was exactly the kind of interaction that the sociologists, either they couldn't detect it with their questionnaires or understand how it could be there. And there it was, there it was. It was fascinating.

KN: Yeah, you know one of my favorite sections in *South Street* is when Rayburn has his little routine that he does when nobody's there, but then he has that dream later where, after his wife has left him, and he thinks about his revenge. That had me laughing out loud. That was great.

DB: The wife was real. She was a piece of work. Nobody liked her. She was not welcome in that place.

KN: I imagine not.

DB: Yeah, there were a couple women who were younger and who float-ed through that South Street bar. One of them was actually also a bartend-er. Her name was L———. L——— was the sexiest woman I had ever seen in my life. One time I was sitting there and she had this thing she would do; she'd wink and say, "Hey, Buddy, got a quarter?" She got showered with quarters, which was a lot of money in those days. One day she said to me, "You a college boy?" I said, "Yeah." And she said, "You go to college?" I said, "Yeah, I ain't messing with you." She said, "You go to Temple?" That was the sort of middle-class school. I said, "No, I go to Penn." She said, "Penn. Don't worry, I won't tell nobody." And I never could never figure out whether she was setting me up or she really meant that.

KN: I dig what you're saying about this ambivalence toward the institu-tion itself. I don't think there's a way around it as a black person.

DB: You don't want a way around it because it's so crazy. . . . The institution has a desire for pathology. An audience will see that Bigger Thomas satisfies that desire, that a character who does something that's counterproductive or risky or whatever word we're using now, it proves a stereotype that already exists. The street lit novels that you're talking about were preceded by a whole bunch of middle-class black novels where the effort was to present a different life that was equally false. . . . It fell to white people to tell about Porgy. . . . I mean, why shouldn't we tell the story of the people that we are? Ain't nothing to be ashamed of that you're poor. You know, and ain't nothing to be ashamed of that because you're poor certain things happened. Maybe you should be ashamed if you're the person that made them poor. . . . The whole street thing, yeah, you run a risk. There's people willing to say, "Aha! She's a whore. I knew they were all whores!" But you know, whores are people, too.

KN: So, there's so much sociology, and so much opinion, just all wrapped around it, wrapped around our existence as black Americans; how do you write your way through it?

DB: Yeah, when I wrote *South Street*, I was just trying to write a book. All this other stuff was floating around in my mind. I was pissed off about sociology. But fundamentally, it was just a story about the people, and the people told the story themselves. Once you've created the characters with certain situations and certain personalities, they're going to tell you what they'll do and what they won't do. . . . The question then becomes, what is out there that people are writing—I don't even think it's restricted to publishers—let's talk about record producers and what stories would people like to tell that will not be seen by the public. What about that? The art that you see is the art that you're allowed to see. I once went on a tour for the U.S. Information Agency in 1986. This was Reagan money, believe it or not. It probably doesn't exist anymore. They would actually send you around the world. They sent me around the world. And people asked me question[s], and the questions that they asked me shocked me in some cases. One was, what are black writers writing in America today? I said, "You know, I don't know. Nobody knows; we only know what's being published. Some of what's published isn't even good. But it seems to conform to a certain pattern or a certain expectation." And then he said, "Well, there's probably a story out there that somebody's writing, as well as this story, but it doesn't fit the expectation or hasn't found the right place, so we don't know that story." The more I get involved working in publishing, working with the movie industry, the more I'm aware of what the art that we see says about the society rather than the individual artists, that the rap that we hear is the rap that we're supposed to hear and I'm not so sure about the people making the decisions.

KN: I guess that's what initially drew me to street lit. I could see that there was all this work that wasn't getting published, wasn't getting forwarded and wouldn't. And the people who were making the decisions about that came from a small coterie—that's my nice way of putting it.

DB: Mmhmm. That's a nice way of putting it. That's accurate. It's not that they necessarily look the same way, not ethnically identifiable in some ways; they're not, but they're educationally identifiable. What we were talking about [off record], about how much money, or about how little people get paid in publishing at the entry level, which is still true, certainly means that the decision making at the top is not going to change that much because you know, unless you have a little money behind you, you went to a good school, you're not going to get a job as a secretary, to make your way up to become an assistant editor. The women that I worked with in publishing were young girls with family in New York and whatnot and so forth, who made their way into the business, and it was a respectable business for a woman to get in. There weren't a lot of women in publishing in those days. They formed a group, women in publishing something or other. And you know different books started getting published. That's the way it works.

KN: You're describing a spoil system.

DB: Yeah, in a sense.

KN: I don't mean that with a negative connotation.

DB: No, and most of the people I know or knew in publishing were socially concerned. Maybe at the upper levels you were going to encounter Rupert Murdoch, but there were a lot of levels before you got to Rupert Murdoch. It was a pleasant place to be, but the time inevitably came to say, What book are we going to publish? How much money are we going to put behind it? What do we expect that book to do? Books are made. They don't find their own level; maybe they do now more with the Internet, but in those days it was what you put in bookstores. And those were decisions that were made, and your fight was to get a book by a black person where they talked about a different kind of story, get somebody to believe that it would sell, and if they believed that it would sell, then it would start to sell. Alice Walker would be an example. Toni Morrison would be an example. . . . People don't want to admit it in publishing, but it's a self-fulfilling prophecy. You look at something like

A Million Little Pieces. That's when the bones show, because somebody decided this would sell packaged one way, but it wouldn't sell packaged another way. But the packaging didn't have a damn thing to do with what was inside. It's like dropping a CD. They're very up front about their marketing. Literary people tend not to want to be. They want to think there's some invisible hand that will control whether it sells. It don't work that way. It don't work that way.

KN: "The invisible hand." I've heard that somewhere else.

DB: Yeah, I bet you have. It's a myth that keeps people going. You write what you write, and it's in the hand of God, or Satan.

KN: Now, speaking of market expectations and stereotypes—I don't remember if it was what [William] Faulkner wrote or what Ellison wrote about Faulkner, but one of them said that Faulkner begins with a stereotype and then there is, in certain cases, not in all parts of his work, but he starts there and then works past the stereotype he's been given and that he initially only passively received.

DB: Susan Straight is sort of a counterexample to all this stuff. It took a lot of people a long time to believe that Susan was for real, and for real not as a writer but for real in the people that she wrote about, in part because she was writing from the inside; she didn't write about the other. And you know, that was something that I detected the first time I met her, not the first time I read her, but the first time I met her. I said, you know, "If you close your eyes, you're talking to a black woman. Never mind the package that this comes in." And you know, it was okay; once you get over that, then you don't expect anything else. But she still comes as a surprise to a lot of my students. They say, "How did she do this?" I said, "You don't understand. She was there. It's not other to her." She's a different kind of writer. For someone who is coming in, I don't know . . . Kathryn Stockett's *The Help*: to her it was a book. She isn't of that. And maybe this was as close as she could get at that time. I thought there was some wonderful, wonderful things, some very honest things that she had either projected or absorbed or whatever. So what do you get down on the poor girl for? Because she made a lot of money?

KN: I dig what you're saying. And to a certain extent, as writers, we're all a little bit different from our communities even if we are of that community, right?

DB: Oh, we're so weird.

KN: I mean, even Malcolm was different. Hell, the guy who cuts my hair, he told me he grew up in Terrell, Texas. And I said, "There's a famous person from Terrell, Texas." He said, "Oh yeah, that's Jamie Foxx. You know his mama kept him in the house while we were all out on the field every day, kept him in the house playing piano every day, and when he'd come out, we'd slap him upside the head because he didn't have to be out in the fields with us."

DB: Oh yeah, we're all crazy. The truth of the matter is that those of us who are concerned with putting it in a package and shaping that package and making it do something are weird. Most people who I grew up with in my hometown were content to sit there and tell a story, slap their thigh, and go about their business. They didn't do revisions. They might tell it differently the next time depending on the audience, but they didn't do revisions.

Part III

Contemporary Street Lit, 1990s and 2000s

Saratoga Avenue

Arisa White

I

You smell like Saratoga Avenue.
Morning comes with no police sirens,
the sun escapes entanglement
from the *how do I begin* tragedies
of project buildings.
The sunlight cuts the curtains,
a machete through bone,
we lie like sky and water.
Your sleeping face,
betrayed by a smile,
uncovers the moon in your teeth.
I fall back to sleep dreaming
hurricane kisses, monsoon tongue.

II

You smell like Saratoga Avenue,
when the night wipes away
the afternoon's sweet with a rag.
A breeze like rubbing alcohol
comes quick and cool—
the train makes your body tremble;
love feels like chewing on rocks.
Quiet doesn't stay,
and you can hear the heart's rhythms
before your left nipple sucks it up.

III

You smell like Saratoga Avenue
when Heineken kisses
make you dance on invisible waves
and crack severs chords
of your adagio breathing.
In a syringe the symphony concludes,
the virus slips you into vertigo;
like rain clouds the concrete looks,
for the sun you wait at the corner.

IV

You smell like Saratoga Avenue
when words wet with Olde English
converge at the corner: brothers weave
worries into hip-hop. He steps out
the streetlight with the light skin
and wavy hair your mama likes,
persuasively spins his game around you
to custom fit like the leather jacket
you always wanted; you ride his hip
like a .45; he aims, fires, and creates
wounds, plunders the openings,
and leaves you with a bullet-pierced sky,
barely breathing in your project box.

V

You smell like Saratoga Avenue's
beaten sidewalks when dreams
are forsaken and prayer stains your hands;
where women find wings from bedsheets,
envisions freedom with the *I*'s of suicide.
Men bleed like unfertilized eggs
while the moon completes its cycle.
Wailing walls are called Tilden
and there's no time to write letters to god.

The History, Power, and Graffiti Art of Brazilian Hip-hop

Ana Lúcia Silva Souza and Jaqueline Lima Santos

For the world of hip-hop culture in Brazil, the turn of the twentieth century to the twenty-first was punctuated by a series of questions: Where is hip-hop going? What are the changes affecting hip-hop culture? Could it be that hip-hop is losing its essence? What are the effects of hip-hop's proximity to governmental departments? How does hip-hop keep its autonomy solid in the midst of nongovernmental organizations? What is the future of hip-hop? Of course, now entering the second decade of this century, not only these questions but also others continue to echo, instigating the battle in search of answers.

However, given the intensity with which hip-hop moves amid a political, economic, and cultural scenario in transformation—that provokes and destabilizes the certainties—the answers have always been only temporary. Perhaps for this reason, hip-hop remains alive and vigorous, and following the dictates of the culture, we can work to ask the questions as the propellers of a process of dialogue and formation and thereby continue producing the knowledge that serves us.

Accordingly, the purpose of this chapter is to contribute to introducing another look at trying to understand a part of this history still little told in Brazil. Therefore, investing in contextualization brings aspects of the history and recent memory and, finally, prepares an exercise in prospection based in the involvement in discussions, reflections on social practices with which we involve ourselves and our studies.

With a focus on the hip-hop movement, we emphasize that in the festivity, the rhythm, the colors, and the uses of languages—gestures, speeches, readings, writings, and images—made with specific purposes in various contexts reveal ways of producing knowledge about Afro-Brazilian history and culture. Even though it cannot be absolutely generalized, this is the predominant viewpoint in the universe of hip-hop, a viewpoint that by means of the production of "local hip-hop scenes" (Morgan and Bennett 2011) helps to invent and inventory the literacies of existence in which the black population has always involved itself (Souza 2011).

Since the 1980s, hip-hop culture has established itself in all Brazilian regions, through its discourse and performance that, in different ways, emphasizes and critiques the effects of experienced social exclusion and racial inequalities on people's lives, to the dramas produced by the tense relations established in contemporary society.

Hip-hop has been touted as an important urban phenomenon in the present sociopolitical scenario of the country that draws attention because it involves the black segment of the population, mostly young people from low-income families who live in the suburbs of big cities. The culture attracts attention from the positive aspects that it provokes, contradicting the statistics of all sorts of violence accompanying the daily lives of black men and women and showing the potential of generating identification and articulation around the universe of black culture, adorning itself to a cultural and political space of development of social practices of self-affirmation.

On the walls of the cities, the reference of hip-hop culture is present on posters of concerts and CD releases, on the programming of lectures and workshops of principal cultural centers, in radio and television advertising presentations, and in special articles in newspapers and magazines.

Its Brazilian story is sung, told, and written by many voices and hands that cite the origin of hip-hop in Jamaican and New York culture and re-create in their territories a musical style that, initially with festive characteristics, earned contours of resistance, protest, and denouncements against social and racial inequalities experienced in society. Here, downtown São Paulo, recognized as the birthplace of hip-hop, saw emerge a growing number of young people coming from the peripheries and choosing it as a meeting point where dance championships, with elaborate steps to the sound of half-sung, half-spoken songs later known as rap, occurred.

From the 1980s until now, hip-hop has spread itself throughout the country and strategically affirmed a discourse of denouncement and propositions through expressions materialized into four elements: break-dance moves; graffiti art in colorful designs with diverse techniques and support; the sung word of the MC, the master of ceremonies who delivers messages to the public; and the DJ's manipulation of electronic equipment responsible for the sound.

HIP-HOP AND ITS PRODUCTION OF LOCAL SCENES: THE BRAZILIAN CASE

As stated by Paul Gilroy in "Wearing Your Art on Your Sleeve" (1993), the Atlantic triangle (America, the Caribbean, Europe, and Africa), formed by the black diaspora, mobilized struggles and promoted mutual exchanges, contacts and confrontations, images, and symbols. This phenomenon made possible the tense circulation of black personalities, books, values, and beliefs and demonstrated the transnational power of black music, which has exceeded the boundaries of the national state. Amid so many other aspects, the author also states that, what could be trivial, in the musical universe gained significant dimension, such as album covers that are transformed into objects of knowledge and, circulating in various parts, were used to address aspects experienced by the black population and allowing the sharing of styles and symbols that constitute the idea of blackness. It was, and continues to be, the musical universe that puts into circulation ideas, generators of pleasure and desires; music is the element that exceeds the commercial impact to be configured as an important political tool.

African American culture (jazz, soul, funk, hip-hop, and other elements), according to Gilroy, has provided a political language for the public universe of blacks:

> The formations and transcendence of the market for "race records" is there to behold. The secularization of black music which led to soul, the civil rights struggles and, in particular, the Black Power movement, can all be apprehended by this means. The ebbs and flows in black political culture have been faithfully transcribed through the text, imagery and artwork of the record sleeve. (Gilroy 1993, 244)

"First the rhetoric of rights and justice, then the discourse of Black Power crossed the seas and enabled Black folks here, there and everywhere to make sense of the segregation, oppression and exploitation they experienced in their countries of residence" (Gilroy 1993, 251). The creation of solidarity ties among those that share a historical memory of utopias aiming for inherent transformations in their condition become audible in the words of Paul Gilroy, through music. We read much that suggests blacks of the West founded their identities from the modern experience of racialization, giving rise to political and historical constructions organized by the exchanges established in the Atlantic. However, their condition produces a double consciousness. The feeling of being inside and outside of the Western world demonstrates how the paradigm of modernity upon the nation had influences on black political thought, producing an invariant identification between the experiences of racial terror and belonging to a state. The result of this would be the affirmation of diasporic nationalist forms.

An example of nationalized diasporic forms is hip-hop, which, according to Gilroy in "The Black Atlantic" (2001), is configured as a mechanism for expression of black and poor Americans, the result of hybridization present in the interactions of the South Bronx.

African American music, carrying a strongly racial discourse and exalting black pride, traveled around the world. And in the midst of this, hip-hop, one of the elements of African American culture created after the civil rights era, has continued this journey, reaching the borders of dozens of countries on five continents. The political discourse of hip-hop captured the world.

According to Marcyliena Morgan (in Morgan and Dionne Bennett's 2011 article "Hip-hop and the Global Imprint of a Black Cultural Form"), "global hip-hop" emerged as a culture that encourages and integrates innovative practices of artistic expression, knowledge, production, social identification, and political mobilization. Hip-hop transcends and challenges conventional constructions of identity, race, nation, community, aesthetics, and knowledge. Although, according to the authors, the term is not official; the use of "hip-hop nation" to describe citizens of the hip-hop community in the world has become increasingly common.

> The hip-hop nation is an international, transnational, multiracial, multiethnic, multilingual community made up of individuals with diverse class, gender, and sexual identities. While hip-hop heads come from all age groups, hip-hop culture is primarily youth driven. Citizenship in the hip-hop nation is defined not by conventional national or racial boundaries, but by a commitment to hip-hop's multimedia arts culture, a culture that represents the social and political lives of its members. (Morgan and Bennett, 177)

Looking at Brazil, we agree with Morgan and Bennett when they affirm that this culture has empowered individuals from various economic classes, encouraging them to become artists in their own right and develop critical thinking skills that can be applied to every aspect of their lives. This perspective also recalls Derek Pardue's reflections in reference to São Paulo hip-hop in *Ideologies of Marginality in Brazilian Hip Hop* (2008) that activists see hip-hop as a sociocultural system through which they self-empower themselves, construct a critical sense of reality, and find possibilities of transformations in their lives. Hip-hop produces aesthetic, social, political, and intellectual identity, beliefs, behaviors, and values, establishing itself as a form of identification, worldview, and lifestyle.

Hip-hop as a diasporic cultural production has circled the globe and created what Morgan and Bennett called "local hip-hop scenes," where activists practice the elements of hip-hop and debate, represent, and critique social systems and the effects on their lives, establishing a form of hip-hop as a movement in which scenes produced locally are engaged in political and social causes. Understanding the presence of hip-hop in its different contexts and complexities is like, according to the authors, assembling a puzzle, since in many diverse places this culture only recently began to be documented. The stories are in the bodies of the people—many of them 1980s youth who, although over thirty years of age, and no longer so young, are still acting young through hip-hop and other ways—helping to put together the strands of a story from the Afro-Brazilian point of view. This is an important perspective for understanding the strategies for coping with life, an apprenticeship to which black men and women in Brazil dedicate themselves daily in festivity and musicality, a safe haven for exercising citizenship.

Constructions of Blackness: Points and Contexts of Departures and Arrivals

According to Márcio Macedo in "Baladas black e rodas de samba da terra da garoa" (2007), in Brazil, in the early twentieth century there already existed black parties that, as a reflection of how society was organized, were segmented by ethnic/racial groups, making it possible for one to speak of the black parties, Spanish parties, Italian parties, and so on. The restrictions caused by the value of access or by group boundaries meant that blacks would create means for their enjoyment, such as backyard and garage parties that were later made possible with the popularization of gramophones and the phonograph market. In São Paulo, for example, these community festivals slowly exited from homes and started to occupy the ballrooms in the city's downtown and, as João Batista de Jesus Felix affirms, "The parties reflect the densely present racialization in São Paulo society; in other words, they markedly reelaborated spaces consisting of traces of inclusion and exclusion" (2005, 18).

The Brazilian context of the second half of the twentieth century is marked by structural and economic changes that spurred the growth of the country and at the same time intensified social inequalities. In this contradictory scenario, where growth is not accompanied by the redistribution of income and economic concentration and wage inequalities become even greater, social movements emerge, with specific characteristics and identities in contrast with other movements of civil society that even then were characterized, in their majority, as movements in which class identity predominated. The impact that the inequalities had on different groups had impelled the emergence of sectored movements, with specific demands, which take into consideration the social reality and forms of oppression experienced by each one, such as blacks, women, Indians, and so forth (Souza 2011). These new social movements (black, feminist, artistic-cultural, environmental, etc.) sought to intervene in political decisions, constructing an increasingly participatory model.

According to scholars like Lélia Gonzalez (in "O movimento negro na última década"), high levels of inequality in the 1970s directly affected the black population, which resulted in increased racial disparities. The social contrasts generated by this exclusion contributed to the questioning of the myth of racial democracy,[1] which came to be denounced by black social movements.

Black men and women that until then claimed a national identity began to take an increasingly Africanist stance in their discourses and sought elements to construct an African diasporic identity. The experiences in the diaspora, the struggle for African liberation, Pan-Africanism, and international solidarity became references, Gevanilda Santos states, and black dances were configured as one of the principal realms where these new groundbreaking ideas were being spread by activist groups.

In a 2007 study, Macedo postulates that, already the 1950s and '60s in Brazil were marked by a strong influence of black culture and greater access to electronic goods such as turntables and vinyl records, means by which blacks of São Paulo in particular, but not only blacks, would come to have contact with American artists, which impelled the recreational practices of sociability and leisure with new formats. During the 1960s and '70s, when the first DJs and sound teams emerged (and were responsible for popularizing the black dances of São Paulo), these environments were already more professionalized. In São Paulo, teams like Chic Show, Zimbabwe, and Transanegra Black Mad were teams that occupied large nightclubs in the downtown region, spreading rhythms like funk, soul, and jazz, among other rhythms.

Also, according to Spency Pimentel's "O Livro vermelho do HIP HOP" (1997), these dances "presented the projection of slides depicting scenes from movies about black Americans, along with photos of famous black people, Brazilians, and foreign musicians or athletes." Also divulged were ideas of Africans and blacks of the diaspora, such as in the book *Soul on Ice* (1971) by Eldridge Cleaver that became fashionable and a reference.

As Felix mentions in "HIP HOP: Cultura e Política no Contexto Paulistano" (2005), the black dances became the political spaces because in them identities were negotiated and constructed, and their patrons sought something more than dancing and listening to music; they sought a space where they could feel themselves amongst equals, "in which entertainment is experienced as an alternative moment to everyday racism, because in this place one does not bring the racial hierarchy present in everyday life" (18).

Within the invented space was circulated information of a political and cultural movement that was consolidated in the ghettos of the United States: the hip-hop movement, the starting point for young blacks who attended the dances, began to occupy the streets of downtown, spreading the new style.

Hip-hop Invades the Scene: Parties, Streets, and Neighborhoods

The possibilities of access to videos allowed, even without completely understanding the lyrics in English, an interaction with images and discourse gestures about prejudice, racism, discrimination, and police violence, a reality we also faced here in Brazil. Among other aspects, the moment was striking because it happened in dialogue with the intensification of people's reaction to the brutality of the military dictatorship regime then in power. The musical style that served as an instrument for socioeconomic and racial emancipation among black Americans fit into the lives of blacks in Brazil. The dance steps broadcasted in the videos were re-created by dancers who came on the scene and began to occupy spaces of the downtown area for the start of school: the Old School of Hip-hop.

Starting from the black dances, they took the stairs at the Municipal Theatre of São Paulo, continued to Rua 24 de Maio Street in front of the Shopping Grandes Galerias and then to São Bento and Roosevelt Squares. In the circulation between one break dancer and another, they refined their techniques. It is also worth mentioning that São Bento Square is the site of the birthplace of Brazilian rap, which was sung over handclaps and beats made with the mouth, which imitated the sound of the beats (Geremias). For years this was the territory of public presentations of breaking and battles between groups from different neighborhoods in the city, and where individuals and groups of national hip-hop—such as Nelson Triunfo, considered the first breaker; Back Spin; Racionais MCs; Lady Rap; Nino Brown; Jabaquara Breakers; Thaide; MC Jack; and DMN, among many others—made their start as young people and who today are the teachers of many other groups.

Gradually, hip-hop in Brazil started to organize itself through meetings held by young people, mostly black, in São Bento and Roosevelt Plazas in downtown São Paulo. One of the points debated was violence and police repression, as well as the racist police stops that they received on the streets in the downtown area of the city. By understanding this reality, they could search for ways of reacting to such conditions. At these meetings, MCs, dancers, and street intellectuals sought knowledge about the elements of the hip-hop movement and had access to magazines produced by American hip-hoppers that were translated, as KL Jay says: "A guy got a magazine, translated in that broken English, took it to the people" (Geremias, 44).

It was also in downtown São Paulo, Roosevelt Plaza, in 1988 that the first posse of the country appeared, the Sindicato Negro (in English, Black Trade Union) that, as Felix points out, already demonstrated concern with the racial question through its name. In "Voz ativa" (2001), Osmundo Pinho defines "posses" as collective groups who organize themselves locally, in their neighborhoods or regions, with the aim of promoting self-esteem and the respect of local youth and promoting political consciousness. Felix states that it is in the posses that hip-hop is experienced fully and critically and where hip-hop activists make their critical and ideological reflections. For a posse to be recognized, it was enough for a group of people who practice elements of hip-hop to get together.

Eventually, the distance separating the militants of the posse Sindicato Negro, in the city of São Paulo, and the existent ideological differences in the organization led to its extinction in 1995. And it was from there that local collectives emerged, other posses on the outskirts of the city. From downtown, these young people began to take to their neighborhoods elements of the hip-hop movement and build local organizations. Even with performances centered in the suburbs, downtown remains a space of reference and information exchanges.

The posses corroborate that the elements of hip-hop spread through the city of São Paulo and took specific forms. Rap, for example, beyond "rhythm and poetry," can mean many things. Due to its political nature, it was gaining new meanings throughout the streets of the world and was already translated by hip-hoppers themselves like Revolução através das palavras (Revolution through the Words) and Ritmo Alternativo e Protestante (Alternative and Protesting), among others (Santos, 2011).

The first rap album released in Brazil was *Kaskatas—A Ousadia do Rap made in Brazil* (Kaskatas—The Audacity of Rap Made in Brazil) in 1988, followed by the compilation *HIP-HOP. Cultura de Rua. O Som das Ruas* (Street Culture: The Sound of the Streets) in 1989. Both contained songs from various groups (Santos, 2011).

Graffiti, which had already been on the streets of São Paulo since the 1970s, initially as poetic graffiti, gained traction in the 1980s through the stencil art technique in hip-hop, especially when the movie *Beat Street* influenced break dancers who occupied the downtown area and showed the interaction of the four artistic elements, experiencing all at the same time and strengthening the elements by combining them. It then started to have a communicative role within the culture, spreading its elements and characters, and contributing to sustaining the voice of protest against inequality, police brutality, and many other social problems.

Knowledge in Brazilian hip-hop has worked mainly through the performance of posses of hip-hop.

> The posses have contact with entities of the black movement, participate in events, symposiums, and conferences promoted by these entities, inserting themselves into the racial question, poverty, drugs, and violence of Brazilian society; encouraging and seeking to discover biographies of black personalities, preparing pamphlets with short biographies and distributing them in meeting points of black youth. (Magro, 73)

According to Viviane Magro (2002), organizations of the hip-hop movement create a space of reference and identification based on social, cultural, and ethnic experience.

> In the periphery, all meet on the street, at the dances, and there the posse appears bringing together two or three groups of rap. It's a way of exchanging ideas about music, art, and the problems of the periphery, to study our origins—African-ancestry—that the school doesn't teach. It is also our union to fight for space in society, demand locations for our rehearsals and performances. (Magro, 70)

These young hip-hoppers seek historical references and construct a social critique that goes beyond the school environment. Its performance in communities incites political ideas and actions for social interventions.

"Hip-hop represented a social, historical, and political construction that was being 'translated' into the Brazilian space" (Felix, 79). A space transformation occurred in several sectors, political, economic, and social. The musicality of hip-hop is the conductor of a time that makes and breaks itself around a project of the Brazilian nation.

THE RECRUITMENT POLICY IN THE ELEMENTS OF BRAZILIAN HIP-HOP

It is around these four elements that participants develop a series of actions with the growing concern of subsidizing the work, especially the development of rap lyrics. Many young men and women join in discussion groups to organize events and shows, think about, and discuss the dynamics and transformations of hip-hop and important emerging issues of the community in which they live, as well as forms of intervention. In this process of self-education, they create many and varied opportunities for contact and handling of written, oral, graphic, and digital language, social practices that, based on the cultural background they have, insert them into a collective process of investigation and of exchanging and promoting learning that enhances the skills and knowledge that meet the needs created in the makings of a rapper (Souza 2011).

It should be emphasized that in these groups young people play an educational role that not only responds to but also goes beyond the social demands around reading, writing, and speaking, densifying the process of integration into the literate world. More than knowing how to read, write, and speak, there is interest in knowing how and why people do it, with what meanings and how these uses of languages interfere in their ways of dealing with situations that are typical of our social time.

Be it in music, dance, or image, all languages mix together, a hybridization without the abandonment of the search for affirmation of black identities, in Brazil or outside of it. The hip-hop movement is an important narrative about another story, emphasizing the collective power over the individual, presenting popular leaders of several countries who seek or sought to create a history in favor of groups that were made into social minorities.

Popular biographies in the hip-hop universe include those of Malcolm X, Martin Luther King, Che Guevara, and Zumbi dos Palmares, which are, directly or indirectly, important for accessing other approaches and different views of what is learned in textbooks. Other popular works, such as books, song lyrics, alternative newspapers, fanzines, comics, and other materials are stored in friends' homes, public libraries, used bookstores, and online. All are important for supporting and helping to engender a discourse in order to convince and draw attention to the need for consciousness, participation, and social transformation.

If the value attributed to the language may be perceived with more power at the time of singing—in the ways that MCs use speech publicly, with agility, studying the tone of the words, and imprinting emphasis on metaphors—we know that the same value gives life and health to all the artistic elements of hip-hop. Next, we look in more detail into how graffiti is used.

The production of graffiti, another entry into the multimodal world of letters and images, requires a project that encompasses research, trade of ideas for the very sustainability of the design, the choice of colors, and support. It involves reading and writing images and circulating different materials in order to structure the set of ideas that comprises this type of text and that can still be done, individually or collectively, learned and taught, through workshops that currently take place inside and outside the peripheral communities. Generally, workshops, and other events involving graffiti—DJ, dance, and MC—require preparation to define the locations, formats, scripts, alliances, support, and numerous aspects related to production. We recall that currently hip-hop events do not always occur in isolation but are sometimes in the midst of other events that require negotiation and dialogues that are not free of tensions.

An example of the complexity of such actions would be the work of the group of graffiti artists OPNI (Objetos Pixadores Não Identificados).[2] Formed in 1997 by a collective of twenty young people from the outskirts of São Paulo, OPNI is currently composed of only three members, Cris, Val, and Toddy, who perform six-handed works and enjoy prestige on the art scene of the streets, murals, museums, and galleries.

Members of OPNI affirm visualizing "the soul of the ancestors" in their art that is "a cry for freedom and revenge." They have already performed various works in art galleries, on city walls, in theater, newspaper, cinema,

TV, magazines, commercials, TV series (*Antônia, Cidade dos Homens*), doc-umentaries (*Quanto vale ou é por Kilo*), and so forth. The magazine *Manifestação*, recognized in the Brazilian artistic universe, is one of the publications organized by the group OPNI.

The group usually paints scenarios that seek to express aspects of every-day reality and create in their drawings elements of social criticism like the symbol Sociedade de Fantoche, a pair of scissors that appears in some of their works representing the intention of cutting the invisible wires by which the world manipulates individuals like dolls; scissors would liberate from the values imposed by society, media, and industry. In the work of OPNI, sce-narios are always accompanied by characters who reflect the diversity of the people who dwell in Brazil; however, it is the black population that appears most expressively. Moreover, they usually paint portraits of black Brazilian personalities and those from the African diaspora who became a reference in the periphery, in the black movement and in hip-hop.

With a resume full of social activities and community work, especially in the field of art, four years ago OPNI opened the space São Matheus em Movimento, where they develop workshops that expand community access to cultural goods such as capoeira, graffiti, percussion, recycling, various events, and so on. They also developed the project ConVida through which they invite artists from around the world to make graffiti on the shacks, streets, alleys, and narrow streets of Vila Flavia, the neighborhood in which they live.

This group is also a part of the hip-hop posse DRR (Domínio, Ritmo, Rua or Domain, Rhythm, Street), one of the oldest in the city of São Paulo. To understand their work more, we explored the exhibition *A vila como ela é* (The village as it is), opening on 16 January 2010, that led to the AEIOU space, in Vila Madalena, a middle-class neighborhood and "the face" of one of the peripheries of São Paulo. Frames, cardboard boxes, wheels, wood, and walls were made into graffiti to express everyday life in Vila Flavia, the east zone neighborhood of São Paulo.

Although the group OPNI exposes frames and miscellaneous objects, the wall space is preferred for the performance of the work of a hip-hop graffiti artist. Cris, Val, and Toddy plunged into the extensive walls of AEIOU and performed amazing six-handed works. See figures 7.1 and 7.2.

There are several works in the exhibition *A vila como ela é*, and among them we chose one to initiate a discussion about the iconographical and the iconological in the productions of the group OPNI.

Erwin Panofsky provides a definition of the iconographic and iconologi-cal as reading tools in the visual arts. Iconography is the branch of art history that deals with the theme or message of the artwork in composition of its shape, and iconology requires more than familiarity with specific themes or concepts transmitted through literary sources. It is a method of interpretation

Figure 7.1. Montagem da Exposição—Espaço AEIOU OPNI

Figure 7.2. Montagem da Exposição—Espaço AEIOU OPNI

that comes from synthesis rather than analysis. In summary, the iconographic works with the scope of the image, and the iconological works with the scope of contents.

For a more complex analysis, we must not remain only in the world of shapes; it is necessary to interpret the extra artistic elements that are brought by the works of art. What generates the meaning of a specific shape? It is necessary to seek those answers in the interpretation of the works. To find the meaning, one has to find the genesis of the meaning. Equally important are the levels of the sensible and the intelligible that necessarily complement each other.

Didactically thinking, figure 7.3 provides not only a picture of reality but also the critical manner in which the OPNI group expounds upon it.

If we start from an iconographic analysis, the painting in figure 7.3 presents a scenario with different characters. There is an image of a man looking over the community, from left to right; a police car; police; and some people being stopped. The scene shows wooden shacks huddled in a progression toward the hill, hanging clothes in the front of houses, someone in the window, and a child riding a bicycle. But why was this scene one of those chosen by the group OPNI? The exhibition *A vila como ela é* shows the reality of Vila Flavia through the eyes of these graffiti artists and is a critical look at the scenario in which they live, as well as other members of "global hip-hop" that produce "local hip-hop scenes," referring back to the expression of Morgan and Bennett.

Making an iconological analysis, one perceives that alongside the image of the man looking from above is written the message "Olha por nóis" (Look

Figure 7.3. Quadro de parede—*A vila como ela é* Jaqueline Lima Santos

for us), which reminds us of the Christian expression "Cristo, rogai por nós" (Christ, pray for us), expressing a belief in something beyond the material world that can look after the residents of Vila Flavia. Look for us: that call for something or someone distant in contrast with a speech more of intimacy and in a more everyday registry; look for us, as one says to a parent, to a grandparent, someone in whom we trust. Ancestry!

Still to the left side of the painting the image of the earth ends, and it seems that Vila Flavia is released into the air, giving the impression that it is a world apart, detached, alienated. The crammed shacks demonstrate the periphery architecture with self-constructions without urban planning and infrastructure required, which makes people live in precarious conditions in relation not only to housing but also to other rights and services—health, transportation, quality education, and the like.

In the graffiti in *A vila como ela é*, the presence of the police in peripheral neighborhoods is almost always seen and felt as abusive and unable to maintain security and life as the statistics show us when they insist on denouncing the high number of deaths of young blacks at the expense of whites. Still more we perceive that the same picture bears the image of a boy kneeling in front of a police officer who directs the weapon toward his face in broad daylight (there is a child on a bicycle) while others are against the wall with hands in the air with another police officer aiming a gun at them. The scene leads us directly and indisputably to a denouncement against the police violence, violence that, as it appears in the same scenario, coexists with a child playing on a bike and people in the window, surviving between danger and leisure. All this contradiction configures life in Vila Flavia.

The narratives of and in the hip-hop universe, the various forms of languages in all elements, echo some of the realities of the different neighborhoods with their topographies, photographs, and peculiar characteristics. The prints are never the same but have recurring themes, among them the violence suffered by the black population, especially black youth, that leads to deaths.

The study "Map of Violence 2012: The Color of Homicides in Brazil" was conducted by the Brazilian Center for Latin American Studies and the Latin American Faculty of Social Sciences—FLACSO Brasil and analyzed data from 2002 to 2010 (www.mapadaviolencia.org.br). It shows that while there was a decrease in the number of murders of whites, down from 25.5 percent, for the black population there was an increase of 29.8 percent. According to the same study, among youth twelve to twenty-one years of age, the number of deaths among whites fell 33 percent while among blacks it increased 23.4 percent. It is a fact that the segment most susceptible to violent death is the youth, but blacks, men, the poor, and residents of periphery neighborhoods and villages are those at the highest risk of violent death.

The narratives of rappers, in spite of the transformations, new technologies, increase of public policies, and other signs of new times, continue to denounce the statistics and insist on saying that death has a race and an age. "Look for us!"

FINAL CONSIDERATION

As Morgan and Bennett presented in "Hip-hop and the Global Imprint of a Black Cultural Form," although hip-hop culture has been marginalized and treated in a trivial form by the dominant discourse, it has demonstrated its power of political regimentation among young people around the world and produced local scenes that respond to local demands and contribute to the empowerment of the social subjects involved. In hip-hop, culture is a political cause.

Besides the local impact, hip-hop, as one of the manifestations of contemporary African diasporic culture, has offered a language that connects youth of postcolonial contexts and enables them to build common political references.

The Brazilian dynamic noted thus far translates itself into a political process of resistance and creativity, which increasingly emphasizes the importance of the presence of hip-hop in the various spaces of political participation. In the case of the group OPNI, we can observe how they manipulate graffiti as a tool to read a particular reality, Vila Flavia, while connecting themselves to something bigger, the hip-hop nation.

Participation in public spaces and departments connect these groups to others, in order to construct alliances and present demands, general proposals, and specifics relevant to the broader agenda of diversity—racial, social, ethnic, age, cultural, gender, and environmental issues—which tends to strengthen its members.

Hip-hop culture transformed itself into movement by showing itself capable of involving different people and groups in a network of events that for many signifies imprinting significant changes in their way of acting and positioning themselves before the production and circulation of knowledge about the world, bringing new ways to gestate, organize, and implement practices that ensure learning and teaching for life.

There are many new voices that echo, showing that the youth, through means of black gestures, extend the translation and do much more than shake (hop) the hips (hip). They are young, black men and women or white men and women who live the same reality and are making, art, history, and culture.

NOTES

1. This ideology masked racial inequalities and contradictions in Brazil under the false idea that there is a harmonious encounter (mix) between different races.
2. OPNI (Objetos Pixadores Não Identificados), home page, accessed 25 July 2013, www.grupoopni.com.br.

WORKS CITED

Barbosa, Marcio, and Esmeralda Ribeiro. *Bailes: Soul, samba-rock, hip hop e identidade em São Paulo*. São Paulo, Brazil: Quilombhoje, 2007.

Cardoso, Ricardo, and Ana Christina Ribiero. "Dança de Rua." Campinas, Brazil: Editora Átomo, 2011.

de Jesus Felix, João Batista. "Chic Show e Zimbabwe a construção da identidade nos bailes black paulistanos." PhD diss., University of São Paulo, Brazil, 2000.

———. "HIP HOP: Cultura e Política no Contexto Paulistano." PhD diss., University of São Paulo, Brazil, 2005.

Geremias, Luiz. "A Fúria Negra Ressuscita: as raízes subjetivas do HIP HOP brasileiro." PhD diss., Federal University of Rio de Janeiro, 2006.

Gilroy, Paul. "The Black Atlantic Modernity and Double Consciousness." PhD diss., Universidade Cândido Mendes, Rio de Janeiro, 2001.

———. "Wearing Your Art on Your Sleeve." In *Small Acts: Thoughts on the Politics of Black Cultures*, 237–57. London: Serpent's Tail, 1993.

Gonzalez, Lélia. "O movimento negro na última década." In *Lugar de negro*, edited by Lélia Gonzalez and Carlos Alfredo Hasenbalg. Rio de Janeiro: Marco Zero, 1982.

Guimarães, Alfredo. "A modernidade Negra." *Teoria and pesquisa* (São Carlos, Brazil), nos. 42–43 (2003): 41–62.

———. "Notas sobre raça, cultura e identidade negra na Imprensa Negra de São Paulo e Rio de Janeiro, 1925–1950." *Afro-Ásia*, nos. 29–30 (2003): 247–70.

Macedo, Márcio. "Baladas black e rodas de samba da terra da garoa." In *Jovens na metrópole: etnografias de circuitos de lazer, encontro e sociabilidade*, edited by Jose Guilherme Cantor Magnani and Bruna Mantese de Souza. São Paulo, Brazil: Terceiro Nome, 2007.

———. "Warming the Black Soul through Vinyl Records: Media, Black Identity and Politics during the Brazilian Dictatorship." Lecture in Trabalho Final da Disciplina, Media and Social Theory. New School for Social Research, New York, Fall 2009.

Magro, Viviane Melo de Mendonça. "Adolescentes como autores de si próprios: cotidiano, educação e o hip hop." Campinas, Brazil: CEDES, 2002.

Morgan, Marcyliena. *The Real Hiphop: Battling for Knowledge, Power, and Respect in the LA Underground*. Durham, NC: Duke University Press, 2009.

Morgan, Marcyliena, and Dionne Bennett. "Hip-hop and the Global Imprint of a Black Cultural Form." *Daedalus* 140, no. 2 (2011): 176–96.

Panofsky, Erwin. *Studies in Iconology*. New York: Oxford University Press, 1939.

Pardue, Derek. *Ideologies of Marginality in Brazilian Hip Hop*. New York: Palgrave Macmillan, 2008.

Pimentel, Spency K. "O Livro vermelho do HIP HOP." PhD diss., University of São Paulo, Brazil, 1997.

Pinho, Osmundo de Araújo. "'Voz ativa': Rap—notas para leitura de um discurso contra-hegemônico." *Sociedade e cultura* 4, no. 2 (2001): 67–92.

Santos, Gevanilda. "Relações Raciais e Desigualdade no Brasil." São Paulo, Brazil: Selo Negro, 2009.

Santos, Jaqueline Lima. "Negro, Jovem e Hip Hopper: História, Narrativa e Identidade em Sorocaba." PhD diss., Universidade Estadual Paulista (UNESP), Marília, Brazil, 2011.

Souza, Ana Lúcia Silva. "Letramentos de (Re)existências." São Paulo, Brazil: Parábola, 2011.

Waiselfish, J. J. *Mapa da Violência 2012: A Cor dos Homicídios no Brasil*. Rio de Janeiro: CEBELA, FLACSO, 2012.

gun(n)

Arisa White

For Sakia Gunn

Sakia, if you had the weapon of your last name,
I would not know you. This steady scrape
against paper to transport fecund lament, never.
If in your hands the pearl handle gun,

my stepfather kept in the broom closet,
I'll give you the aim I practiced at twelve.
Head: "Home is where the heart is."
Trashcan: knees; the crack between the two
matters most.

If you brought me roses in high school,
wrapped in newspaper to protect me from thorns,
I would take them, wash ink from my fingers
in the jeans and jersey flood of your girl/boy body.
Let me be your girl.

4-evah 2 eternity onto my back,
your finger's ballpoint end, again and again
practices the heart over i, and into the morning
we stash whispers where over thread, thread crosses.
I promise

I have impeccable aim.
Pulling a trigger loosens mustangs
in your veins. Pee into my mortar, an old war
recipe makes bullets complete. Let your shower
wash an asshole from the streets.

If blood quickly betrayed its avenues
for Newark's sidewalks, his shirt tired of its thirst. . . .
If his buddy drove him to the hospital
or left him to watch the night unspool—
what a Jacob's ladder he could have made. . . .

If you're shocked your life required this exchange,
let me hold you. Enter the rooms I keep.
If we listen, you'll hear *Take off your coat*,
my threshold demands no bend—no ifs about it.

Comparing the Available Female Roles and the Social Contexts of *Sula* and *The Coldest Winter Ever*

Keenan Norris

"Female freedom," Toni Morrison writes in her 2004 foreword to *Sula*, "always means sexual freedom . . . especially when it is seen through the prism of economic freedom" (xiii). "Outlaw women are fascinating," she asserts, "not always for their behavior but because historically women are seen as naturally disruptive and their status is an illegal one from birth if it is not under the rule of men" (xvi). Morrison, here, has triangulated a set of assertions regarding womanhood and autonomy generally that can be applied specifically to the conflict at the heart of *Sula* (the fundamental opposition between Sula's absolutely disruptive and inviolable individuality and the superstitions and prejudices deeply rooted in the customs of Medallion's black community). The first of these assertions is that female freedom and sexual freedom are inseparable. The second is that women have historically been seen at essence as disruptive beings whenever they act as individuals as opposed to mechanisms within a marriage, family, or community. The last is that women have been accorded illegal status when not under the rule of men. All three statements, when examined in their proper contexts, are true: (1) Because most societies are administered by a primarily male government and economic hierarchy and because the governing ideology of our societies, as expressed in our religious documents and cultural faire, is typically centered around the concerns of men, women's roles in their social worlds are defined by men at the level of ideology and generally at the level of governing practice. Men have separated themselves from women and raised themselves above women economically, politically, and ideologically. Therefore, female freedom is inseparable from a radical relationship to the female sexual role. More specifically, the female sexual role must be changed for women to be free from male authority. (2) Because Western ideology largely derives from a book wherein the world's first woman breaks the bond between man and God, women are historically seen as disruptive figures. Moreover, because men have a freedom of movement, decision, and economic autonomy that is universally accepted, the disruptions that men bring about are understood not as disruptions but as the way of the world; because women have relatively less freedom, their disruptions are seen as discordant with the way of the world, and women are identified with that which is problematic to human societies. (3) Because women are understood as naturally disruptive and because men generally maintain ideological, economic, and political control over determining social systems, women who do not accept male rule place themselves outside the governing principles of their social worlds and become anathema to those worlds.

Morrison writes that she conceived of the women of *Sula* spatially:

> Hannah, Nel, Eva, Sula were points of a cross. . . . The nexus of that cross would be a merging of responsibility and liberty difficult to reach, a battle among women who are understood as least able to win it. Wrapped around the arms of that cross were wires of other kinds of battles—the veteran, the orphans, the husband, the laborers, confined to a village. . . . And the only triumph was that of the imagination. (xiii–xvi)

At the center point of Morrison's design is a difficult goal, the merging of responsibility and liberty; this point of merger is the ideal democratic secular society, the near antithesis of Medallion's black community. As a morally righteous, racially segregated, economically deprived burg, Medallion's Bottom is emphatically not a liberatory zone. The fully deprived black women of the community are least able to attain the ideal way of being so prized in their fitfully democratic nation. Only their most heroic attempts will draw them closer to that nexus ideal.

Just as distant from this idealized state of being are the other black folks in Medallion, the scared and judgmental church women and the disapproving men with no ground to stand on, the compassionate but trauma-shocked Shadrack, the unemployed laborers, and the undifferentiated orphans. Their confined existences "wrap around" and further confine the existences of Hannah, Nel, Eva, and Sula. As Trudier Harris, in her chapter on *Sula* in *Fiction and Folklore: The Novels of Toni Morrison*, explains, Hannah, Eva, and Sula Peace are "unacceptable except as reflections of a community that is dying. Sula carries no values that would sustain a society; Hannah would chip away at any established values; and Eva is too harsh . . . to create any but a very narrow world" (79). Contrary to Harris's alignment, it is the dying world of Medallion that is ultimately the root of the problem and not the Peace women. Just as blood will have blood, confinement creates confinement and cinches close confinement. The restrictions imposed on the black townsfolk in general and black male townsfolk in particular (primarily inter-generational unemployment enforced by the racist hiring practices of Medallion employers) function to deepen the restrictions placed upon the most restricted of persons, the black women of the community. The wires cinch closer and closer, tighter and tighter, turning round themselves, and eating into that which they purport to protect. On the cross, the four women struggle against, or accept, their bonds. Closest to the nexus ideal is Nel, who is free enough to love Sula deeper than she does anyone save her children, her husband, and her God. Nel loves women, men, and her community. She willingly bears the responsibilities that come with loving people. She becomes a pillar of the community and a heroically devoted wife, mother, and friend. Even after Sula has betrayed her by sleeping with Nel's husband, Nel seeks to reunite with Sula at Sula's deathbed and weeps and keens at Sula's grave. Nel is instinctively compassionate and responsible, and her passionate, devouring attachment to Sula indicates a certain freedom from the confines of Medallion that is unusual among the women and the men of the town. Contrasted with Nel, Sula Peace is the furthest from the nexus ideal: she is an absolute individual, with no love or care for her community, a force disruptive of the male-female power dynamics and the religious and moral certitudes held dear in Medallion. Sula, "an active, destructive artist," to borrow Harris's formulation, ultimately refuses the consolations of marriage, economic solvency, and community approval (54). Her destiny is, thus, pre-ordained. Living within social matrices of the community, she is subject to its governing logic and must, therefore, die impoverished, despised, and alone, impaled at the sharpest, most distant point on the cross.

This is perhaps the most powerful theme of Morrison's first major work: the archetypal conflict between this insular and entrenched small-town community in collision with an individual unreconciled to its dictates. "Sula," Harris writes, "simply is. . . . She is simply in the community; what it does or how it responds to her is of no consequence to her" (78). Sula's self-created and self-willed existence is, paradoxically, the centrifugal force in the novel, around which all else rotates, and yet is strangely without gravitational pull because Sula has no care for her community. This paradoxical nothingness around which the whole novel orbits has drawn much critical attention. Barbara Hill Rigney points to the silence that attends Chicken Little's drowning, the "closed place in the water" where he goes down, as well as the "soundlessness" of Sula's orgasm and the decisive departure, absence, and nothingness that becomes of her romance with Ajax, the painful recognition of which quickly kills the force that is Sula (23–24). This and other similar critical interventions have been validated both directly and indirectly by Morrison herself in her own critical work. *Playing in the Dark: Whiteness and the Literary Imagination* is predicated upon the importance of those silences and omissions that obscure African American presence in canonized American literature from Melville to Twain, Faulkner, and Hemingway. In her 1988 lecture "Unspeakable Things Unspoken: The Afro-American Presence in American Literature," she tells us that "a void may be empty but is not a vacuum . . . certain absences are so stressed, so ornate, so planned, they call attention to themselves" (16).

The first half of Morrison's novel calls attention to the insanity of a WWI veteran returned to Medallion's black village, the childhood of Sula and Nel, and the many sudden, violent tragedies that mark these years, including Sula and Nel's accidental drowning of Chicken Little. The randomness and inexplicable shocks of the novel's first movement become juxtaposed against the allegorical narrative of the second movement: Sula, ushered along by a plague of sparrows, returns from ten years away at college and from traveling between America's great metropolises to The Bottom. Shadrack tips his cap to her, and Dessie decides that this is a salutation shared between Satan's disciples. Almost immediately her behavior and eventually her very presence spark animus amongst the black folk. Sula puts on airs, wearing attention-catching clothes; she unabashedly sleeps with other women's men, takes Jude (Nel's husband) to bed, and is rumored to be so promiscuous that she even sleeps with white men, so that she fast comes to embody, for the black people of Medallion, the essence of the Devil's mischief.

The last of these offenses, her rumored relationships with white men, is an explicit challenge to black male authority over black women. Sula is transgressing the ideological line that would keep her under the control of black men. This transgression is soliloquized in one of the novel's more memorable passages: upon meeting Nel's husband and hearing him complain about how he and black men in general are conscripted into menial service at the beck and call of powerful white men, Sula counters that black men are not oppressed but rather "the envy of the world" (104). Everybody, she says, desires and loves black men. White women want them, and white men want to be them; sisters love them, and brothers love themselves well beyond the limits of healthy self-esteem. Sula's boldness leads Jude to comment that Sula is unmarried because, while she can stimulate a man's mind, she is too intellectually assertive and domineering to stir his body. Contrary to Jude's admonition, Sula's appeal proves stronger than Jude would admit when Jude cheats on his wife and sleeps with Sula, an act that at once reinforces Sula's thesis that black men are sexually desirable as well as the fact of her absolutely anarchic, transgressive character.

"As always," Morrison writes, with hard eloquence, "the black people looked at evil stony-eyed and let it run" (113). They "said [Sula] was a bitch" and evil as well (112). Medallion's black community scorns Sula and only tolerates her presence in the patient yet thoroughly close-minded way that they abide all things they count as evil. Because God "was not the God of three faces they sang about," they are so compelled, for "they knew quite well that He had four, and that the fourth explained Sula." They lay broomsticks across their doors at night and sprinkle salt on porch steps, to ward off the evil that they perceive. "There was no creature," Morrison writes, "so ungodly as to make them destroy it. . . . The presence of evil was something to be first recognized, then dealt with, survived, outwitted, triumphed over" (118). This complex relationship to perceived evil, and by extension to Sula, is interesting for its divergence from mainstream Christian religious responses to that which is taboo or considered evil. "She is," Rigney writes, "that last unexplained quadrant of the crossed circle symbolic of mandelic wholeness, the fourth face of the Holy Trinity, without which Father, Son and Holy Ghost are incomplete" (55). Whereas mainstream Christian responses would include either the banishment or outright annihilation of the evil subject, the black folks tacitly tolerate that which they despise. In fact, as Rigney argues, the first three faces of the Trinity cannot be understood without knowledge of a fourth, and that fourth face provides wholeness to a material life so powerfully impacted by despair and deprivation. God, as black Medallion perceives him, is dually good and evil. I read God's fourth face not with Rigney as some quadrant inexplicable without excursion into Buddhism (i.e., "the crossed circle symbolic of mandelic wholeness") but rather as the lost angel Lucifer, selectively silenced and erased in more tame forms of Christian religious practice but everywhere present in the black Medallion world. This fierce Christianity, like the concept of mandelic wholeness, can be objectified by a four-quadrant symbol, but in Morrison's own formulation, where "Hannah, Nel, Eva, Sula were points of a cross," this symbol is the cross repurposed to a black folk culture design (xiii–xvi).

This black folk culture spiritual design accommodates the Devil, Sula, and a thousand natural shocks, inexplicable deaths, and sudden tragedies. For the black people to banish evil from their presence and therefore *take control* of their environment by subduing it would be to fabricate an unnatural lifeway wherein the work of God would be replaced by the fears of men and women. Such an escape, even if desired, is impossible due to the racial segregation and economic deprivation that the community faces on a daily basis. At its best, the black community confined to The Bottom, barred from good jobs, and forced to live on the town's leftovers exists beyond fear and beyond consolation, in a state of stony-eyed knowledge, endurance, and courage.

When Sula meets Ajax, she falls in love. He appreciates her mind as well as her body and willingly holds conversations with her, which she values more than their physical relationship. Ajax sees in Sula a woman reminiscent of his mother, an "evil conjure woman" strange in appearance and incredible in her talents. Where before Sula, Ajax "had never met an interesting woman in his life," save his mother, his curiosity is suddenly sparked (126). Sula's uncanny effect on men intensifies with her relationship with Ajax, and Ajax has an equal effect on her. For the first time, Sula begins to work her way toward the nexus of the cross where liberty and responsibility intersect. In the attempt, of course, she tangles ever more tightly in the wires that represent the community wrapping round the ambitions and emotions of women.

"Sula," Morrison confides, "began to discover what possession was" (131). Her need for Ajax is so surpassing, it astonishes and overwhelms and changes her. Where until his arrival, Sula had been a kind of inviolable individual impervious to the pettiness, possessiveness, and neediness of town and city, after Ajax her sentiments become more mainstream. When Ajax leaves her, with seemingly typical masculine indifference, Sula is broken. As if in acknowledgment that she has succumbed to love and heartbreak and is no longer the uniquely impervious self of all her previous days, Sula soon after falls ill and dies.

In her deathbed argument with Nel, Sula reasserts her radical female authority: "I know what every colored woman in this country is doing . . . dying. Just like me. But the difference is they dying like a stump. Me, I'm going down like one of those redwoods. I sure did live in this world." When Nel asks what Sula has "to show" for all her living, Sula responds, "Show? To who? Girl, I got my mind" (143). This assertion, reminiscent of Ellison's Invisible Man happily sequestered in a forgotten basement by novel's end, is also in keeping with Morrison's rhetoric in the 2004 foreword: "The only triumph was that of the imagination" (xiii–xvi). Fiedler's *Love and Death in the American Novel* was perhaps the first critical work to identify and extensively document the centrality of antisocial male characters in the canon of American literature, noting, among other observations, the American rejection of the European novel of manners, its dramas of family and community relations, and its reliance on custom, ritual, and acceptable behavior in favor of an antiheroic narrative mode that fetishizes individual freedom of mind and body above all else. Sula's elevation of individual intellect and desire above the wants, needs, and customs of the community is in keeping with male heroes from Huckleberry Finn and Ishmael to Victor LaValle's mentally ill ecstatic, Percival Everett's Thelonius "Monk" Ellison, and Junot Diaz's wondrous Oscar Wao. Precisely what draws Nel and Ajax and the reader to Sula is that she is, if not the only interesting woman in Medallion, at least an exceptional female figure indifferent to patriarchal authority and community customs, a woman willing to assert her own individuality and freedom.

Sula's presence is anarchic, and her actions far from unproblematic—a "despicable user," Harris avers (54). In her behavior, Sula not only exposes the town's bigotry but also plays games with the genuine companionship and loyalty that is offered her. The most dubious of her acts is sleeping with Jude, Nel's husband. "But what about me?" Nel wonders during the deathbed scene. "Why didn't you think about me? Didn't I count? I never hurt you" (144). This plea, moving, heartfelt, and morally unambiguous, rings true. Sula has hurt Nel without cause or thought to the consequences of her actions. Nel is right to look askance at her old friend, even on her deathbed. The conflict between the individual and the community, between liberty and responsibility, is a thick, fraught one. Neither Sula nor her community is necessarily right or good, nor is either necessarily wrong or bad. Their conflict is an inevitable moment in the progress of a society, a tipping point at which old values are challenged, dubiously upheld, and ultimately found wanting. When Sula is buried and the black people of Medallion shun her funeral, leaving it to the white people, this is a comment less on Sula's character than on the character of the townsfolk and their governing ideologies. Where even the white people of Medallion are willing to acknowledge the universal moment and tragedy of death and cross racial lines to send Sula on, the black folks are conspicuous for their mean-spirited refusal to do so. The old values of Medallion's community, at least those that relate to the female role within the community, having been challenged and dubiously upheld, are finally found wanting.

That Sula is labeled as bad and even evil due to the misogynistic ideology informing the townsfolks' judgments is wrong. If Sula were a man, her betrayal of Nel would have been forgiven in time and, more important, would have been seen as a natural aspect of her male character. To brand a man as evil or rail endlessly against his promiscuity is understood as a waste of time and a denial of nature, but women are afforded no such forgiveness. *Sula* speaks powerfully to the untruth of such ideology. As in Matthew 10:34, Sula has not come to make peace. Rather, she has returned to Medallion as the embodiment of difference and change. She has asserted her individuality and freedom by taking control of her sexual life and by disregarding the male-dominant ideologies of both the men and women among whom she lives. In the "Unspeakable Things Unspoken: The Afro-American Presence in American Literature" lecture, Morrison calls her "new world black and new world woman . . . improvisational. Daring, disruptive, imaginative, modern, out-of-the-house, outlawed" (33). *Sula* is a major complication and progression in American literature's approach to women's lives. Roderick Ferguson posits that the novel "offered black lesbian feminists an opportunity to formulate a politics that could negate the gender, racial and sexual regulations of nationalist formulations" (111). Certainly the novel acknowledges an expanding range of available female roles, in part by dramatizing just how limited and irrational are the gender, racial, and sexual boundaries that Sula transgresses. *Sula* at once presages the many commercially and artistically successful novels by and about black women over the past three decades and marks a high point in the radical representation of black women, upsetting unexamined notions and challenging the literature itself to deeper examinations and explorations.

Read in relation to *Sula*, Sister Souljah's *Coldest Winter Ever* signals both progression and regression. Published twenty-six years after Morrison's radical novel, *The Coldest Winter Ever* is today one of the most popular books among young black readers, male and especially female. Simone Gibson notes, in "Critical Readings: African American Girls and Urban Fiction," that it is "the novel accredited with the reinvigoration of the genre from its original popularity in the 1960s and 1970s" (565). So it makes sense that I've known many young people, especially young black women, to insist that the novel is the best thing they've ever read, their most favorite novel, even that they have read it three and four and five times.

The main character is Winter Santiaga. Winter covets her mother's many marital possessions and shows no compassion for her mother when she loses the man and the looks that garnered those goods. Winter betrays her girlfriends, fucking their men and double-crossing them in business. She steals donation money from HIV-infected patients, beats and robs an old woman with a sock full of rocks, spends money with staggering frivolity, ignores the advice of legitimate mentors, is absolutely uneducable, and seems to find value only in a life inundated with predatory, rapacious thugs. The novel, however, is bigger and more complicated than Winter, and its vision of black womanhood is important and multifaceted.

Winter is the daughter of Ricky Santiaga, one of Brooklyn's most notorious and successful drug dealers. As the novel opens, the Santiagas find themselves at the tail end of a long reign as a drug kingpin family in the ghettos of Brooklyn. Sensing that they are no longer safe within the city, Mr. Santiaga moves his family to Long Island. But when his impatient, greedy wife grows bored with her new suburban home, things go wrong. Mr. Santiaga takes her with him on a trip back to Brooklyn, and she is shot in the face, destroying her appearance and sense of self-worth. Santiaga, enraged, retakes a hands-on approach to his business, mandating a war on the streets of Brooklyn. In the ensuing madness, law enforcement gets involved and Santiaga's entire crew of drug pushers and assorted thugs are apprehended, jailed, charged, and eventually convicted of conspiracy and drug trafficking. "It was apparent it was a total wipeout. One by one," Winter recalls, "women's voices filled with fear, rage, and hysteria called demanding Santiaga rescue their husbands, brothers, sons" (93). Santiaga meets the same fate as well. His family scatters. His house and all his assets are seized and redistributed; his wife falls into crack addiction; his youngest twin daughters are placed in the care of Midnight, the only man in Santiaga's crew not to be imprisoned; and his eldest daughter Winter is remanded to foster care until she turns eighteen.

Winter articulates a rational argument against the policing of drug trafficking: "People don't understand Santiaga's world. It's business. Nobody kept a drug dealer's business in check but the dealer himself and the team he set up. There has to be punishment for those within the team who test too much and step out of line. There has to be punishment for outsiders who attack the business. Violations have to be responded to." Winter is not wrong. Drugs should be legalized and regulated throughout the country, thereby eliminating the need for those who sell drugs to protect their product and locations of sale. Law enforcement, Winter argues, "shouldn't be able to barge into our business and force their rules on us" (117–18). In a true free market system, unencumbered by misplaced morality and selective competition, law enforcement would only interrupt business that directly endangers the public health and welfare. Drug abuse, not drug use, would be policed. Where Winter and her father have it wrong is in their unwillingness to bend to settled law: until the laws change, they risk their freedom by dealing drugs, or even by living in the same house as a drug dealer. By idolizing her father and rationalizing his stubborn, destructive behavior, Winter sets a life path for herself that is similarly doomed.

Winter's only male attachments are to men who remind her of her father. She seeks out strong-willed young men involved in drug dealing. This explains her crush on Santiaga's employee Midnight. Midnight's assertion of discipline, poise, confidence, and control impresses her. She describes his voice as having "that masculine authority that made me hot" (41). Note how Winter's romantic and sexual impulses depart from Sula's: while both are promiscuous, Sula and Winter are attracted by different characteristics in men. Where Sula is drawn to Ajax for his masculinity, self-confidence, and self-control, she has no desire to see Ajax dominate other people, least of all herself. Winter states that her man "would need to own the world to win [her]" (10). Where she takes pride in imagining Midnight beating down other men just to impress her and sees proof of manhood in Santiaga's murder of two fellow inmates (she figures they are weak men who deserve to be done away with), Sula doesn't care to see her man dominate everything in his path. Where Winter wants her man to own the world, Sula is not possessive or ego driven and is not attracted to men who are highly acquisitive or egotistical. Where Sula is "new world black and new world woman," Winter is cut from an old and confining cloth that limits the possible lifeways for both women and men (Morrison, 33).

Winter wants to dominate and humiliate other women, hence her constant talk about being the baddest bitch, the finest-looking, best-dressed chick in Brooklyn. Where Sula and the Peace women locate themselves within a small but complex "woman-centered consciousness" that "defies syllogistic equations," as well as traditional logic, morality, and spirituality, Winter lives in a vast but tightly tied and simply drawn world (Harris, 75, 71). Hers is a world without the dark unknowable beauties of spirituality, cut off from supernatural fantasy and power. It is a world of material, man-made hierarchies, with everyone's worth determined by whether they are more or less attractive, wealthy, and so forth, than their peers. Because her thinking is so oriented around a simplistic ethics of dominance and submission, she cannot understand why the men whom she wants to be dominated by should be humble before women or before the world. Sister Souljah points out in her excellent explanatory notes for the novel, "If a man cannot be humble, it is likely that he cannot be still. To be still is to be silent, without motion. Every man needs to have or develop the ability to be still at some point in each day. It is the time when he can consider or reconsider his past actions. It is the time when he can think or pray. It is the time when he can allow his conscience to do its job." Obviously, these truisms apply as aptly to women and girls as they do to men and boys. Winter, in particular, shares these faults with her male counterparts. "There are many grown men today," Souljah writes, "who never even consider going to a library or bookstore, or opening a book to read. . . . Their lack of humility convinces them that there is no need to read. Their arrogance reminds them that they already know everything. As a result, they can never grow or change." She points out that, in contrast to Winter, Midnight is contemplative, bookish, loyal and humble, willing to take direction and able to learn from his mistakes. "Midnight," she writes, "was able to be still" (497–98). Winter and Midnight would have been incompatible at every level. Where Midnight, despite his profession, fulfills many of the ideals of masculinity (and gives up drug dealing, moves to Maryland, raises Santiaga's youngest daughters, and opens a barbershop after Santiaga goes to prison) by ceding authority and dominance, Winter's desires remain too base to allow her to recognize the deeper strength that comes from humility, silence, and study.

One might, however, look at Winter in a different light. *Salon*'s Sean Elder categorizes Winter as a "dead-pan narrator in the Huck Finn mode." Elder takes gleeful pleasure in Winter's fast-tongued mockery of everything and everyone around her—from overweight activists to AIDS patients in need of "fashion rescue" (Souljah, 272). Seeing Winter as a ribald, Huck Finn–type character groups her not only with Twain's famous child but also with an array of canonized antiheroic American youth figures portrayed in literature, including J. D. Salinger's Holden Caulfield (*Catcher in the Rye*) and Hemingway's Nick Adams (the Nick Adams stories), as well as more recent antiheroic central figures such as Cormac McCarthy's kid (*Blood Meridian*) and, in fact, Sula Peace herself. Such an analysis exposes a surprisingly strong connection between Morrison's seminal novel and Souljah's famous street lit story. As antiheroic and antisocial female outlaws, Sula and Winter are reminiscent each of the other. While very different in the ways they approach their womanhood and their given societies, Winter does share with Sula a visceral lack of regard for propriety and nicety. Winter is the narrator of her picaresque so she usually expresses this antiheroic streak in misanthropic interior monologues, whereas Sula is "off stage" for large portions of *Sula* and therefore expresses her antiheroic style through a compilation of sexual exploits, rumored doings, and singularly memorable encounters. (The scene in which Sula cuts off the tip of her finger to scare the white boys who have harassed Nel and her on the way home from school comes to mind, as does the famous scene in the kitchen with Nel and Jude.) Despite even this formal difference in how their cavalier attitudes are presented to the reader, it is probably the case that Sula and Winter stand as the two most well-known black female versions of a classic American literary type, the solitary, journeying, experiencing antihero.

"Precocious, babacious and as tough as a hollow-point bullet," Winter predictably bucks at the curfew and other restrictions placed on her at the all-girls foster home (the House of Success), which she is required to enter after her father is incarcerated (Elder). She sets up a scheme by which a girlfriend on the outside steals clothes from department stores and supplies them to Winter, who then sells them to the girls at the house. Along with doing hair and nails for the girls, this scheme nets Winter some decent money with which to indulge herself. Perpetually on the search for eligible young drug dealers and rappers, Winter attends a party with some of her old friends. When she flirts with her girlfriend Natalie's boyfriend, there's a falling out that ends with Winter unable to return to the House of Success without being attacked. On the run, she ends up living with radio personality and purveyor of black uplift rhetoric Sister Souljah and Souljah's friend, a young black female doctor who owns the house in which Souljah lives and from which she ministers to various disadvantaged groups. Winter hates Sister Souljah on general principle ("She the type of female I'd like to cut in the face with my razor" [1]) and dismisses the doctor as an overeducated, unmarried failure. Completely dismissive of the material aid and advice both young black women try to give, she lies about her identity, her past, and her family situation and attempts to use Souljah to gain access to the popular rappers with whom Souljah organizes benefit concerts and charity events. When Winter learns that Souljah has a vague relationship with Midnight, she works as doorwoman at an event for HIV-positive New Yorkers at which Souljah is speaking, steals the event's donated monies, steals Souljah's letters (including her correspondence with Midnight), and leaves for Maryland, where she has learned Midnight lives. The strict moral logic that overgoverns the plot and intent of the novel makes for a severe dichotomy here, between Winter—mean, dishonest, hapless, and uneducable—and Souljah and the doctor, who are both generous, fair dealing, professionally successful, and well educated. Winter's rejection of these women and the bond that they offer presages her ultimate downfall.

Before she can make it to Maryland, Winter meets an old sex mate, Bullet. Bullet has become a successful drug dealer since last Winter knew him. He satisfies Winter's ego, telling her she's beautiful and taking her on vacation to Key West. Winter figures she's finally returned to the life she was always meant to lead, now supported by a man as able and calculating as her father. It quickly becomes apparent that Bullet is practicing psychological control over Winter, sequestering her in an apartment, marking her movements, and punishing her whenever she disobeys him. In one chilling episode, he lets three pit bull dogs loose in the apartment, effectively confining Winter to her bedroom for days without food or water. Bullet keeps his drugs in the apartment, leased under Winter's name. He transports the drugs in a car, rented under her name. And when law enforcement busts the criminal operation, Bullet is not even charged while Winter is given a fifteen-year prison sentence. After her first year incarcerated, her old girlfriend Natalie is imprisoned in the same unit on similar charges. The novel ends with brutal determinism: at the funeral for Winter's mother, Midnight, the symbol of right masculinity, arrives with Winter's two younger sisters; Santiaga and Winter, the symbols of America's imprisonment age, attend as well. "[My father] wanted to hug me," Winter recalls, "but his hands were chained, and so were mine" (426). At book's end, father and daughter are state property no different than if they were slaves.

In her 2010 essay "Reading Street Literature, Reading America's Prison System," Kristina Graaff observes that "a particular important facet of the genre is how it is inextricably linked to the US penal system on multiple levels. . . . Imprisonment is also a central theme in most storylines" (1). *The Coldest Winter Ever* closes within the prison system, in this powerful final scene. But the specter of incarceration haunts the entire novel. In a sense, the book begins with incarceration when Santiaga is convicted on drug charges. Shortly thereafter, Winter enters a form of juvenile confinement, if not incarceration, at the House of Success. The possibility of jail and prison time stalks every movement of the criminal enterprises that pervade the narrative. Graaff speaks to the shadowing omnipresence of prison, which is a feature not only of Souljah's novel but also of the vast majority of street lit novels:

> In a rather pessimistic, though one might say also more realistic stance, prison is integrated into numerous Street Lit narratives as an inevitable and recurring part of the characters' life. In what might be termed *stagnation narratives*— referring to the African American migration narratives that usually depict the *move* from the South to the Northern cities—characters permanently oscillate between streets and prison, without ever managing to escape the vicious circle between the two worlds. (Graaff, 2)

In this startling formulation, Graaff not only describes the role of prison in much of street lit but also is able to link it, in ironic contrast, to the Great

Migration that is an essential component of African American history deeply impactful upon American life ever since WWI. Isabel Wilkerson explains that the migration's "imprint is everywhere in urban life. The configuration of the cities as we know them, the social geography of black and white neighborhoods, the spread of the housing projects as well as the rise of a well-scrubbed black middle class"; all were the product of the migration. Perhaps even more importantly, the migration created "people who might not have existed, or become who they did . . . James Baldwin and Michelle Obama, Miles Davis and Toni Morrison, Spike Lee and Denzel Washington" (Wilkerson 10). Perhaps Winter Santiaga would not exist in the way she does without the migration having happened, but she is the product less of the migration itself than of inner-city social patterns that postdate it.

By contrast to the epic agential movement across American space in quest for freedom, safety, better-paying work, and the fulfillment of human potential that Wilkerson narrates in *The Warmth of Other Suns*, the stagnation narrative that Graaff identifies within street literature presents us with documents that are almost exactly opposite in their content. The stories are tightly bound within their urban confines. The story subjects are never fully free, for they "permanently oscillate between streets and prison"; they lack the basic bodily safety that comes with the knowledge that one is highly unlikely to be incarcerated, as well as the more general safety that a life outside illegal and penal spaces obviously affords. Those who are put to any sort of work provide labor with scant remuneration, probably compensated at a rate lower than the inflation-adjusted real wages received by plantation sharecroppers after Reconstruction. The stagnation narrative also recalls Ruth Gilmore's observation that the principal effect of modern mass incarceration is not spectacular violence or even covert punishment but *"incapacitation"* (14). Gilmore avers that theorizing mass incarceration of black and brown Americans cannot properly be termed a "new slavery," nor linked to Patterson's social death concept that is more correctly seen as the effect of slavery, not incarceration, because "very few prisoners work for anybody while they're locked up" (21). Rather, Gilmore writes, from the perspective of the prison system and from the perspective of the society that has brought it into being, modern American prisons are nothing more than a "simple-minded . . . geographical solution that purports to solve social problems by extensively and repeatedly removing people from disorder, de-industrialized milieus, and depositing them somewhere else" (14). From the perspective of the incarcerated and the potentially incarcerated who populate street lit texts (not to mention the fact that many authors of street lit novels can claim personal experience of incarceration), the absurdity of a penal system that simply seeks to periodically relocate people into immobile situations is obvious because, by its very nature, such a system negates personal development and moral and social evolution, and reinforces a cyclical lifestyle that turns between dubious freedom and stagnating confinement. There is no rehabilitation here, let alone progress beyond recurrent criminality and imprisonment. Street lit's stagnation narratives reflect criminologists' findings that mass incarceration as a system of crime regulation is a self-perpetuating practice: "Prison time doesn't exactly prevent crime and it doesn't exactly cause crime. Its public safety benefit," Paul Butler writes, "depends on our ability to calibrate how much to use it. . . . Most scholars believe that the increase in incarceration in the 1990s lowered the crime rate by around 20 percent"; however, "after that, most criminologists agree, the crime reduction benefit of incarceration levels off" due to the combined effect of prison and jail overcrowding, social disorder, family disruption, the routinization of the prison experience, and there being too many unemployable young men (32–33). Central to the objective value of street lit, Graaff argues, is precisely that it makes such an issue of mass incarceration in America. Mass incarceration and the prison system that is its operating mechanism is a kind of socially silent yet omnipresent, hugely powerful institution in America. "[Street lit] embodies and illustrates the omnipresence, magnitude and repercussions of the prison apparatus like no other literary genre or artistic expression" (3).

Graaff terms *The Coldest Winter Ever* "a cautionary tale," chiefly because Souljah has structured her story so as to "illustrate the destructive outcome awaiting those involved in the crack trade, but also to represent prison as a just punishment for those partaking in criminal activities" (2). This moral structure is, additionally, ethnicized and racialized: Winter's last name, Santiaga, suggests her Latino heritage. Winter's mother is African American, and her father is Latino or black Latino. Mr. Santiaga's mistress, Dulce Triminestre, is Puerto Rican. If Winter is the product of these crime-corrupted unions, the message seems to be that inner-city black and brown youth have been tragically corrupted by the processes of the drug game and the felonizing of possession and conspiracy charges. In particular, her story demonstrates the impact of the drug culture on poor communities and the dubious way in which law enforcement builds cases against socially marginal people, exploiting the weakest members of a criminal enterprise, and punishing them for not colluding against their friends, family, and close associates.

Distinguishing her novel from the glorifications of street life inundating hip-hop and Hollywood, Sister Souljah, in her notes to the novel, asks, "But who was going to tell the story that focused on the fall of a drug kingpin, and of how he descends into poverty and slavery? How the state places him back in chains naked and pinned in, chained to another slave just like him? . . . How the world pimps his unprotected daughters and dwarfs then devours his sons?" (437). *The Coldest Winter Ever*, she implies, is the answer to these questions. If the novel is understood as a statement, or a series of exposés, it is the predictable answer to these questions.

Conceived as an utterly determinist and naturalist fiction wherein each character, save Midnight, fulfills a destiny determined by his or her socioeconomic position, the novel is less a piece of art than a social and political statement and, as such, is completely effective. However, when placed against Morrison's *Sula*, *The Coldest Winter Ever* appears a sad, limited expression. I am not making an artistic judgment; rather, because Souljah's novel eschews traditional literary aesthetic concerns around lyricism and narrative experiment as consciously and determinedly as do Stephen Crane's *Maggie: A Girl of the Streets* and Dreiser's *Sister Carrie*, I am noting the social openness, hope, and beauty of women like Sula, and the comparative closedness and pettiness that characterizes Winter's life. Winter is much more kin to abused and abusing characters like Crane's Maggie, Dreiser's Carrie, and Ann Petry's Lutie Johnson. Like Carrie, Winter's avarice is its own prison, and like Maggie and Lutie, Winter is forsaken by the world, condemned by its logic of power. In fact, one can find parallels between the way Carrie is seduced first by Charlie, then by Hurstwood, only to part disastrously with both men, and the way Winter binds herself to the degenerate rapper GS and then allows herself to be seduced and betrayed by Bullet. I refer to Carrie's parting from both her lovers as disastrous despite the fact that Carrie herself ends up a famous woman in the entertainment world. This is not only because both men gutter out when their relationships with her fall apart but also because at the book's conclusion, Carrie is materially successful but, like Winter, lacks the close relational bonds that are so crucial to psychic wellness.

Comparing Souljah's story with Stephen Crane's naturalistic novel of New York renders similar parallels: Winter is marginalized by the state after her father is arrested and the family's assets frozen; poverty and intergenerational alcohol abuse force Maggie out of doors and into street prostitution. Maggie's marginalization and eventual squalid demise resembles Winter's imprisonment and consequent erasure from free society. Like Lutie Johnson in *The Street*, whom after killing Boots realizes that she has misdirected her rage and despair at an average black man instead of at the landlord, club owner, and police who have variously targeted her son and her, at book's end Winter finds in her imprisoned father the symbol of personal, familial, and racial defeat.

The Coldest Winter Ever can be located within this sphere of urban naturalism and determinism and shares with other novels of this type a certain moralizing as well. The logic of *The Coldest Winter Ever* is a strictly dichotomous world of right and wrong (the doctor is good; Santiaga is bad. Midnight is good; Bullet is bad. Souljah is good; Winter is bad, etc.). Whereas *Sula* challenges traditional moral and artistic strictures, *The Coldest Winter Ever* reinforces a deeply conventional moral system and falls back on a cumbersome literary style. Perhaps because the consequences of transgressing moral codes in the world of contemporary street literature are no longer a bad reputation and a case of the clap but death from AIDS, imprisonment on drug possession charges, or execution in the streets, there is little room left for the political and poetic risks characteristic to the world of Morrison's women.

Sula, for one, lives her life with a sense of its human potential: she lives to the utmost and, against their conscious will, enlivens all those around her, friends as well as enemies, lovers and haters. Because she has stepped out of her "proper" place and imagined herself differently, those around her react to her uniqueness and discover new capacities within themselves for fear, love, and imagination. Sula's willingness to transgress the boundaries of her social world stands in stark and depressing contrast to the determinism that rules Winter's society, actions, and ultimate fate. Where Sula is free, Winter is figuratively and literally a slave to her father's world, her ghetto upbringing, and the state itself.

We might speculate that one reason for this regression is the unsustainability in modern America of the black folk culture that Sula at once revels in and so flamboyantly disrupts. Sula's story itself is the sign of a dying community; black Medallionites are unable to get jobs or make money and cannot protect their land from annexation into a golf course by the hostile dominant society. Medallion is precariously preserved in its pre-WWII state by a mish-mash of Christianity and folk spirituality, by endurance and insularity. It is a doomed world just as Sula, though the free artist of herself, is yet a doomed woman in her dying world. Perhaps Winter Santiaga is the inevitable progeny of the death of black and Latin folk cultures in modern America.

Sula ends in sorrow, but it is told in love. By contrast, *The Coldest Winter Ever* records a bleak regress into intellectual, spiritual, and physical confinement. However, it must be recognized that if the novel is read not against its predecessors in black women's literature but by itself, it is valuable. Taken for what it is, the scathing record of an American crime involving equally drug addicts and dealers and a misguided corrupt judicial system, the novel serves its purpose. It is a tour de force. And if it is in some sense time bound to our specific environment and our passing way of things, readers will come to it years from now knowing themselves lucky and will read with awful wonderment about this world.

WORKS CITED

Birkerts, Sven. "The Surreal Thing." *New York Times*, 9 May 2004.
Butler, Paul. *Let's Get Free: A Hip-Hop Theory of Justice*. New York: New Press, 2009.
Collins, Patricia Hill. *Black Feminist Thought: Knowledge, Consciousness, and the Politics of Empowerment*. Boston: Unwin Hyman, 1990.
Dreiser, Theodore. *Sister Carrie*. New York: Oxford University Press, 1900.

Elder, Sean. *"The Coldest Winter Ever*: Sister Souljah Gives Herself a Starring Role in Her First Novel." *Salon*, 12 April 1999. www.salon.com/.

Ferguson, Roderick. *Aberrations in Black: Toward a Queer of Color Critique*. Minneapolis: University of Minnesota Press, 2004.

Gibson, Simone Cade. "Critical Readings: African American Girls and Urban Fiction." *Journal of Adolescent and Adult Literacy* 53 (2010): 565–74.

Gilmore, Ruth Wilson. *Golden Gulag: Prisons, Surplus, Crisis and Opposition in Globalizing California*. Berkeley: University of California Press, 2007.

Graaff, Kristina. "Reading Street Literature, Reading America's Prison System." PopMatters, 12 February 2010. www.popmatters.com/.

Harris, Trudier. *Fiction and Folklore: The Novels of Toni Morrison*. Knoxville: University of Tennessee Press, 1991.

Morrison, Toni. *Sula*. New York: Vintage, 1973. Reprinted with a new foreword by the author. New York: Vintage International, 2004.

———. "Unspeakable Things Unspoken: The Afro-American Presence in American Literature." Lecture presented at the Tanner Lectures on Human Values, University of Michigan, Ann Arbor, 7 October 1988.

Petry, Ann. *The Street*. New York: Mariner Books, 1946.

Rigney, Barbara Hill. *The Voices of Toni Morrison*. Columbus: Ohio State University Press, 1991.

Souljah, Sister. *The Coldest Winter Ever*. 1999. New York: Pocket Star Books, 2006.

Wilkerson, Isabel. *The Warmth of Other Suns: The Epic Story of America's Great Migration*. New York: Vintage, 2011.

In Their Own Words

Street Lit, Code Meshing, and Linguistic Diversity

Nikia Chaney

EBONICS, A FOREIGN LANGUAGE?

In 1996, the Oakland Unified School District declared that African American Vernacular, or Ebonics as it was called, was a separate language from English. The school district stated that this language was the primary language of the majority of Oakland students. The district further claimed that Ebonics was "genetically based" on "West and Niger Congo African Language Systems" (Original Oakland Resolution on Ebonics, 1996). The school district asked for federal funding to support Ebonics educational programs that were equivalent to existing bilingual programs. They wanted a raise in salaries for teachers who were fluent in both Standard English and Ebonics, and they wanted mandated instruction in Ebonics for students. In essence, the school district wanted to legitimize this "foreign" language, Ebonics, in order to help their struggling students master Standard English.

At the time of the resolution, half of all children in the school district were African American. Approximately 52 percent of all students enrolled in the district were African American. Yet these students' grade point averages were only 1.8 percent, far lower than other minorities such as Asian, Hispanic, and white students who attended the same schools and sat in the same classes. These other minority students, however, were entitled to federal funding from the Department of Education, Title 7, for bilingual education for the fiscal 1997 budget because English was not their native language. If "Ebonics" was characterized as a foreign language, then African American students in the district would be entitled to this same funding. Perhaps the Oakland school district in drafting this resolution looked at the measure as a

creative educational approach for both the disparity in their students' performances and the survival of the majority of their struggling students, or perhaps the motive has more to do with a need for extra funding. Regardless of
their intentions, one fact remains clear: this was a legitimate attempt to
recognize African American English separate from Standard English in the
classroom.

Undoubtedly, there was massive negative publicity resulting from this
resolution. The Oakland School District was criticized by the news media
and local governing boards. Curiously, African American organizations and
prominent African Americans also spoke out about the resolution. As detailed in a 1996 *New York Times* article, the poet Maya Angelou said, "The
very idea that African American language is a language separate and apart"
would encourage African American students not to learn Standard English.
Jesse Jackson also spoke against the resolution. He said, "I understand the
attempt to reach out to these children, but this is an unacceptable surrender,
border-lining on disgrace." He compared teaching Ebonics to teaching
"down" to the children and barring them from higher education and jobs. The
outcry against Oakland by members of the African American community
added to the contention surrounding the issue. Finally, the Georgia State
Senate passed a bill against Ebonics being taught in public schools. In 1997,
the federal government denied federal bilingual funds for African American
students.

The school district then amended the resolution and sought to emphasize
the idea that instruction was not to teach instruction in Ebonics. Rather, the
school board insisted, the instruction would serve to translate Ebonics into
Standard English. This attitude showed a few things: (1) the administrators of
the Oakland school district were quick to back away from their previous
convictions; and (2) the Oakland administrators and teachers had a distinct
view of "home" language and a student's right to that language that was, in
fact, not that different from the conventional ideas. These ideas contend that
students should be taught composition through correctness toward the standard. Oakland administrators accepted that the only way to help students
become proficient in the standards was through translation and code-switching. While these events served as a major catalyst for the recognition of the
pluralization of language and language diversity in the classroom in the
United States, they betrayed a serious lack of understanding of linguistic
diversity and multicultural pedagogy.

African American Vernacular (AAV) is characterized as a dialect of English. AAV is rule governed, with different phonological patterns of sounds.
AAV has a specialized system of syntax and semantics, as well as specialized
systems of negation and marking the past (Green). However, AAV is not a
separate language. Rather, it is a different dialect used by individuals based
on particular social settings. This distinction is key. Much of the discourse on

world English and pedagogy has examined the use of AAV in the classroom. Many of the issues surrounding the use of AAV have stemmed from issues of racism and identity, as well as class and socioeconomic characteristics of our society. The problem of AAV and AAV use in the classroom is a problem of race, identity, and class (Edwards, 175).

When we talk about linguistic diversity, we cannot and should not separate it from racial, cultural, and socioeconomic diversity. It is incorrect to place all student academic failure in composition on student language and dialect. This is the major mistake that the Oakland school district made when it decided that a way to ameliorate its African American student failure would be to declare AAV a completely different language. Rather, student failure to thrive in composition should be viewed through both the lens of the student's material concerns (including socioeconomic factors) and the context of their composition abilities. The classroom is a social environment, and we cannot hope to become good composition teachers without addressing these kinds of concerns beyond standard grammatical patterns.

In order to address those concerns, educators need to be frank and open about the differences in these social settings and the implications of those differences. John Edwards argues that the negative attitudes and positions educators take on the different use of dissimilar dialects by students has a range of consequences. The difficulties experienced in the classroom by the use of black English (AAV) exposes serious complications of language diversity and pedagogy. Students who spoke black English were routinely classified as remedial and discriminated against. Teachers cannot hope to be successful with these kinds of complications if they do not address the bias that speakers of AAV can and do experience, as well as their own biases and expectations.

HOME LANGUAGE, NOT ALLOWED HERE

One very distinct teaching practice that directly addresses the use of AAV in the classroom is that of code-switching. Code-switching pedagogy is described as teaching students how to recognize the difference between home speech and school speech. Students are taught to choose the language style most appropriate to the time, place, audience, and communicative purpose. The type of lessons that supporters of code-switching can use would explore the idea of language being taught in lessons that require metacognition about language usage from the students. For example, a student would be taught how to translate a sentence in dialect: "I be walking," to "I am walking," a Standard English counterpart, as part of a composition lesson. Code-switching has enjoyed some measure of success.

Rebecca Wheeler and Rachel Swords (2006) created a guide to code-switching in the classroom, *Code-Switching: Teaching Standard English in Urban Classrooms*, that provides instructions and reproducible classroom charts. Because teachers are "building on the linguistic knowledge that children bring to school," they are less apt to label different dialects as "wrong" and inferior and label the student as unskilled. The goal of code-switching pedagogy is to teach students how to use different dialects in appropriate social settings, audiences, and communicative purposes (Wheeler and Swords, 54–58). In many ways, this strategy would seem like a perfect solution to the problem of AAV in the classroom. Students would not be barred from using their "home" language; rather, they would limit AAV discourse to spoken literacy, and use Standard English for academic reading and writing. Good, right? Well, not quite.

Vershawn Young (2011) argues that in order to be effective, code-switching pedagogies exaggerate the differences between AAV and Standard English. These exaggerations do not pertain to real-world usage of both dialects. AAV and Standard English are both dialects of a common language that is related and, when used, intermix and overlap. Switching between two "languages" is still prescriptive and discriminatory because it seeks to separate linguistically the different experiences of one student. In practice, these students would come to the realization that "home speech" is unacceptable in a school setting. They would be forced to characterize these different dialects by using ideas of "rightness" and "wrongness" without exploration of creativity, expression, and personal identity. This would be further impressed by the lack of literacies in "home" language. Where should students go to find material in their own speech patterns and vernacular?

In my own experiences, I have found that code-switching has had a negative impact on my own education. Although I grew up speaking AAV, in elementary school I discovered that there was a different way to speak. While I was fascinated by the existence of this difference, I was not so happy with the idea that the words in my head were wrong if written outside of this "school speech." In order to succeed, I needed to switch between the two dialects. Not only did teachers expect me to accept this without question, but also I was praised for being able to "forget" my home dialect in the classroom and identify with literature that both sounded foreign and described foreign cultural settings to me. While I am grateful that I was introduced to experiences and dialects outside my "home," I was not able to easily find my own identity, let alone language, in those early literacies. Unfortunately, I found myself internalizing these early lessons by considering my "home" experiences somehow less worthy.

I navigated my academic world by changing, violently changing, the way I spoke from one context to the next. In school I tried my hardest to speak "properly" with perfect grammar and pronunciation. At home I relaxed and used the AAV and dialect of my parents. But this splitting in two left me feeling lonely, dispirited, and unfulfilled. I could not translate one experience from the other. I could not tell a joke at home about an academic experience, nor could I share or express my experiences at home in my papers, with my teachers, or to my peers. In the end as I continued my academic career, I made an unconscious decision to leave my "home" dialect, AAV, behind. While I had no explicit instruction to do so, the subtle messages about AAV usage in my education had an impact.

Sonia Nieto (2004) argues that the most successful education is one in which the student is central (274–78). Multicultural education, then, is education that seeks to recognize, validate, and appreciate the different cultural experiences of each individual student. No one experience or one culture should be placed above the other. If we consider dialect as intrinsically connected to culture, then appreciating different dialects is essential to providing students with an educational experience that is as inclusive as possible.

CODE-MESHING

What, then, are some alternatives to code-switching? How do we, as educators and writers, celebrate the multiplicity of the English language without prescribing merit for one dialect over the other— especially in this time when cultural boundaries, economic status, and academic inflexibility directly affect the learning experiences of each student? Many educators believe that a "standard" must be taught in order for students to succeed in a world that values one dialect, Standard English, over others. The inherent bias in that pedagogy must be accepted because there is bias in the world. Standard English is the norm, the accepted, and these teachers feel they would be giving a disservice to their students if they did not show them how to adhere to this standard. However, this seems very much like the criticism that the Oakland school board received for trying to classify Ebonics as a foreign language. Again, there is an assumption that "home" language and nonstandard dialect is somehow "wrong" and that students must move away from nonstandard dialects in order to succeed.

Code-meshing can not only serve as an alternative to these issues but also answer some of the deeper questions on multicultural literacies and education. Code-meshing is a strategy that allows for the intermingling of nonstandard dialects, in the classroom and through composition with Standard English. A good example of a text that uses code-meshing can be found in an excerpt of Young's essay "Should Writers Use They Own English?":

> Yet even folks with good jobs in the corporate world don't follow no Standard English. Check this out: Sam Dillon write about a survey conducted by the

National Commission on Writing in 2004. He say "that a third of employees in
the nation's blue chip companies wrote poorly and that businesses were spending as much as 3.1 billion annually on remedial training." (64)

What is fascinating about his text is that even though it intermixes Standard
English with AAV, there are few comprehension difficulties. If anything, the
text betrays an intricate understanding of both dialects and a creative flair
that not only expresses explicitly the author's personality but also makes an
explicit illustration about what the intermixing of dialects in academic writing can do.

Code-meshing seeks to do more than just translate or teach a standard.
Suresh Canagarajah (2009) views code-meshing as "a strategy for merging
local varieties with standard written englishes in a move toward gradually
pluralizing academic writing and developing multilingual competence for
transnational relationships" (1625). Min-Zhan Lu's (1994) definition for
code-meshing sees it as an intermixing of different dialects into a whole body
of work (455). Canagarajah's definition implies that the use of code-switching can be political, while Lu's definition leans more toward the creative.
Both definitions, however assume that code-meshing is a choice, not a ploy
used to ascend to Standard English. These definitions show that the act of
code-switching assumes without prejudice that all languages and dialects are
equal.

This connection between personal expression and the exploration of
equality in language diversity is something that educators should be able to
share with students. Students should learn how to navigate the world of
linguistic diversity with fluency. They are robbed of self-esteem and creativity by the presumption that there is only one "standard" and that academic
success is characterized by achievement toward this standard. Code-meshing
calls for us to put in question, and allow our students to put in question, these
preconceived notions about the world.

One of my first introductions to the world of literature was a science
fiction novel by Ursula K. Le Guin. I loved her work because she was not
afraid to explore different cultures and societies, something sorely lacking in
the school readings I was assigned to at the time. I can vividly remember
being surprised that one of the main characters in one of her stories had black
skin and dark eyes. Just that small connection to my own experiences en-
deared me to Le Guin and pushed me to read more. I craved recognizable
markers in the literary world that would validate my experiences. Yet literature that featured characters that looked like me but did not sound like me
would not have been enough. I had already learned that my language was not
to be found outside of a small social setting. Standard English, however, is
everywhere. Therefore, I assumed that a part of me, a real and valuable part,
should not be found outside of a particular social setting either.

I struggle with this understanding even now. When I hear others speak, internally I seek to "correct" their English, even as I appreciate the creativity of different dialects. When I entered college, I was introduced to Zora Neale Hurston's *Their Eyes Were Watching God*, a novel that uses Southern black dialect within the narrative structure. I found reading her novel difficult and uncomfortable. I couldn't help thinking that Hurston should not be telling this story in this way. How much better would the story be, I thought at that time, if she had used Standard English and Standard English only to tell the story. As an African American woman, I internalized the misrepresentation and lack of cultural representation as something that is "improper" for the mainstream, and I carried that attitude for many years. Yet, paradoxically, I became deeply interested in expressions of English beyond conventional modes. I am a poet now because I love the malleability of language that poetry demands. Even in my poetry studies I tended to gravitate toward the unconventional, the experimental, the thing outside of any type of "standard" that pushes boundaries. Yet, I had been a successful student, and I attributed that success to the acceptance of the expectations of the discourse of the classroom. I did not honor or explore my different dialects except in carefully controlled settings. Nor did I seek to actively challenge these notions.

John Edwards in his discussion on Ebonics asserts that students identify with perceptions of their language usage. Negative perceptions bring about negative feelings of self-worth. Linguistic diversity through social stratification is universally destructive because it carries with it negative associations that can and are extremely persistent. Only when I rejected my early experiences of linguistic instruction did I feel better about using, reading, writing, and experiencing different dialects. And I find it sad, perhaps, that only now have I discovered a genre of literature that can be used to help my own students discover linguistic diversity without such a devastating blow to self-esteem.

STREET LIT AS LINGUISTIC CANON

We cannot deny that there is value in cultural connection in teaching. Nor can we deny that students are more apt to connect with literacies that show them a reflection of their own lives. For African Americans, this hunger has sparked a culmination of spoken work, hip-hop, and urban literature (street lit). These genres are predominately African American, and they routinely explore the culture and language of the urban landscape. These works do this in both setting and, more importantly, language.

One clear example of this is the novel *Pimp* by Iceberg Slim. Written in the '70s, the novel describes an urban landscape with a kind of frankness and starkness that is startling. The novel also describes a world of abuse, prostitution, and exploitation. So terrifying is this vision that it is easy to overlook brilliant moments of code-meshing and linguistic diversity. For example, the narrator of the novel says of his mother, "He treated Mama like she was a princess. Anything she wanted he got for her. She was a fashion plate" (4). Or later on when he reveals his mother's betrayal to a loved stepfather: "For him she was brown-skinned murder, in a size 12 dress" (5). Like Hurston's novel and Young's essay, these statements do not mirror the kinds of grammatical correctness of Standard English. Instead, they characterize the kinds of language patterns, phonetic spellings, and idiomatic phrasing that students find outside of academic settings.

Urban literature can also be very important in composition pedagogies because the types of linguistic diversity that urban literature offers are authentic. Code-meshing is not static. As we have seen in the above examples, the interpretation of authentic language use is subjective to the author. In urban literature there are no universal phrasings, no set grammatical usage, no prescribed word choice, or style. This mirrors actual language use. Code-meshing recognizes that language is fluid, and street lit in its various forms celebrates this fluidity.

More contemporary street lit such as *The Coldest Winter Ever* (1999), by Sister Souljah, and *Gangsta* (2003), by K'wan, are good examples of this in their broad range of code-meshing usage. Like Iceberg Slim's novel *Pimp*, both *Gangsta* and *The Coldest Winter Ever* describe an urban setting that exists outside of mainstream society. While all three novels use stark characterization and plot to drive the story, *The Coldest Winter Ever* uses a more explicit type of code-meshing that is closer to the linguistic tendencies of *Pimp*. "I hopped on the train and jetted back to Sterling's house. I had to take off my dress and switch my bag before I met Momma or else she'd be pissed that I spent her money on clothes" (Souljah, 127).

Words like "pissed" and phrases like "jetted back" are embedded in the text of the narration. In *Gangsta*, however, the text of the narrative adheres more to Standard English even as the dialogue is written in dialect:

> He knew that the only way for him to possibly get any further rest was to simply listen to her and not argue.
> "Damn, fool, you dead?" she shouted as she burst into the room. "I been calling you 'cause you got a phone call." Martina tossed him the phone and went back the way she came. "And tell your stupid ass friends to have some respect when they call my house." (K'wan, 2)

The Coldest Winter Ever and *Pimp* are written in first-person narrative mode, while *Gangsta* is written in the third-person narrative mode. This is significant because it can be argued that code-switching in practice is more a rhetorical movement of speech. This highlights ideas of polyliteracy, a mixing of oral and auditory qualities in writing. The act of speech helps in the act of writing; since speech has many rhetorical qualities and expressions, and spontaneous fluidity, speech can be harnessed for writing (Elbow). Street lit can be a very valuable tool in this kind of multimodal approach to teaching composition in that much of the work is created by individuals who come from oral traditions.

Because street lit offers different types of code-meshing, street lit is useful in illustrating the different ways that dialects can be blended, the creative use of voice, and the stylistic choices writers can employ. These choices are important in allowing speakers of different dialects the ability to better express their own personal experiences. Santiago Vaquera-Vasquéz, in Young's compilation (2011), in defining the term "mercacirce," fully embraces the intermixing of Spanish and English, and Mexican and American, culture. He asserts that "Spanglish," neither English nor Spanish, is his dominant tongue and that we, who live between two dialects, should all embrace both languages, not choosing one over the other. He contends that multilingual individuals and by extension individuals who speak different dialects should never be prescribed to switch between the two but should exist on the borders (Vaquera-Vasquéz, 89–97).

This is where I find the most comfort: on the border. I cannot fully embrace AAV as my native tongue, nor can I contend that Standard English is my dominant language. Like Vaquera-Vasquéz, I identify my language as something that is complex and intermixed. As an educator it is my hope to share my understanding of that complexity and linguistic variety with my students through the use of street lit as both a tool of linguistic diversity and an example of composition written in their own words.

WORKS CITED

Canagarajah, A. Suresh. "The Place of World Englishes in Composition: Pluralization Continued." In *The Norton Book of Composition Studies*, edited by Susan Miller, 1617–42. New York: Norton, 2009.

Edwards, John. "Black English as Ebonics." In *Language Diversity in the Classroom*, 170–85. Bristol, UK: Multilingual Matters, 2010.

Elbow, Peter. "What Is Speaking on the Page and How Does Freewriting Teach It?" In *Vernacular Eloquence: What Speech Can Bring to Writing*, 147–64. Oxford: Oxford University Press, 2011.

Green, Lisa. "A Descriptive Study of African American English: Research in Linguistics and Education." *International Journal of Qualitative Studies in Education* 15, no. 6 (2002): 43–57.

K'wan. *Gangsta*. New York: Triple Crown Publications, 2003.

Lu, Min-Zhan. "Professing Multiculturalism: The Politics of Style in the Contact Zone." *College Composition and Communication* 45, no. 4 (December 1994): 442–58.

Nieto, Sonia. *Affirming Diversity: The Sociopolitical Context of Multicultural Education*. 4th ed. Boston: Allyn and Bacon, 2004.

Slim, Iceberg (Robert Beck). *Pimp: The Story of My Life*. Los Angeles: Holloway House, 2004.

Souljah, Sister. *The Coldest Winter Ever*. New York: Pocket Books, 1999.

Vaquera-Vasquéz, Santiago. "Meshed America: Confessions of a Mercacirce." In *Code-Meshing as World English: Pedagogy, Policy, Performance*, edited by Vershawn Ashanti Young and Aja Y. Martinez, 89–97. Urbana, IL: National Council of Teachers of English, 2011.

Wheeler, Rebecca S. "Becoming Adept at Code-Switching." *Educational Leadership* 65, no. 7 (April 2008): 54–58.

Wheeler, Rebecca S., and Rachel Swords. *Code-Switching: Teaching Standard English in Urban Classrooms*. Urbana, IL: National Council of Teachers of English, 2006.

Young, Vershawn Ashanti. "Should Writers Use They Own English?" In *Writing Centers and the New Racism: A Call for Sustainable Dialogue and Change*, edited by Laura Greenfield and Karen Rowan, 61–72. Logan: Utah State University Press, 2011.

Young, Vershawn Ashanti, and Aja Y. Martinez, eds. *Code-Meshing as World English: Pedagogy, Policy, Performance*. Urbana, IL: National Council of Teachers of English, 2011.

Crucial Churches

Tristan Acker

Men with great plans conspire and
tinker under your nose at the
local bakery with low-fat milk and
thin-coated plastic book
receipt, passport photo
wallet

Storefront Churches, brown men
leaning on cars, in the business
district

cars are death machines

weed is lubricant

at best I'm lovable in a million thorny ways
not for money but for a good time
I know where I'm at
A city under spur camera
twelve dollars per capita
Oreos in my lungs

we share something crucial, we
are here

The Art of Storytellin'

Hip-hop Music and Its Cousin, Street Lit

Khalid Akil White

African American storytelling has deep historical and cultural roots. Those roots extend back to West Africa, where entertaining, enlightening, informing, and educating, through storytelling, was the job of the "griot."

The translation of the term "griot" means "the keeper of tradition." Being a griot was to be in a position of power, influence, and status in the villages and communities in Africa. The griot (male) or griotte (female) had the prestigious position of being revered, respected, and feared, all at the same time, for their intelligence, their wisdom, and their undeniable talent for making words come to life in the stories, parables, and proverbs they told. Through the art of storytelling, the griots educated, motivated, and captivated their audiences.

The art of storytelling has, and always will be, a part of who African Americans are, collectively. It's one of the many vestiges of the African diaspora that we've held onto. Storytelling is a mainstay in African American culture. It's provided us with a collective voice. Storytelling's been a tool used for our collective survival. The art of storytelling is, arguably, a black thing.

In our history, our griots and griottes include some of the most impactful and influential people in African American culture. Our pastors and sociopolitical leaders, singers, spoken word artists, writers, poets, and yes, even our rappers carry the tradition and spirit of the griot in them.

As African American and urban American culture has evolved with the times, the subject matter that our griots touch on has evolved as well. Once upon a time, past griots and griottes entertained, enlightened, and informed our people about demanding their full citizenship, to deny being counted as three-fifths of a human. In our past, griottes wove words together to paint pictures and educate our people about the strange fruit that hung from the poplar trees in the South.

Still, some griots held our collective attention captive, spinning stories of shining cities like Chicago, Philly, and Harlem. Their stories told of magical places of promise, hope, and prosperity. But in the next breath, their stories also warned us that in these same places life wasn't a crystal stair. These were cities where many a dream ended up deferred.

Other griots from our glorious past captivated audiences discussing dreams they had. In those dreams, the griot told us that, someday, we'd be free at last. And, as a people, we'd make that dream a reality, by any means necessary! Lest we forget, it was one of our more modern-day griots who shared a simple, yet divine, message with his people. Simply put, this divine message warned the world not to push him, because he was close to the edge.

As an '80s baby, and a young man who came of age in hip-hop's "golden era" (1988–1993, roughly), I've watched hip-hop culture's trek through the gangsta rap era (1993–1997, roughly). I survived hip-hop's bling bling era (1997–2004) and am currently witnessing hip-hop's evolution into Generation Y.

Throughout these various stages, hip-hop culture and rap music (the language of hip-hop culture) have remained cornerstones in my life. Over the years, I've loved most things about rap music: its competition, the lingo coming from the culture, the clothing and hairstyles, and the icons it's created. But most importantly, I love the wordplay. I've fallen in love with the art of storytelling in hip-hop culture.

I've fallen in love with the ways in which an artist can stimulate my intellect, my interest, and my imagination, and the ways in which the music is relevant to situations I've experienced as a young black man. It's the storytelling, the urban legendry, the cleverness, the innovation involved, and the juxtaposition of hip-hop's conscious thoughts against the seeming capitalistic foolishness of making it rain in a local strip club. This music that I love so much has long served as a form of "edutainment." Again, it's this historic art of storytelling that constitutes the lifeblood of rap music.

So, to me, it seems organic that the literary genre street literature or urban literature is emerging as a viable, popular, and widely accepted contribution to the African American literary canon. In the same way that the storytelling in rap music comes from the self-expression of urban and inner-city African Americans, street lit arises as the artistic "cousin" to rap music. The two artistic forms are undoubtedly related. Street lit comes from the same "family" as rap music. As with most of our cultural expressions, both descend from our collective past as storytelling griots, as keepers of African tradition.

Street lit incorporates many of the same experiential tales, the wisdoms, the warnings, the anecdotes, the bravado, and the foolishness that its cousin, rap music, entails. It's just that street lit expands on the thoughts, themes, and images that we hear in rap music. Whereas a rapper's storytelling is usually reserved to four minutes per song, the street lit author gets the opportunity to tell the same story in four hundred pages. And, very similar to rap music, the street lit audience tends to include the youth and young adults, the hip-hop generation. Hell, these days many of your successful rap artists have delved into full-fledged authorship of street lit novels themselves. The good ol' art of storytelling exists in both artistic forms.

Not only an avid, lifelong fan of rap music and hip-hop culture, I too am an avid reader. In addition, professionally, I am a professor of African American studies at a community college in the San Francisco Bay Area. I sometimes have to reconcile with the fact that I love hip-hop and I read street lit to unwind. But I am expected to teach in an academic environment where these forms of artistic expression are often devalued. It's no secret that many of my students, black, white, Latino, and Asian, too love hip-hop culture and read street lit. I see the books they read. I hear the music they play. Hip-hop and street lit traverse ages, races, and ethnicities, for sure.

As an educator today, I have competition in the classroom. I have to compete day in and day out with students' digital addictions to texting, web browsing, social networking, and even sexting in the classroom. Students are often tuned out, plugged in, and more interested in the day's trending topics than in topics of discussion in lectures and in textbooks. So, how do I ensure their attention is paid to their education as opposed to their status updates? By using the art of storytelling!

Hip-hop culture, rap music, and street lit helped me to navigate my world as a young man, a college student, and now, a professional. These forms of self-expression have also been useful to me when I'm able to incorporate them into my classroom. Whether it's Tupac, Sister Souljah, or Langston Hughes's use of "black English," the universality of hip-hop culture and its cousin, street lit, have enabled me to make inroads with my college students today. In order to compete with everything digital, and everything going on outside of their academics, I have to draw them in with something relevant. Street lit and hip-hop have been a go-to.

I incorporate the art of storytelling infused in hip-hop and street lit. I've found that these artistic genres will get students to read, discuss, and think. They are relevant, often timely, and poignant, if utilized right. If it's breaking down Lupe Fiasco's lyrics in the song "American Terrorist," if it's discussing the context of African history found in Nas's song "I Know I Can" (my six-year-old daughter, Khaliah, loves that song), or if it's comparing the images of African American women in Omar Tyree's *Flyy Girl*, the students seem to grasp the material more readily. Hip-hop and street lit have been helpful in keeping them engaged and coming back to class.

I know there are critics of both rap music and street lit. I know that the themes within them can be misogynistic, stereotypical, violent, negative, and depressing at times. I know that, when taken out of context, the ideas within these genres could be downright detrimental. I understand that. However, I am advocating for the relevance and practicality that these forms of self-expression have with our youth and young adults. When trying to get young people to read, they will gravitate more toward subject matter that they enjoy.

I've seen the pull that street lit and rap music have with our youth and young adults, with my own two eyes. In fact, I'm living proof of it. I am an unabashed purveyor of hip-hop culture, rap music, and street lit.

These artistic forms draw from our collective, shared experiences as African Americans. Both art forms are inclusive of the spirit of the griots and griottes of our great past. Both art forms are based on the art of storytelling.

As African Americans, hip-hop and street lit are our art forms. These are our artists. These are viable means of expressing our collective voice. And like it or not, just like African American culture, both street lit and hip-hop culture are here to stay.

Street Literature

A Contextualization, Historiography, and Personal Narrative

Celena Diana Bumpus

The original doctrine of the Zulu Nation stated the following: "We believe in power, education in truth, freedom, justice, equality, work for the people, and the upliftment of the people" (Universal Zulu Nation). The Zulu Nation would later be internationally known as the Universal Zulu Nation. By the late 1970s, the culture had gained media attention, and it would only continue to grow as a musical and cultural force throughout the 1980s, '90s, and 2000s. Within hip-hop's roots of storytelling, songs describing the harsh realities of urban city life would give rise to the controversy-causing subjects of sex, drugs, and violence embedded within some of their most popular songs. Hip-hop's description of urban city lifestyles also includes the concepts of redemption, freedom, protest, social awareness, lessons learned, and education.

These autobiographical, biographical, cultural awareness, and storytelling songs that emerged from the hip-hop culture about the trials, tribulations, redemption, and escape from the cruelty of the urban, city lifestyle would give rise to literature that expanded upon those same themes, especially as more individuals yearned to share their fictional and nonfictional books. These books would be placed under the genre of street literature, which is also known as urban fiction.

Urban fiction is a literary genre, where the stories take place within an urban city and describe the realities and culture of the socioeconomic structure of its characters. The view of life from the underbelly of the city prevalent in most of its books gives street literature an impression of being "dark" themed. While the explicit and liberal use of profanity and the depiction of sex and violence may be prevalent in some books, the writers describe the lives of their characters with animation, energy, and enterprise.

Most contemporary urban fiction has been and is currently known as a genre written by and for African Americans. Author W. E. B. Du Bois, in his essay "The Souls of Black Folk," described a "veil" separating the African American community from the communities outside its real and imagined borders. Du Bois therefore concluded the other cultures existing outside of the African American societal borders could not, in all likelihood, relate to the people, settings, and events experienced by the African American culture. Conversely, people who resided outside the veil of urban, inner-city, and African American life could not write fiction about that culture.

However, in her book *The Readers' Advisory Guide to Street Literature*, author Vanessa Irvin Morris lists books, currently considered canonical literature, that have components of urban fiction or "street lit." The precursors to modern-day urban fiction would include Stephen Crane's *Maggie: A Girl of the Streets* (1893), Charles Dickens's *Oliver Twist* (1838), and Paul Laurence Dunbar's *Sport of the Gods* (1902). I would also include Upton Sinclair's *Jungle* (1906). Morris concludes from her observation, "Urban fiction is not just an African American or Latino phenomenon, but rather, the genre exists along a historical continuum that includes stories from diverse cultural and ethnic experiences" (18).

American novelists have written about urban communities describing sex, drugs, and violence within their narratives for many years, most iterations of which are independent of African American characters. One of the most popular books describing a generational criminal family is Mario Puzo's *Godfather* series, beginning with series' first book, *Godfather*, published in 1969. Puzo's book, which was adapted into a series of movies, also titled *Godfather*, would herald the flood of novelists wanting to immortalize a criminal culture of sex, drugs, and violence in fictional and nonfictional accounts. Many autobiographies and biographies also imitated its contextual structure of a "criminal family." I would conclude, at its very core, Mario Puzo's *Godfather* series was the impetus to the emergence of street literature.

During the 1950s through the 1980s, many African American and Latino authors tried to maintain the conventional literary quality of their books, despite their personal stories of exploration and ascension from the grips of a large city's urban despair. Their books of poetry, essays, novels, biographies, and autobiographies helped to set the stage for the literary genre that would later become known as street literature or urban fiction.

In 1962, Amiri Baraka stated in his article "The Myth of a 'Negro Literature'" that "A Negro literature, to be a legitimate product of the Negro experience in America, must get at that experience in exactly the terms America has proposed for it in its most ruthless identity" (Jones, 170).

The Autobiography of Malcolm X (1965) and Claude Brown's *Manchild in the Promised Land* (1965) offered nonfictional, realistic, coming-of-age stories that captured the lives of young African American men living in urban cities. Eldridge Cleaver, author and political activist, was one of the early leaders of the Black Panther Party. His 1968 *Soul on Ice*, a collection of essays, received excellent reviews. In *Soul on Ice*, Cleaver, "a reformed serial rapist and racist," states, "If a man like Malcolm X could change and repudiate racism, if I myself and other former Muslims can change, if young whites can change, then there is hope for America" (483).

Nikki Giovanni, poet, author, and activist, recollects that her early books of poetry *Black Feeling, Black Talk*(1967), *Black Judgment* (1968), and *Re: Creation* (1970) were inspired by the civil rights and black power movements, African American activists, and artists. Her book *Love Poems* (1997) was written in memory of Tupac Shakur, and she has stated that she would "rather be with the thugs than the people who are complaining about them" (Barnes & Noble). And in the 1970s, a convicted African American criminal named Robert Beck wrote the book *Pimp*, under the pen name Iceberg Slim. Written at the climax of the black power movement, Slim's book depicted the ruthless street life of the "inner-city underworld." Slim received an international readership with his subsequent books.

At the close of this past century (at the end of the 1990s), there was a rebirth of urban fiction as demands for literature about the inner-city lifestyles increased. With the advent of improved computer and social media technology, new writers gained more confidence in bringing their manuscripts to the publishing markets. Author Omar Tyree was in the forefront as a writer in this rejuvenation of urban fiction, reprinting his novel *Flyy Girl* in 1999, after its initial publication in 1996. Sister Souljah's 1999 bestseller *The Coldest Winter Ever* also received critical acclaim. The model that set the standard for contemporary urban fiction's entrepreneurial publishing and distribution community was Teri Wood's book *True to the Game*, also published in 1999. These three books—*Flyy Girl, The Coldest Winter Ever*, and *True to the Game*—were instrumental in the renaissance of urban fiction and are considered classics in the genre.

Street literature today is progressing. Nonfiction books from producers, singers, and artists in the hip-hop genre have been widely and openly received. The memoirs of Russell Simmons, Kevin Liles, LL Cool J, 50 Cent, and FUBU founder Daymond John are filed under nonfiction street literature. On the heels of the high sales from his memoir, 50 Cent created G-Unit Books. Authors Carmen Bryant, Karrine Steffans, and "shock jock" Wendy Williams have also written nonfiction bestsellers for the genre.

Cash Money Content, the publishing branch of the hip-hop music label Cash Money Records, was established in 2010. Cash Money Content recruited a cadre of the best-known street literature authors to actively publish and promote street literature novels in print and adapt the stories for film. Wahida Clark, husband-and-wife team Ashley and JaQuavis Coleman, K'wan Foye, and Treasure E. Blue are some of the authors recruited by Cash Money Content.[1]

Other street literature authors have worked to encourage "street teams" to enter the hip-hop literary community. Those authors, K'wan Foye, Nikki Turner, Kole Black, and Relentless Aaron, are also credited with bringing musical promotions to the hip-hop literary community. These authors have joined with hip-hop artists, such as 50 Cent, to coauthor the real-life stories of the musicians.

Urban fiction novels featuring other ethnic cultures have sprung from the successful foundation laid by African American authors in building and maintaining the genre's readership. Urban Latino fictional authors have secured a solid foothold in the genre of street literature. Jerry Rodriguez's novel *Devil's Mambo*; Deborah Cardona's novel *Chained*, written under the pen name Sexy; Jeff Rivera's novel *Forever My Lady*; Richard Rodriguez's novel *Always Running*; Piri Thomas's novel *Down These Mean Streets*; Yxta Maya Murray's *Locas*; and Junot Diaz's *Drown* and *The Brief Wondrous Life of Oscar Wao* are examples.

The first known Urban Islamic fiction novel, *The Size of a Mustard Seed*, was written by author Maryam "Umm Juwayriyah" Sullivan (2009). Sullivan, as a multigenerational, inner-city American Muslim, wanted to fill the void of urban fiction, portraying the lives of characters who share her ethnic and religious background. Palestinian American Suheir Hamad is a spoken word poet and memoirist who has written several street lit–style books, including *Drops of This Story* and *Born Palestinian, Born Black*.

In 2009, author Tamika Newhouse landed a major book deal merely nine months after self-publishing her classic street lit saga *The Ultimate No-No*. The same year, Newhouse founded the AAMBC Literary Awards, a highly respected award amongst the urban genre. Rahiem Brooks, noted for originating the Urban Literary Awards, is the author of *Laugh Now* (2010), its sequel *Die Later* (2011), and *Con Test: Double Life* (2011), a mystery novel.

Sister Souljah, Sofia Quintero, Elisha Miranda (aka E-Fierce), Heru Ptah, Ferentz Lafargue, Saul Williams, Abiola Abrams, Felicia Pride, Marcella Runell Hall, and Martha Diaz are all authors who take a more academic approach to street literature by applying the use of metaphor and signifying. These books can be used as teaching or socialization tools as they preserve the love and positivity of hip-hop music and its culture.

Founder and CEO of the publishing company Triple Crown Publications Vicki Stringer (an urban literature author) has published forty-five novels and thirty-five writers as of 2008. According to *Kirkus Reviews*, author Treasure E. Blue sold sixty-five thousand copies of her self-published book before signing on with Random House Publishing.

Besides utilizing hand-to-hand sales and word of mouth to increase readership, the Internet has exponentially increased both author and publisher efforts and abilities to reach out to street literature readers and hip-hop culture aficionados. Rasheed Clark, a self-published author, was honored with fourteen Infini Literary Award nominations for his first two best-selling novels—*Stories I Wouldn't Tell Nobody but God* and *Cold Summer Afternoon*.

African Americans comprise approximately 13 percent of the entire population of the United States. The white population comprises approximately 73 percent of the remaining 87 percent of the country's entire population and accounts for the majority of sales in street literature books.[2] As a result of the increased readership of white Americans of street literature, I have noticed an interesting phenomenon within my city and neighborhoods: information has become more accessible for other ethnic groups to read about the various struggles and difficulties African Americans and Latinos face, living in heavily impacted urban communities; outside ethnic groups are obtaining a better appreciation of the strength of the families living within those communities; and other ethnic groups are approaching African Americans and Latinos with confidence to discuss the stories they read within street literature novels and autobiographies.

On a global level, foreigners are sharing their stories about their experiences and lives, residing and surviving in heavily impacted urban cities, in the form of songs, which emulate the hip-hop genre, and in fictional and nonfictional novels in the genre of street literature.

The future of hip-hop literature and culture lies in maintaining its early direction as a vehicle for social change and promotion of inner-city peace through creative and artistic self-expression. The expanding youth readership of street literature and aficionados of hip-hop culture and music have encouraged modern researchers to utilize the genre to increase urban literacy. Secondary school teachers in suburban and urban school districts have considered integrating urban literature into curriculums. They are referring to it as "'multicultural young adult literature,' to expose students to 'authentic' voices representing urban life" (Gibson).

My personal experience with the phenomenon of hip-hop, rap, and street literature has been varied and international. Moving from the suburbs of Seattle, Washington, to "the Jungle" in Los Angeles, California, I was first introduced to hip-hop and rap by my older cousin, who was a big fan of the band N.W.A. The first hip-hop song that mesmerized me was "Rapper's Delight" by the Sugar Hill Gang. I memorized the lyrics to "Rapper's Delight" to share with my mother and grandmother. My cousin took me to my first rap concert for my eighteenth birthday at the Hollywood Bowl, in 1987, to see Run-DMC and the Beastie Boys. In the days before the concert, she took me shopping to find the perfect "hip-hop outfit" to wear to the concert—a pair of loose-fitting, navy-blue pants that gathered at the waist and had suspenders that fit over my layered half shirt and sports bra, with Nike tennis shoes. She teased my long hair into fluffy bangs and a side ponytail. As a fan of the famed rock group Aerosmith, I was especially excited to see the band's spectacular comeback in their collaboration with Run-DMC in the hip-hop modernization of their song "Walk This Way." In the subsequent years I attended more rap concerts with my cousins and friends, featuring LL Cool J, Digital Underground, Grandmaster Flash, De La Soul, amongst other bands.

At the University of California, Riverside, between 1989 and 1992, I studied and obtained my degree in psychology and sociology, with an emphasis in perception, personality development, and social psychology. Within the field of personality development, I also took a class on the "Personality Development of the African American Child" and a class on the "Personality Development of the Mexican American Child."

Back then, a college girlfriend, studying to be a teacher, and I would spend our weekends listening to hip-hop and rap songs, translating the lyrics in order to better understand our teenaged students and clients. It was like learning a foreign language. We both adopted the rule with our students and clients, allowing them to express themselves in the language in which they felt most comfort in order to maximize their reintegration and socialization back into the mainstream cultures. We taught the students and clients the importance of being adaptable enough to carry discussions in the established norm as well as maintaining their culture individuality by speaking in hip-hop and rap genre.

Twenty years later, in 2006, I would visit Egypt, during a several-month vacation, and discover avid fans of Eminem, Jay-Z, Snoop Dog, and Sean Paul. This time, I found myself translating modern hip-hop and rap lyrics into words, ideas, and concepts that would resonate with the Arabic adults between the ages of eighteen and thirty years old, while I lived in the suburbs of Cairo. Several of the Egyptian men shared their love of Eminem's music with me as his lyrics resonated with their desire to expand their self-identity and individuality.

Throughout my career, I worked with teenagers and young adults in a variety of settings, such as the California Conservation Corps, a work development program for young adults located at Patton State Hospital, San Bernardino, California; Inland Empire Job Corps, a federally contracted vocational training program for young adults administered through the U.S. Department of Labor, located in San Bernardino, California; Helicon Youth Center, a closed mental health facility, located in Riverside, California; in-home family counseling through Family Services Association of Riverside County; Riverside County Juvenile Hall, a juvenile correctional facility; Court Dependency Unit Investigations, Riverside County Department of Social Services, Child Protective Services; and Lutheran Social Services, community outreach and after-school programs, in Riverside, California. In these roles, I counseled high-risk gang members and teenagers who often used the popular slang terms in the latest hip-hop and rap music to express their feelings, experiences, and emotions.

Throughout my research for this chapter, I discovered hip-hop utilized in other artistic and educational genres: in 2001, Robert Townsend directed a musical film produced by MTV entitled *Carmen: A Hip Hopera*. The film stars Beyoncé Knowles, in her debut acting role, Mos Def, Rah Digga, Wyclef Jean, Mehki Phifer, Da Brat, Joy Brant, Jermaine Dupri, and Lil' Bow Wow. The musical is based upon the 1875 opera *Carmen* by composer Georges Bizet. The film takes place during modern times in Philadelphia and Los Angeles. The "film is a hip counterpart to the most famous film version of the opera, 1954's *Carmen Jones*, with an all-African American cast featuring Dorothy Dandridge, Harry Belafonte and Pearl Bailey in place of Bizet's opera" (Braxton). In the song "A Glorious Dawn," creator of the PBS series *Cosmos*, Carl Sagan, and renowned scientist Stephan Hawking provide narrative lyrics (spoken word) to Sagan's beat-box sounds and syncopated rhythms. It encourages listeners to learn about modern science through imagining and conceptualizing the vastness of the universe.

Also, while researching for this chapter, I discovered two innovative programs within the Inland Empire region of Southern California, where I reside: the "Cup of Happy Program," with "Riverside SafeHouse" in the city of Riverside, and "Desert SafeHouse," in the city of Thousand Palms, provide a program that teaches high-risk and homeless teenagers how to positively express themselves through creative writing, utilizing rap and hip-hop as a genre. I was welcomed as a guest speaker during their creative writing class in October 2012.[3]

In this chapter, I focused upon several key aspects of street literature in verse (music) and novels: examining the origins of American novels based on life in the urban cities of the United States and their use of sex, drugs, and violence in their story lines, which are independent of African American characters; comparing the aspects of African American lifestyles to the present-day phenomenon of street literature as an African American literary genre; discussing the readership of street literature; and finally summarizing the similarities in the needs of hip-hop and street literature to give voice to the experiences of protest, redemption, freedom, and social awareness with the similar missions of other genres of music and literature.

NOTES

1. Cash Money Content, "Authors," accessed 26 July 2013, http://cashmoneycontent.com/.
2. U.S. Census Bureau, "2010 Census Data," accessed 26 July 2013, www.census.gov/.

3. Safe House, "Cup of Happy and Depression Treatment," accessed 26 July 2013, http://safehouseofthedesert.com/.

WORKS CITED

Barnes & Noble. "Meet the Writers: Nikki Giovanni." Accessed 20 May 2013. www.barnesandnoble.com/.

Braxton, Greg. "'Carmen' Gets Hip." *Los Angeles Times*, 6 May 2001.

Bynoe, Yvonne. *Encyclopedia of Rap and Hip-Hop Culture*. Westport, CT: Greenwood, 2006.

Cleaver, Eldridge. "From Soul on Ice ." In *The Portable Sixties Reader*, edited by Ann Charters, 478–83. New York: Penguin Putnam, 2003.

Gibson, Simone Cade. "Curriculum and Instruction." In *Critical Engagements: Adolescent African American Girls and Urban Fiction*, 23–24. PhD diss., University of Maryland, 2009. Proquest (UMI 3359273).

Honig, Megan. *Urban Grit: A Guide to Street Lit*. Genreflecting Advisory Series. Santa Barbara, CA: Libraries Unlimited, 2010.

Jones, Leroi (Amiri Baraka). "The Myth of a 'Negro Literature.'" In *Within the Circle: An Anthology of African-American Literary Criticism: From the Harlem Renaissance to the Present*, edited by Angelyn Mitchell, 165–71. Durham, NC: Duke University Press, 1994.

Kirkus Reviews. Review of *Harlem Girl Lost*, by Treasure E. Blue. 1 August 2006. www.kirkusreviews.com/.

Morris, Vanessa Irvin. *The Readers' Advisory Guide to Street Literature*. Chicago: American Library Association, 2011.

Universal Zulu Nation. "The Beliefs of the Universal Zulu Nation." Accessed 20 May 2013. www.zulunation.com/.

Street Literature and Hip-hop's Ties to Slave Narratives and the Sex Slave Trade

Alexandria White

Oakland. An urban ghetto; a gentrified space of opportunity; a city with much potential; an ethnically diverse city with a radical and revolutionary past; and a city full of rolling hills, redwoods, oaks, bay laurels, and cemented creeks that is a hard-to-define locality. Yet, that first description urban ghetto certainly qualifies it to fit into a broad discussion of street literature and its musical counterpart hip-hop. According to law officials, Oakland's reputation creates a haven for street culture with an "endless victim base." Alongside drug crime and gang violence, Oakland is now also heavily "associated with the sex trade" (CBS San Francisco News). That Oakland is associated with the prostitution that occurs within its borders—particularly the blocks of High Street and International Boulevard on down to the lower avenues—is an understatement and obscures the true nature of what is occurring in these areas. What is really going on is not anything less than human trafficking and I daresay sex slavery. Many of the girls in Oakland's red-light district are noticeably young and look like they belong in school, not on the street being sold for sex by ruthless pimps. The literary genre of street literature deals precisely with the real-life, inner-city realities of prostitution, drug crime, addiction, and black-on-black violence—but does it deal with the human trafficking of female children and adolescents that is on the rise in Oakland?

As a literary genre, street literature stems from urban realism, social realism, and of course the slave narrative. The literary genres of social realism and urban realism date back to the 1930s and 1940s and attempt to provide insight into and reflect upon the lowest rung of our society—not just

135

for entertainment but for purposes of encouraging the audience to be motivated to help fix the societal ills that create a sociopolitical space for the lower classes. Social realist narratives were meant to move readers to do something about the detrimental and exploitative social conditions featured in these stories. Richard Wright's *Native Son* became an instant classic in the genre of urban realism and led to Wright being the first African American to "receive both critical and commercial success" in the white literary establishment (Gates and McKay, 1357). Set during the depression in Chicago, Wright's character Bigger Thomas, a "prototypical delinquent victim caught in the unforgiving straits of urban blight and poverty," allowed Wright to give insight into the sociological factors influencing black juvenile delinquency and criminality in urban America (1358). Wright's compelling novel centers on the male character Bigger Thomas and is from his perspective—the two primary female characters in the novel, Mary (white) and Bessie (black) are murdered by him. Mary is accidently killed by him, whereas Bessie is first raped by Bigger and then brutally murdered. Bigger's actions are justified in the book because of his social conditioning and environment. This book squarely touches on sexual violence toward women—which is an important theme permeating throughout much of street literature. The theme and reality of sexual violence against women in urban literature, street literature, and hip-hop is not only prevalent but also somehow normalized. Wright's seminal text allowed for other black writers to gain "recognition and prestige from a predominantly white literary world" (1357). In some ways, it is through Wright's *Native Son* where the genre of urban literature becomes lucrative for black writers looking for success and fame.

Street literature is also rooted more generally in the African American literary tradition—as we know that "urban" is often a euphemism for "black." (We tend, however mistakenly, to generically associate the inner-city and urban environments with black and brown folks, just as we associate suburban and rural areas with white folks.) Since street literature is also rooted in the African American literary tradition, it cannot be disassociated from the slave narrative—a literary genre created and utilized by enslaved Africans in America before blacks were even given a formal education. Much like the social realist texts of white and European writers, the slave narrative's purpose was to provide insight into the horrible realities of society's most downtrodden people. The slave narrative proved the humanity of blacks as well as revealed the haunting experiences of those suffering within the peculiar institution, the so-called necessary evil and uniquely American institution of slavery that held the majority of African Americans in bondage for much of this country's existence. As Beth Coleman has illuminated in her essay "Pimp Notes on Autonomy," the institution of slavery helped to create the pimp, who like the slave master, generates economic profit from commodifying and selling human beings. As Coleman puts it, the pimp is specifically selling sex—but how can that be separated from the female's body? Sex becomes a commodity precisely because the female human being is alienated from her body and lacks power over her own body (Collins, 145). The pimp has complete control and domination over the prostitute. Is it ironic that the figure of the pimp is often glorified and glamorized in street literature, hip-hop, and popular culture? No. The practice of controlling, exploiting, and profiting from women's bodies in the black community and even in the mainstream white community has gained a certain level of acceptance and normalcy.

Many of us know the enormous wealth that slavery generated for white Southern American planters, runaway slave catchers, and slave traders. The international enterprise of human trafficking was and still is quite lucrative. The purpose and goal of the slave narrative and abolitionist texts was to call on the conscience and moral principles of the audience and readers—these narratives written by people like Frederick Douglass, William Wells Brown, and Harriet Jacobs were meant to combat the propaganda against blacks that relegated us as subhuman and only fit for slavery. Both Jacob's and Brown's texts reflect on the sexually exploitative nature of the institution of slavery—Douglass himself was a product of sexual intercourse between a slave woman and her master. The inferiority of blacks and the practice of slavery were deeply embedded within the American imaginary and economy. Much of white America (and probably many enslaved blacks) believed that the social order that rendered blacks to the status of property was perfectly normal and natural. The slave narrative acted as a direct challenge to that assumption and ideology while attempting to alter the prevailing societal norms of the day.

Where are the modern-day slave narratives of the young females held in bondage and repeatedly sold for sex slavery by ruthless, profit-driven opportunistic pimps? Some of these stories are captured in the news. In 2010, NPR on the show *All Things Considered,* aired a story called "Trafficked Teen Girls Describe Life in 'the Game,'" which interviewed two young girls from Oakland who had been sexually exploited from the age of fifteen until they were seventeen and twenty years old, respectively. The interviewer explains that Oakland has been "named one of the hot spots for child prostitution. . . . And like most kids in the Bay Area, [the girls being interviewed] listened to music by Oakland rappers whose lyrics about pimpin' glamorized the game." Girl 1 had been introduced to prostitution through what some call a Romeo pimp, a boyfriend who used the combination of domination and affection to manipulate the young girl into selling her body.

However, girl 2 was actually kidnapped by what law officials call a guerilla pimp, the type of pimp who abducts young girls from the street so that he can raise and groom them to be the type of product he desires. These kind of pimps use violence and fear to control the females. Girl 2 had her phone confiscated, was gang raped, brutally beaten, continually drugged, and often only fed once per day during her experience.

The brutality surrounding the modern phenomenon of prostitution in Oakland stems from the fact that many pimps nowadays were former drug dealers, and they have transferred the viciousness of the drug trade into the sex trade. As Barbara Grady from the *Oakland Tribune* writes,

> When selling crack cocaine became a tougher way to make money at the beginning of the decade because of increased police pressure, many drug dealers turned to pimping instead. . . . By selling young girls for sex, street hustlers were less likely to get caught. They didn't have to carry the commodity in their pocket or stash it in their homes, as they usually did with crack cocaine. They could use cell phones and laptop connections to the Internet to conduct business with customers while simply posing as boyfriends walking down the street with their girls.

Former drug dealers–turned–pimps see the sex trade as more lucrative because they can keep selling the same product repeatedly with little investment or risk involved. Sex and human trafficking laws are far less severe in terms of sentencing than current drug laws; maybe California Proposition 35, which bans human trafficking and sex slavery, will begin to redress this misplacement of priorities. Also, in 2012, although times have changed so much since the era of slavery, street literature can still be compared to the slave narrative. The intersection, or should I say collision, of Africans with American slavery undoubtedly creates literary roots in the slave narrative (amongst other literary origins, i.e., the folk tradition). Inner-city ghettos and projects are modern-day plantations where the slave masters do not belong to an aristocratic planter class. Does human trafficking still exist within the black population? Certainly. The prevalence of modern-day human trafficking in the black community is a horrible reality that hauntingly harkens back to the days of slavery.

Is the contemporary literary landscape of street literature interested in fostering social change? Yes, the origins of street literature also lay in the folk and oral traditions of blacks in America and so some street literature stories also serve as moralistic and cautionary tales of warning for young people about the dangers of inner-city street life (Morris et al., 19). Does the genre also exist to glamorize and romanticize the harmful and detrimental activities of drug dealing, drug addiction, and pimping and promiscuity very much associated with urban ghetto culture? Yes, this is also true. In today's highly commercialized literary and artistic industries, whatever sells does not have to contain moral or ethical content, nor do the authors and artists hold any obligation to the community they are from or the community they are depicting in their respective artistic mediums. In earlier historical moments, art about blacks and created by blacks nearly always contained the element of social protest, and economic profit was not the primary goal.

Obviously, the audience, readership, and purpose of the slave narratives and street literature differ quite dramatically. Street literature is read primarily by young people of color who tend to be predominantly inner-city black females between the ages of sixteen and thirty (Morris et al.). The purpose of street literature varies depending on which author is being read; some street writers do warn their audiences about the perils of street life in order to encourage inner-city young people to make more responsible decisions and choices. Sister Souljah, author of the widely read street novel *The Coldest Winter Ever*, is a hip-hop artist and social activist very much concerned with the progress and condition of the black community. Young people reading her book have expressed being woken up to the realities of life by the actions and behaviors of the main character in Souljah's landmark book (Brooks and Savage, 52). However, street literature, like its musical counterpart hip-hop, does not necessarily challenge stereotypes about black inner-city culture. Perhaps these genres reinforce negative assumptions about black and brown people; this may largely be due to the primary audience of street literature and the logic of a commercialized entertainment industry controlled by whites. The slave narrative's audience was Northern whites and antislavery sympathizers abroad. Most blacks during that era had no access to education and were largely illiterate, so they were certainly not a target audience.

Although it would be inaccurate to say that today's inner-city youth are illiterate, they certainly are not reading enough; I often find myself exasperated when students in my English literature and composition classes declare that they hate reading and avoid the activity as much as possible. Not surprisingly, inner-city, low-income black and brown youth are reading at levels below the national average. Some research also suggests that what young people read when they are at home during their leisure time greatly impacts their academic achievement (Hughes-Hassell and Rodge, 22).

Despite these problematics, the genre of street literature could offer a solution for making inner-city youth more enthusiastic about reading since recent scholarship, not to mention book sales, has demonstrated that contemporary street literature greatly resonates with young urban black and brown teens. However, some critics believe that teenagers reading this genre could result in further moral and social crisis because of the confusing messages it sends about sex, drugs, and violence. Tellingly, real-life girls who have been rescued off the street are often lured into prostitution because of the glamorization of the lifestyle through hip-hop and popular media.

One of the obvious points of attraction for inner-city black and brown people to the genre of street literature is the connection of that literary genre to hip-hop/rap music. Contemporary street literature and hip-hop are deeply intertwined with one another—similar to the relationship free jazz had with the black liberation movement of the late '60s and '70s. Some scholars feel that contemporary street literature emerges from hip-hop, but I believe that hip-hop, like street literature, springs from the well of the black oral tradition. Perhaps some dominant themes found in hip-hop actually emerged from street literature. (Many rappers such as Nas, Kool G Rap, and Tupac were inspired by famous street literature author Donald Goines.) All black American art has a direct lineage to the sociohistorical conditions that uniquely allowed for the African to exist in America. However, many consumers of black art, including blacks themselves, lack a critical and historical lens when engaging with these media. Black art is simply experienced as entertainment, and little attention is paid to how motifs and themes permeating through street literature and hip-hop connect to a trajectory that extends all the way back to the institution of slavery. Street literature and hip-hop are artistic media and tools that reflect the experiences, the triumphs, the obstacles, the struggles, and the obscenities, atrocities, and contradictions of inner-city ghetto, urban life.

Art reflects culture, yet art also shapes culture. Hip-hop and street literature have a reciprocal relationship with each other and also influence the audience that engages and interacts with these artistic forms. Undoubtedly our young people are exposed to the music of hip-hop much more so than the books of street fiction. What some consider the hyperbolic, braggadocio, and violent content of hip-hop is actually grounded in a grim, nihilistic reality that can be observed in any given inner-city in America. The brief examples of the two teenaged girls caught up in the sex trade reflect a hellish inner-city social reality and a brutal economic opportunity that thrives in Oakland and in every American city as I write these words. The prevalence of sexual violence against women and misogyny found in contemporary hip-hop demonstrates how stereotypes about black women created during antebellum times have been internalized by the black community. In the broader category of black-on-black violence, rape is often a tool used by pimps to gain domination and control over women so as to render the female profitable. This dynamic certainly parallels white slave masters' treatment of slave women where enslaved African women were raped for the "pleasure and profit of their owners" (Collins, 135). Street literature and hip-hop certainly deal with pimps and prostitution—but how realistically and accurately do these media portray this phenomenon? Iceberg Slim, a well-known urban fiction writer, began his literary career in 1967 with his autobiographical book *Pimp: The Story of My Life*. Famous rappers such as Ice Cube and Ice-T claim they were influenced by his stories (hence the Ice prefix in both of their names; see Cash Money Content). An online *Time* magazine article published in 2006 points out how pimps have become cool in popular culture. Rap group Three Six Mafia's *It's Hard Out Here for a Pimp* actually won Best Original Song at the 2006 Academy Awards!

Author Bryan Bennett describes how the depiction of pimp culture in fictional and nonfiction films and documentaries is also serving as a pedagogical tool for pimps:

> In the hit movie *Hustle & Flow*, the life of a fictional pimp became mainstream entertainment. In several other movies about pimps, their real-life exploits are serving a more dismaying purpose: as vocational instruction, according to detectives and prosecutors in several U.S. cities. The law-enforcement officials say that pimps are using widely available movies to teach minors how to be prostitutes. The documentaries available online and in video stores explain the vocabulary and rules of pimping in the words of real people in the trade. Produced to give the public a window into an illegal and degrading business, the films are now serving the unintended function of instructing vulnerable juveniles how to work with a pimp and indoctrinating them into the world's oldest profession.

What does it mean that pimps have crossed over into mainstream culture as a form of entertainment? What does it mean that so many of our young people admire the concept of the black pimp and aspire to be pimps, while despising the concept of the white slave master? Why are pimps glorified and popularized so much in hip-hop and the larger media? Is the approval of pimps in black urban culture predicated upon the acceptance of or apathy toward the abuse, domination, and exploitation of women? All of these questions hint at disturbing answers. The genres of street literature and hip-hop can provide solutions instead of being a part of the problem, if the media and entertainment industry allows them to.

But don't hold your breath. "Demythologizing Oakland's Pimp Culture," written by Eric K. Arnold, creates hope in changing the attitudes existing within black and urban communities regarding the glamorization and grim reality of pimp culture—specifically in Oakland. His article historicizes how Oakland became infamous as a center for pimp culture starting with the release of the "blaxploitation" film *The Mack*, which takes place in Oakland and is loosely based on a real-life Oakland pimp named Frank Ward. His analysis also describes how Oakland rappers Too $hort and Dru Down as well as other rappers like Outkast, Jay-Z, and Dr. Dre used *The Mack* as inspiration for lyrical content and album sampling. Arnold also points out many grim statistics, noting that African American women are four or five times more likely to be sex workers when compared to other ethnicities and that the average age of a girl initiated into the sex trafficking industry is only twelve years old.

Fortunately, the main point of his piece is to bring attention to grassroots community efforts that have been made in Oakland to address the issue of child trafficking, while directly linking this issue to glorification of Oakland's pimp culture. Recently, Rocky Seker and Black Cinema at Large organized a panel addressing child trafficking. Arnold, a moderator for the event explains:

> The venue was Geoffrey's—which, legend has it, ironically hosted more than one "Player's Ball" in its heyday, some proceeded over by Too $hort himself. . . . Our panel included Holly Joshi, supervisor of the Oakland Police Department's Vice and Child Exploitation Unit; Nola Brantley, a former sex worker who's currently the Executive Director of MISSSEY, a non-profit which provides holistic services for child victims of domestic human trafficking; Nkauj Iab Yang, Program Manager for Banteay Srei, a youth development organization focusing on young Southeast Asian women who are at risk of or engaged in the underground sex trade; Pat Mims, the Coordinator for the Sexually Exploited Minors Program for Bay Area Women Against Rape (BAWAR); and Casey Bates, head of the Alameda County District Attorney's Sex Trafficking department. . . . The idea was to bring advocates together with enforcement officials to contextualize the issue and try to identify some community-based solutions.

Bringing this discussion out into the community and involving multiple non-profit organizations and law enforcement agencies is an excellent step in the process of dealing with this tragic issue. But this alone is certainly not enough. As Arnold notes in his article, it is up to us to be actively engaged as members of any given community or society to determine what is and is not socially acceptable. The time has come for us to glamorize and glorify values and actions that uplift and empower each other—rather than those values and actions that destroy and exploit one another.

WORKS CITED

Arnold, Eric K. "Demythologizing Oakland's Pimp Culture (Analysis)." Oakland Local, 4 January 2013. http://oaklandlocal.com/.

Bennett, Bryant. "Are Pimp Films Too Instructive?" *Time*, 13 March 2006. www.time.com/.

Brooks, Wanda, and Lorraine Savage. "Critique and Controversies of Street Literature: A Formidable Literary Genre." *ALAN Review* (Winter 2009): 48–55.

Cash Money Content, "Iceberg Slim Ebook Collection Released Today." 4 December 2012, http://cashmoneycontent.com/.

CBS San Francisco News. "Child Prostitution Growth in Alameda County Outpaces Police Efforts." August 2011. http://sanfrancisco.cbslocal.com/.

Coleman, Beth. "Pimp Notes on Autonomy." In *Everything but the Burden: What White People Are Taking from Black Culture*, edited by Greg Tate, 69–71. New York: Harlem Moon Books, 2004.

Collins, Patricia Hill. *Black Feminist Thought: Knowledge, Consciousness, and the Politics of Empowerment*. 2nd ed. New York: Routledge, 2000.

Gates, Henry Louis, Jr., and Nellie Y. McKay, eds. *The Norton Anthology of African American Literature*. 2nd ed. New York: Norton, 2004.

Grady, Barbara. "Dealers Turning to Sex Business." *Oakland Tribune*, 24 April 2008. www.insidebayarea.com/.

Hughes-Hassell, Sandra, and Pradnya Rodge. "The Leisure Reading Habits of Urban Adolescents." *Journal of Adolescent and Adult Literacy* 51, no. 1 (September 2007): 22–33.

Morris, Vanessa J., Sandra Hughes-Hassel, Denise E. Agosto, and Darren Cottman. "Street Lit Flying Off Teen Fiction Bookshelves in Philadelphia Libraries." *Young Adult Library Services* (Fall 2006): 16–23.

NPR. "Trafficked Teen Girls Describe Life in 'the Game.'" *All Things Considered*, 6 December 2010. www.npr.org/.

like a woman

Debra Busman

I

The other girls tell me I am going to have to dress "like a woman" if I'm going to make it on the street. "Screw you," I laugh. "I've been fucked all my life, and I've never had to wear a dress yet."

"Just tryin' to help you out, girl," they call out as they walk on down Santa Monica Boulevard, ankles bowed out over wobbly spike heels, popping their gum and adjusting their spaghetti-strap bras as if they had something special going on down there. Don't none of us, 'cept Lisa, have any tits yet and even if I had 'em I wasn't about to go dressin' in no drag shit. For one thing, it costs too much and I've got better things to do with my money. And for another thing, I can't hardly walk in that shit, much less run. Or fight. Some girls can, though. I seen one girl whip off those fuck me pumps and bust some motherfucker trying to get something for nothing across the side of his head quicker than I could have cracked his nuts. Said she fucked up his eardrum cuz she got the pointy part right inside his ear hole and see, check out that blood, girl. I think she was just feeling good cuz she got his wallet, messed him up, and didn't even break a heel.

It was good for me, cuz she made a buy with the joker's money. You had to carry if you wanted to run the serious shit, and it wasn't my style. The other girls all laughed and called me Mahatma cuz I was always reading Gandhi and Thoreau and shit about nonviolence and revolution and civil disobedience, but we was all tight anyway. We watched each other's backs, and they knew I could fight like a motherfuckin' crazy person if I got pushed too far or somebody I hung out with was being messed up. There was no doubt but that I'd kill somebody if I had a gun, so it was better to just stick to dealing pot and reading my books. I had a lot of reading to do.

So, yeah, now I'm working the trade. I didn't particularly want to, but there aren't exactly a lot of career opportunities for fifteen-year-old girls living on the streets of LA. The truth is I was getting fucked anyway so I figured I might as well get paid for it, right. You couldn't sleep anywhere without waking up to find some guy's dick poking around looking for some hole, didn't matter which one. Seems like ever since I can remember I been waking up to find some big hairy thing climbing on or off of me. I got tired of the shit and thought, hell, I can't get any sleep anyway, I'm going to make somebody pay for this shit. At least now I'm calling the shots and making some money. And I was right. Don't need no fancy drag dress. There is plenty of trade. I do all right. Lots of hairy guys just dying to pay for bait. Tell me I remind them of their daughter and then tell me how they want me to fuck them. They got some messed up shit, man, but the money's good. Better than working at McDonald's, right?

II

"Hey, Baby, bring us some more coffee, will ya?" I spit in their coffee. And carry it to their table, talking to my body like it was somebody else, "Now, don't you mess me up here; we can't show no fear, okay. We just go in and out real smooth, no shaking, no tripping, no spilling. We just gonna set this shit down on the table real calm and professional like we're some college girl and then we gonna get back behind the counter." When I get my feet all talked into not stumbling and my hands convinced they gonna set the coffee down on the table and not in the faces or crotches of these motherfucking pigs I got to wait on, then I move. But it's all gotta happen real fast; these jokers don't like to wait. I tried for a while to talk my mouth into smiling like a straight girl, but it wasn't gonna happen so I let it slide. It wasn't ever my mouth they looked at anyway.

So, here I am working graveyard shift at Winchell's Donut House on Ventura Boulevard. Keeps me warm and dry at night; let's me hustle up easy daytime money. I didn't last too long on the night streets. It was okay, I mean, the money was easy, and it felt good to be setting the price and terms for something that was gonna get taken from me anyway. And me and the other girls, we was tight. Got us formed all together like a pack of wild dogs (they called 'em "worker collectives" in the books I read, but I knew what they meant), and for a while nobody messed with us. Some john, dick, or hairy try and pull something too kinky or not pay you or some shit and the other girls would be on his ass like white on rice. For some of 'em, that was their favorite part of the trade.

Yeah, we had some good times. Those girls never did stop trying to get me into a dress, but, like my smile at the donut store, it just wasn't gonna happen. And they still called me Mahatma and made fun of my books, and I still called them queens and told 'em they'd never look as pretty as the boys round the corner in West Hollywood. We was tight. But it all got fucked up. The shiny boys who dealt and carried wanted a piece of the action. They didn't think no females should be making that kind of money without givin' it to poppa, so we had some problems. Also, we couldn't do nothing about the police. Seemed like no matter how many we sucked and fucked, they just kept coming back round. They fucking multiplied like bunnies. They must have had the whole damn police force working vice and narcotics so they could get laid and stoned and then make some money from the payoffs and the stash they stole on busts.

But, hey, check it out. Here I am again surrounded by the motherfuckers. Come to find out my boss has a deal with the police that if they come around his store a lot for "protection," he (which means I) will give them free coffee and donuts. The truth is I would much rather be robbed than protected; in fact, I was working the last two times this store went down and it was cool. These brothers came in with weapons and all, and I didn't even have to tell my body nothin'. My feet stayed calm, my hands were steady, and damn if my mouth wasn't grinning wide and pretty as I asked them if they'd like some jelly donuts to go with the cash drawer I was emptying for them. But that was just twice. The rest of the time, night after night, I have to serve these pigs coffee and listen to them go off braggin' about the niggers, beaners, spics, and faggots whose heads they've cracked and the hippies, whores, and dykes they've raped and messed up good. Like now they're talkin' right in front of me like I don't even exist except to bring them more donuts, which I guess is good since I belong to a few of the categories they like to fuck with and my friends belong to the rest. But it freaks me out to be so invisible, even though it saves my ass. It's like I'm in some sort of Nazi spy movie and it's only the whiteness of my skin and this thin, white polyester donut uniform that keeps them from recognizing me as the enemy and killing me, too.

I keep thinking I ought to be doing something more than spitting in their coffee. My hands say, just give us a gun and we promise you we will not shake or tremble, and in my mind I see their bodies sprawled out all over the floors I have to scrub each night. But the truth is I just stay invisible and try and keep from showing my fear. It's all I can do to not throw up or piss on myself, and I cannot stop the sweat from running down my back and sides. And so I sweep the floors, wipe the counters, load the glazes, and lay out the chocolate sprinkles in seven crooked rows.

Hard Men of the Street

Black Masculinity and the City in Kenji Jasper's Dark *and* Seeking Salamanca Mitchell

Cherie Ann Turpin

Manthia Diawara defines "black funk culture" within parameters of music and film produced by black men and women seeking to somehow capture the drive or longing for what she refers to as "the notion of a black good-life society (7). To have a "good life" is to experience "material well-being and pleasure." In other words, one could consider such drive in popular black cultural production as a means toward expressing that which seems unreachable for those in our community without financial privilege or social enfranchisement, that is, the means to pursue happiness. Acquisition of wealth and clout bypass those communal "checks and balances" that could temper individualistic impulses expressed in such art: "Both funk and the notion of a black good-life society take ethical decisions away from the church, out of the moral and religious arena, and place them squarely at the feet of material well-being and pleasure" (7).

The black arts movement of the late '60s and '70s was centered by a motivation to empower the collective and to give voice to a disenfranchised black community rendered silent by elitist notions of cultural production. Addison Gayle's call for a black aesthetic in 1970 was grounded in the belief that those who were part of the disenfranchised classes in the black community best articulated authentic, revolutionary art. Here, the emphasis was on the communal rather than individual pursuits of wealth and clout. On the other hand, cultural expression of "black funk culture," or black popular culture, serves as a crossroads of sorts between ideas of culture as primarily commodities for financial gain and ideas of culture as something far too intangible to be used and exchanged as coin. "Black funk culture is the most dangerous and uncompromising element of the black good-life society; it is the poetics of black art which is threatening not only to its adversaries but to itself" (Diawara, 7).

As with any other literary expression, black popular fiction carries the possibilities of rupturing simplistic categorizations and assumptions with regard to cultural production. Key to this movement is an articulation of constraints imposed by social codes already in place with regard to gendered, racialized, and classed bodies. As asserted by Stuart Hall, "There is no escape from the politics of representation, and we cannot wield 'how life really is out there' as a kind of test against which the political rightness or wrongness of a particular cultural strategy or text can be measured" (473).

Kenji Jasper's novels *Dark* and *Seeking Salamanca Mitchell* encapsulate young black men's struggles to escape the limiting, dehumanizing constraints imposed upon them through social boundaries of the city and through a "policing" of their bodies by members of their own community to contain and minimize resistance to dominant perceptions of black masculinity. Patricia Hill Collins notes the significance of the commodification of racist ideological notions of black men:

> The buck, brute, the rapist, and similar controlling images routinely applied to African American men all worked to deny Black men the work of the mind that routinely translates into wealth and power. Instead, relegating Black men to the work of the body was designed to keep them poor and powerless. Once embodied, Black men were seen as being limited by their racialized bodies. (152–53)

Such images have continued to overwhelm popular perceptions and expectations of black men, which in turn continue to replicate more representations of an idealized black "brute." Writing against the grain, Jasper's characterization of black men subverts this ideology by bringing attention to its inability to be successfully replicated or performed as anything but a parody of its own shape. Within this context, Jasper posits the notion of the replication of physical and emotional violence as evidence of this ideology's damaging impact upon the social fabric of African American communities.

The black men who populate Jasper's texts and who attempt to emulate the black "brute" exist as imprisoned bodies incapable of creating or sustaining an existence based on this text. *Dark*'s Thai Williams and *Seeking Salamanca Mitchell*'s Benjamin Baker both exist in a fictionalized rendering of inner-city Washington, D.C., as men forced through violent circumstances from homogenized, docile positions as semicriminalized laborers to outsiders now forced to consider other possibilities of existence and purpose. As outsiders, Thai and Benjamin become both witnesses and participants in shaping a consciousness that resists social pressure to define well-being and happiness through the acquisition of goods, women, or status through brute force or through the equally dehumanizing existence as a voiceless government worker imprisoned by the urban landscape and social stratification.

Jasper's novels challenge idealization of a singularity of urban experience for black men and indeed present a much more disruptive and fragmented landscape of the streets as encountered by young black attempting to embody the "thuggish" or "hard" black criminal superstar looking for the "black good life" and its rewards. His protagonists experience what Stuart Hall refers to as dislocations and antagonisms:

> We are always in negotiation, not with a single set of oppositions that place us always in the same relation to others, but with a series of different positionalities. Each has for us its point of profound subjective identification. And that is the most difficult thing about this proliferation of the field of identities and antagonisms: they are often dislocating in relation to one another. (473)

Jasper's fictional men exist in landscapes already rendered hostile through multiple processes of negations, exclusions, and repositionings that bring attention to the unreliability of singularity of experience, encountering the city, its subgroups, and their respective codes. Further, Jasper's positioning of his protagonists' stories over key familial absences exposes cracks in the imposed script of black masculinity and subsequently reveal it as an unstable series of performances that cannot sustain itself as a reliable, meaningful model of black manhood. As noted by Hall, "The way in which a transgressive politics in one domain is constantly sutured and stabilized by reactionary or unexamined politics in another is only to be explained by this continuous cross-dislocation of one identity by another, one structure by another (473). In Jasper's fictional universe, the streets serve as signs of disunity and fragmentation, rather than as a unified site, politically and culturally.

TYRANNY OF THE STREETS

In *Seeking Salamanca Mitchell*, Benjamin's encounter with the city reveals a contradictory existence as a child of parents who were part of the working-class culture that sustains law and order, as well as being a child lured by what he believes to be both exciting and promising to produce friendship and respect. "I knew nothing of risk, nothing of true danger, other than the echoes of screams and gunfire that came to my window while I slept like a baby. I was neither the hero of rap lyrics nor one who had been schooled in the code of the streets. But I wanted to be. And the desire to obtain something is often all one needs for its acquisition" (4). Benjamin contradicts himself when he claims ignorance regarding "true danger" followed by his recall of the sounds of it. Describing himself as sleeping "like a baby" during gun battles and conflict suggests not only knowledge of its existence but also an awareness of his place outside it, as well as the significance of having a policeman as a father that allowed him to deny or at least delay acknowledgment of its existence. Expressing his longing to be "schooled in the code of the streets," Benjamin attempts to find entrance into what he imagines to be a place of power and status, something he believes unattainable to him because of his father's position as enforcer of the laws of the city. Rather than seeing himself as privileged, socially, he sees himself as lacking and unskilled: "But I was not like them. Because I was my father's child I was never allowed to wander the night, never permitted to forge bonds with those whose parents let them play unsupervised until the early morning" (4). Benjamin associates street knowledge and bravado with "acquisition" of what he associates with dominance and empowerment; moreover, he seeks to "wander" and to "forge bonds" at will, tempering the idea of free exploration with the notion of creating "bonds."

Benjamin's struggles can be understood as a series of misfires in his failure to perform as obedient servant to the city-state as represented by his father the police officer, whose absence leaves him vulnerable to the criminal enterprise with which he becomes entangled, as represented by Alphonse Mitchell. Mitchell has a "respectable" and public face as a community elder but runs a criminal gang of thieves and robbers and is thus sent into the prison system with its own social codes: "I was no longer clean, no longer quarantined by a father's badge and the reputation that stuck out in front of it like a battering ram. The Old Man had fully uneducated me into the daily grind of the streets, and with four yards to show for my efforts. For that I loved him like a father" (33).

Benjamin's loathing of his past as a body marked as taboo to the outside world is punctuated with utterances that seem contradictory; his status as a clean, innocent one is marked by what he describes as "a battering ram," suggesting his body is both sexually virile and a weapon. To be "uneducated" is to be stripped of that weapon, which contradicts what he describes as gaining "four yards to show." Thus, what had been assumed by Benjamin Baker to be freedom from the oppressive law of the state is yet another prison, complete with its own social codes and punishments, as well as a folding over of authoritarian boundaries and containments manipulated through individual and collective will.

Indeed, Mitchell imposes his authority through a commodification of young black men's bodies as expendable laborers who maintain order in the streets he owns through his criminal enterprise; Benjamin's seduction into crime and subsequent betrayal by Mitchell could not have happened without the existing capitalist government structure he uses to punish and banish Benjamin. Michel Foucault's seminal work *Discipline and Punish* asserts the power relations' dynamic that produces and perpetuates domination and control:

> In effect the offence opposes an individual to the entire social body; in order to punish him, society has the right to oppose him in its entirety. It is an unequal struggle: on one side are all the forces, all the power, all the rights. And this is how it should be, since the defence of each individual is involved. Thus a formidable right to punish is established, since the offender becomes the common enemy. Indeed, he is worse than an enemy, for it is from within society that he delivers his blows—he is nothing less than a traitor, a "monster." (90)

As a black man who has been "caught up" in criminal activity and subsequently the penal system, Benjamin performs as to be expected by society, which is that of the "offender" or the "black male perpetrator." Through these same misfires, Benjamin's awakening presents the self that engages in a journey to reposition himself as a man who, in order to escape the criminal landscape as constructed by both Alphonse Mitchell and the seemingly impersonal presence of the power brokers running D.C. and its social strata, Benjamin must dismantle the script that demands his participation in naming himself as a criminal, thug, or "monster." His passion for Salamanca and his young daughter becomes a beacon for him to subvert the paradigm and acquire a sense of personal empowerment, self-knowledge, and spiritual transformation, aspects of his renaissance.

Alphonse Mitchell's attempts to expel Benjamin from both social bodies can be seen as an exercise of the forces and powers endowed to him as an authority figure who is both author and enforcer of those unwritten codes that permit him to treat all bodies in his purview as expendable property. His past in Detroit as an abusive man who murders his wife because of her attempt to escape him remains concealed from Benjamin and his daughter Salamanca until he beats her for becoming pregnant: "Without warning, the fingers on his right hand formed a fist, and that fist traveled upward, into her abdomen and, subsequently into her womb" (Jasper, *Seeking Salamanca Mitchell*, 75). Like the trophies, Salamanca's body, including her sexuality, reflects his status in the community. He punishes her for her "failure" to obey those social codes that assumed his dominance and control over her sexuality. Mitchell's recitation of biblical scripture as he attacks her invokes what he believes to be his right of dominance over her body, as well as his right to punish her for breaking the code: "'Mortify therefore your members which are upon the earth,' he began from memory, a passage he'd taken from the dictionary-size Bible he kept beneath the shelves of trophies against the wall" (75). Her pregnancy altered her status from that of a commodity to be stored like a trophy to that of someone capable of making decisions regarding her body, regardless of what others determined with regard to her position as a single mother.

Similarly, Viola Mitchell's murder in Detroit by a much younger Alphonse Mitchell illustrates his assumptions of women as objects for use, exchange, and in this case, disposal. He justifies his violent acts through social codes and contracts, and uses place as a sign for an entire tradition of patriarchal rule and discipline. Under such codes, he becomes absolute ruler. Under the code of the streets and of the rural south, Alphonse Mitchell creates an uneven, dangerous lineage of oppression and brutality.

> Because he was from Rocky Mount, North Carolina, the South. And in the South, husbands and wives prayed and stayed together. No alimony. No white lawyers and judges trying to tell whom and how much he had to pay to keep his family fed and clothed. She wasn't questioning just his authority, but his whole belief system. As a matter of fact, she was questioning his manhood, and that just could not be. (224)

For Mitchell, the law of "the South" merges with the law of the street and thereby justifies his actions and reaffirms what he believes to be black masculinity. He affirms his definition of empowerment and agency by crushing all opponents to his dominance, regardless of its impact on his household or his community. Stuart Hall notes how mass-consumed ideals of black male subjectivity are often based on the subjugation of others:

> Thus, to put it crudely, certain ways in which black men continue to live out their counter-identities as black masculinities and replay those fantasies of black masculinities in the theatres of popular culture are, when viewed from along other axes of difference, the very masculine identities that are oppressive to women, that claim visibility for their hardness only at the expense of the vulnerability of black women and the feminization of gay black men. (473–74)

Mitchell's violent acts toward his wife and daughter serve as "trophies" and evidence of his "hardness," as performed repeatedly in his history with women. Despite his position as a man of considerable influence and wealth, he is also subject to those same "counter-identities" that delude him into believing that "punishing" the women in his life serves the best interests of his family and his community. He embodies the harshness of the street, while losing those women whom he identifies as evidence of that same "good life" and assuming they are "hard" promised to provide for him.

LOVE AND GUNS

Like Benjamin, Thai Williams in *Dark* becomes entangled in crime and violence and subsequently seeks escape from a script that predicts a violent death or a spiritual death through imprisonment. The monstrous as performed by Thai appears as a ghostlike apparition chasing him from Washington,

D.C., to Charlotte, North Carolina, which he believes to be a safe haven from the vengeful murder he commits in a moment of rage over an ex-girlfriend. As with Benjamin, Thai becomes "unclean" and loses his status as a law-abiding resident; significantly, as a government worker, his fall into the "dark" and into a status as enemy of the city helps to fuel his inner torment.

> "Do you even know what love is?" the shadow of a man asked me as he stood over me in that alley in Congress Heights. The barrel of a gun was right in my face and I couldn't speak. I could only hear his words repeatedly beating against my brain to the faint beat of the Backyard Band. But no matter how hard I thought about what he kept asking me I didn't get it. Then I woke up. (49)

Here, Thai becomes both the shadow and the victim in the alley. The gun serves as a sign of force to induce Thai to speak, but its presence and implied threat induces silence. However, the silence cannot be assumed to be empty of response. The question posed to him in the dream is framed in a manner suggesting he does not "know what love is," but it paradoxically suggests that he does know "love," or of its absence. Knowledge of its absence, or at least its opposite, hate, as well as a repetition of the question becomes apparent with the appearance of the gun. Thai "does not get it" because he was the "shadow" holding the gun to his opponent in the waking world. He cannot see his own process of exclusions and negations that allowed him to not see "love" or humanity in the other he has murdered.

This process of exclusions and negations of what Thai "is not," "what he would not do," and "what he does not know" continues with his "righteous rage" at Yvette, a young woman he meets at a party who almost immediately confesses her abortion to him. "I pictured myself tearing her head off with my bare hands. I wanted to avenge the life she had somehow taken even though it had come out of her own womb" (41). Thai's emotional violence appears as misplaced, in that he positions himself as "avenger" of an unknown dead child whose demise has not been explained or understood. He excludes himself as deserving the same revenge for his own murderous actions while assuming hers to be worthy of death. The absence of the child in her "womb" and his silent eruption could be connected to earlier stories of abandonment: Yvette becomes Thai's absent mother and Sierra the ex-girlfriend in this same space.

Her refusal to carry "life" becomes a retelling of his mother's failure to live, as well as a failure of Sierra to carry his baby to term. The gap between Thai and Yvette is better understood with his recall of his mother as an emptiness: "Absence of mother: I moved on without her. Nothing kissed my bumps and bruises besides Q-tips and peroxide. I wiped my own face in the morning and taught myself to never show any weakness" (69). Without the appearance or memory of a mother or a nurturing female presence, Thai's emotions lack the language needed to build empathy for women, and as a result, his relationship with Sierra fails after her miscarriage. "I never thought about her either. I gave her everything she asked for and took her out and we talked about the future, but all I thought about was the seed in her womb, while she never talked about it at all" (123–24). Sierra's reluctance to connect with Thai can be understood as a fear of losing her own identity and becoming his property. He centers on "the seed in her womb" as evidence of his claim on her body. She and the baby become acquisitions that mark his manhood.

The gap created by his mother's early death renders him vulnerable to absorption of the brute, emotionless ideal of street thugs. The ideals presented to him in the "streets" limit his understanding of empathy, compassion, and affection as essential elements in building relationships and negotiating power between people in relationships. "Girls were an alien race who you entered and left, unless you loved them or gave them your baby" (69). The absence of nurturing as well as the absence of the feminine in his young life produces a man who sees women as lacking meaning or purpose beyond use/ function.

Thai's shift from would-be thug to empathetic being begins with his father's revelation of his mother's death through gun violence and his father's subsequent act of vengeance on the murderer. Thai Williams's transformation from dreamer to cognition and agency of the self can and should be considered a journey toward what would be described in black vernacular terms as "realness." He recognizes his struggle to unravel the script as being a common struggle among black men who have suffered emotional injury:

> As I looked Diamelo the Terminator in the eye all I could see was what I had been. The dark figure in my dreams with the .380 now wore my face. Behind my target's eyes was the presence that had sent Snowflake, Cuckoo, me and my father to the Dark Side. He had come through my door possessed by that dark demon that erased all ethics and reason and thirsted only for blood in exchange for a final closure. (216)

In order to engage in the "funk" of life he comes to recognize that the "shadow" in his dreams is yet another performative of an idealized masculinity impossible to truly embody. He recognizes himself as the gun-wielding gangster in his dreams, as well as the impossibility of sustaining such a performance without destruction of the self and others.

Thus, Kenji Jasper's novels depict painful downfalls and transformative movements by young men who choose to rewrite black male subjectivity, as well as shift ground from myths, both generated and reinforced through black popular culture. For Jasper, the script of the violent, angry black thug masks the pain of abandonment, emotional damage, and spiritual wounds. His protagonists walk through a fictional universe where it is possible to dismantle stereotypes of black men and, through such actions, engage in self-agency.

WORKS CITED

Collins, Patricia Hill. *Black Sexual Politics: African Americans, Gender, and the New Racism.* New York: Routledge, 2005.

Diawara, Manthia, et al. "A Symposium on Popular Culture and Political Correctness." *Social Text* 36 (Autumn 1993): 1–39. www.jstor.org/.

Foucault, Michel. *Discipline and Punish: The Birth of the Prison.* New York: Random House, 2012. Kindle edition.

Hall, Stuart. "What Is This 'Black' in Black Popular Culture?" In *Stuart Hall: Critical Dialogues in Cultural Studies (Comedia)*, edited by Kuan-Hsing Chen, 465–75. London: Taylor and Francis, 2007. Kindle edition.

Jasper, Kenji. *Dark.* New York: Broadway Books, 2001.

———. *Seeking Salamanca Mitchell.* New York: Harlem Moon, 2004.

An Analysis of Omar Tyree's *Last Street Novel*

Keenan Norris

Omar Tyree's *Last Street Novel* is a metafictional contemplation of and commentary on street literature as a burgeoning market force, as a purveyor of popular tropes relating to black folks, and as a self-cannibalizing entertainment genre. The novel's main character is Shareef Crawford, a figure who bears at least initial superficial resemblance to Omar Tyree: like Tyree, Crawford is a best-selling writer of black romance fiction; like Tyree, Crawford desires to write books that appeal to men as well as women; and like Tyree, Crawford is frustrated by the lack of support that his unromantic writings receive. In his open letter straightforwardly titled "An Urban 'Street Lit' Retirement," Tyree identifies as a "hardcore fact" the "urban audience's preference for denigration." He further opines that "after trying to educate and uplift the same young, urban readership who fell in love with *Flyy Girl* with the sequel book *For the Love of Money* . . . the positive and progressive voice that I [had] become so proud of, had lost me the support of my young urban audience." In less elaborate and more definitive terms, Tyree's surrogate in *The Last Street Novel*, Crawford, makes the same point: "*Nobody wants to learn shit. . . . They want blood. They want violence. They want death*" (298). The disillusionment and cynicism at the state of the publishing market and street literature's place within it drives both Tyree's statement of retirement and the novel that is, for now, his curtain call.

Shareef Crawford, a successful romance writer who fears an obsolescence akin to that of his real-life creator, is torn between attempting to ride the rising wave of gritty, violent urban literature, keeping to his stock-and-trade romance writing, or trying his hand at commercially risky, intellectually substantive black fiction. On the current state of black popular fiction, Crawford makes this assessment: "Weak character development, weak dialogue, weak plot points, with a weak buildup, weak chronology, uneven climaxes, and a weak resolution" (32). To an adoring female fan (with whom he happens to be engaged in an extramarital affair), Crawford goes even further in his diatribe: "Mos Def, on his first album, he made the comment that the state of hip-hop depends on the state of the people. He said if the people are doing good, then the hip-hop will reflect it. But if the people are doing bad, then so is the hip-hop. And it's the same thing with books. You can't push something on the people that they don't want and they don't feel." Mimicking the stance of major publishers prior to the rise of street lit, Crawford even says of black people, "Books . . . that's too much work for 'em." He adds the caveat that "if they do read, they only want to read shit they can swallow. Soul food" (59).

The "soul food" desired by a broad black readership, Crawford again and again states, consists of ample doses of titillating romance and ultraviolent crime stories. Urban literature novelists can write about street crime or salacious sex; street lit writers are limited to street crime stories, but either way, according to Crawford, it's all the same unhealthy "soul food" served up repetitiously.

Crawford identifies his audience and the audience for street lit as wholly black American. Moreover, he identifies black buying practices as at the root of the salacious and rapacious content of the fiction. Instead of placing blame with the publishing industry, he blames the audience ("You can't push something on the people that they don't want and they don't feel") for dictating the content of the genre. While acknowledging Crawford's general accuracy as regards the genre's black buying base, it should nevertheless be noted that, first, the appetite and even preference for the salacious and rapacious is prevalent in reading communities of all races and ethnicities and, second, that after a particular group's buying practices have been identified and pigeonholed, industries have a tendency to assume those practices are unchanging and are quite often interminably slow to respond to altered buying habits. This historical lack of corporate foresight suggests that the black book-buying audience's habits can and probably will change, given time, and that the black book-buying audience's habits are not the sole or even main explanation for the narrowness of the subject matter found in black popular fiction. The immediate demands of commercially motivated authors and profit-driven publishers obscure this longer-term reality.

Endlessly hectored by black men who insult either his manhood or his work, Shareef Crawford eventually decides to transition from writing romance novels to penning a street lit novel.

After initially toying with the idea of writing under the pseudonym "the Street King," he is prevailed upon by his New York mistress to visit convicted drug dealer Michael Springfield in prison and interview Springfield for a possible novel based on his crimes and prison renaissance. Springfield's proposal provides the writer with everything he desires: a true-to-life crime saga, a ready-made sequence of events, and a provocative backstory to create buzz for the book's writing and release.

Crawford decides to spend time in Harlem to research the site of his new book idea, leaning on his friends for local contacts and word about the latest hot spots in town. He goes to the penitentiary up north, accompanied by his mistress Cynthia, to speak with Springfield.

The writer is a Harlem native but has not lived in the Manhattan neighborhood in decades. In the narrative's present tense, he, his estranged wife, and his two children live in a ritzy South Florida enclave. Additionally, Crawford has a South Beach villa that he uses to entertain another of the "disrespectful bitches" whom he now prefers to his wife, this one a Dominican American mistress named Jacqueline.

Obviously, the writer has moved far from the hood where his grandparents raised him, and his simple knowledge of Harlem as a living, evolving urban organism is diluted. In the time of the novel, Harlem is ground zero for gentrification of older urban cores. As Jurrell, a childhood nemesis-turned-suave-adult, tells Crawford, "A lot of things are changed in Harlem now. . . . It's about moving on up. And if you're not moving on up, then you're moving on out of Harlem" (144). Once simply a crime-ridden ghetto, "Harlem, New York," an omniscient third-person narrative voice that Tyree fitfully employs in order to relay necessary sociological information explains, "was the most significant microcosm of American economics, culture, and social status . . . in a square radius of less than five miles" (171). In addition to not understanding the extent of Harlem's changes, the writer has also forgotten just how fast rumor, reportage, innuendo, and speculation can spread in the hood's insular space. Less than twenty-four hours after his conversation with Springfield on the prison yard, Crawford is warned by his childhood friend Trap to leave Harlem as soon as possible. Dangerous criminals, Trap says, have heard about the book idea and are nervous that Springfield will divulge their names and deeds given the public forum to do so. Therefore, they are threatening Trap in an attempt to stop his friend from writing his book.

By this point, Tyree portrays his mouthpiece with self-deprecating grandiosity, thinking of his unwritten book as "his Harlem masterpiece," and is unwilling to bow to the rumored threats against himself and his friends (206). Instead of leaving Harlem immediately, the writer roots himself in his childhood home, choosing against advice to stay in his low-grade hotel on Frederick Douglass Boulevard. Indeed, his intransigence is doubly born of the incredulity at the idea that men who do not read books and mock his romance novels would kill him over a book he has yet to actually write, and from a kind of birthright pride. "Harlem don't scare me," he tells his friend Spoonie, "I grew up here" (204).

Spoonie's rejoinder, that "ten thousand motherfuckers who died of bullet wounds in Harlem" could claim similar nativity, falls on deaf ears (204). Likewise, Trap's admonition that street thugs read work where their vital interests are involved and will stop at nothing to protect those interests goes unheeded.

The next morning Cynthia calls Crawford, sobbing, totally distraught: Michael Springfield, she tells him, is dead; he's been murdered, shanked on the prison yard for his anticipated treachery. Suddenly, the speculative has become the real. The jailed drug kingpin is dead, and Crawford's life and work are under threat. Cynthia begs Crawford to relocate downtown as soon as possible and to go back to his wife and family in Florida on the first plane flying. But the writer, stubborn and recalcitrant, seeks out Jurrell, the bully from his youth who now seems to be a reformed businessman. After spending the day with Jurrell scouting Harlem's newly constructed, high-priced condominiums and lofts, the writer insists on returning to his hotel. At the hotel, he's confronted by some of the thugs who want to dissuade him from writing Springfield's story. They want to question him about his intentions with the unwritten chronicle. Despite the fact that Springfield hasn't told Crawford enough information to write an editorial, let alone a novel, the confrontation quickly degenerates into chaotic violence with the thugs chasing after the fleeing writer, shooting at him in the middle of the crowded boulevard.

Almost inexplicably, Crawford is saved when the thugs are met by a separate group of thugs coming from the opposite direction, returning fire. Suddenly, a luxury car drifts up alongside the running writer, and he is made to understand that its driver and passengers are with the crew that has just saved his life and his potential novel. The crew drives Crawford downtown, where a young hustler fresh to the game named Baby G proposes that Crawford write his life story, the story of a living and free Harlem gangster, instead of the narrative of the dead and irrelevant Michael Springfield.

The writer quickly identifies the baby gangster as a boastful but minor Harlem character not worthy of a novel. While he listens patiently to the kid's stories of street mayhem and attention-catching antics, he doesn't seriously consider writing his story. With Springfield dead and his own life in immediate danger, the stubborn writer has almost been compelled to give up on his crime novel project. He is not in the mood to consider new subjects for his novelistic designs. At this point in the novel, Tyree seems to be engaged in a thorough mockery of urban literature as a genre. A rival black writer derides Crawford, informing him that "[Springfield] tried to get other writers to tell his story too, and nobody would go anywhere near him. Until you came." Thus, Crawford is the "sucker" fascinated enough by the allure of imagined ghetto glory and masculine bravado to risk his wealth, reputation, literary career, and very life for the opportunity to novelize commonplace thuggery. As the rival writer tells him, "You should have stuck to writing romance" (255). Indeed, when the confused and conflicted, set-up, and hunted romance writer lectures a young black journalist on the false totems of hood status, he seems to unconsciously critique his own decisions and his own predicament. "And you a damn college student, gettin' caught up in the same bullshit these young rappers get caught up in" (257). Crawford is, by this point in the tale, a best-selling novelist, a man of wealth and prestige, wholly "caught up" in a "bullshit" quagmire of misunderstood motives and fearful and vengeful men. "As much as he talked about the nonsensical lure of urban street life, the danger of it all was compelling him to stick around and prove that something could happen" (272). It can be inferred that among the internal commentaries that *The Last Street Novel* makes is that street lit's purveyors could do so much more with their work than repeat the "bullshit" that "young rappers" have placed in the cultural mainstream, but instead they are prisoners to the compelling dangers of the streets just as thoroughly as the kid who could be studying at home but chooses to sell rocks or pimp girls on the corner. Street lit novelists are figured as "suckers" retelling a set of powerfully overworked stories that have primarily functioned to stigmatize and degrade the black people that are the objects of such narratives.

Tyree implies that the writer's motivation for pursuing his story at such risk to himself is base and simple: Crawford wants to be respected as a man by other men. When his childhood nemesis, Jurrell, praises Crawford's commercial successes, noting that "you a million-dollar nigga with no ball or microphone," the writer nevertheless manages to construe this encouragement as a negative. "You know what I honestly feel like after you say all of that shit to me, man . . . I feel like the guy playing jump rope with the girls while all the guys are playing football and slap boxing." Figuring the feminine (jump rope) as inferior to or incompatible with the masculine (e.g., football and boxing), the writer senses a distance between his profession and the popular tropes of masculinity. To write is to distance oneself from popular understandings of masculinity and thus to feminize oneself. The only remedies are either to give up writing or to masculinize the writing process through refiguring the basis of literature around popularly understood tropes of masculinity and black masculinity. Crawford's writing career is far too lucrative to walk away from, leaving him with one masculinizing option: to write street lit. Unfortunately, the tropes of street lit seem inseparable from prior figurations of black men as irrational, animal, and ultraviolent.

Crawford confides in Jurrell, "It's like you can't really talk to women, man. I feel like I'm talkin' at 'em half the time. . . . So why can't I talk to other guys about the shit that I do as a writer, like an athlete would, or a rapper would, or a thug would? You feel me? That's why this shit is important to me, man" (273–74). Here, the novelist speaks to realities difficult to acknowledge in the formal space of academic critique. Phillip Brian Harper, in his investigation of the anxieties that attend expectations of African American masculine identity, in *Are We Not Men?* uses the term "physical-ization" (120). For Harper, this term describes the way black men's identities are so deeply wedded to our physical attributes, that in fact these attributes, or the social perception of them, often constitute our social selves. I find Harper's terminology very useful, yet I want to take a different angle in my critique.

Crawford wants to connect with men across precisely the space that his identity as a writer seems to shutter him from. The writer is a trope, as is the athlete, the rapper, and the thug. Each is a trope expressing desire. The thug and the athlete use physicalization as a conduit between the subject and the desired object, while the rapper and writer use the abstractions of language. The immediacy and power of athleticism and thuggery make expression visceral. Rap obscures the abstract nature of language through forcefulness of delivery and the raw assertion of prerogative. By contrast, fiction writing, however forceful and raw its real origins, is recognized popularly as a sophis-ticated form resistant to immediacy, resistant to the visceral. The fundamen-tal distance between every man and the tribe of men is eased by the physical and intensified by the intellectual. Crawford seeks to negotiate and ultimately erase this division through literary reenactments of violence.

Upon waking in a swank Manhattan hotel with his luggage lying neatly before him (all courtesy of Baby G's intrepid crew), Crawford's tribal pre-rogative still compels him: "I'm a street nigga," he thinks to himself. "I was *born* to the streets. *Harlem!* I don't even know my parents. So if I die fuckin' with this book, then that's my legacy. But I'm not running" (305). The writer is many things. He is a best-selling romance novelist, an aspiring street lit novelist, an owner of expensive waterfront properties, a father and husband and playboy, an orphaned son, and a child of the ghetto. If he is a "street nigga," that is only one aspect of his self. It is a self-imposed and senseless self-reduction.

After a final confrontation with his pursuers in which the writer discovers that it is his "friend" Trap who has orchestrated the whole thing; a gun battle in St. Nicholas Park; the deaths of Trap, Spoonie, Baby G, and various "soldiers"; and the revelation that Jurrell, far from being a reformed busi-nessman, is actually the deadliest gangster in Harlem, Crawford is yoked into a Faustian business deal with his childhood nemesis. To atone for all the killing he's caused, Crawford must write Baby G's story as well as Jurrell's. He must become "the Street King" of his idiotic ambitions, and he must descend into the depths of Harlem's perpetual underworld even as he pens his best-selling tales from the luxurious haven of his South Beach villa and Fort Lauderdale home. Distributing his street lit via Jurrell's "Underground

Library" imprint, he will line the pockets of Harlem's chief thug. This is one fate of street lit and hip-hop in microcosm: both genres, as they experience commercial success, become materially disconnected from the actual poor and distressed in the inner cities while remaining dependent on the poverty, distress, and subjugation of those subjects for continued profits. The parasite degrades the host *from a distance.*

Far from the nostalgia that he had earlier nursed for his childhood home, the writer now knows that "Harlem [is] one of the most vicious communities not only in America, but in the world" (341). Yet he is contractually obligated both by his corporate publisher and by his underworld boss, Jurrell, to perpetuate and lionize this viciousness in the form of his crime novels. His books, written under pseudonym, detailing the exploits of Baby G and the machinations of a supposed "square" who runs Harlem's underworld from behind the scenes are instant street classics. Along with the new romance novel that the writer also pens, under his real name, these narratives of violence and premature death elevate him to unparalleled commercial success. But the writer is no longer his own man, and his books are no longer the product of his dreams and desires. Shareef Crawford is on the plantation, as it were, and Jurrell and the publishing company are his overseers. As his one surviving friend, Polo, puts it, "That boy Jurrell ain't gon' let you slow down . . . ma-fucka gon' want a private jet off ya' ass next year" (400). The writer decides to console himself with the small victories: the Underground Library might end up employing ten, twenty, or thirty previously unemployable persons and keep their families in clothes and fed. He has reconciled with his wife and can see his children on a daily basis again.

The book ends with some old standards: Crawford can't "stop [his] shine for nobody." He always had been and always would remain "a winner." He was "born to do what he had to do and be who he had to be . . . there was no turning back from it" (399–401). Crawford's final assertions ring hollow, and even the small familial and economic victories that the writer can count pale in comparison to the devil's bargain he unwittingly finds himself in. He is, finally, the prey of forces more rapacious and all encompassing than his mere literary talents, and there is no way out of his contractual obligations.

The Last Street Novel satirizes the psychological and commercial forces behind street literature. The novel critiques the fan base, the writers, and the corporate and criminal partners that together form the supply and demand for this literature. As self-commentary of the genre upon itself, perhaps the novel stands too far outside and too much in judgment of the form to be a truly internal critique. However, it is an important book within the genre in that it does more than simply perform the basic tenets of the genre, going beyond the plot dynamics that characterize street fiction. Even the novel's title seeks to assert control over the genre, claiming its place at the end point of the literary phenomenon. Tyree's title categorically states that the street lit genre is in its death throes and that the novel and its author have the power to bring it to its end. However hubristic such claims may seem, insofar as the title is of a piece with the narrative and the allegorical suggestions of the narrative (the Faustian bargain, the stories of ghetto squalor, and the novelist trapped in his self-made misguided design), the claim is a serious one. How can a genre premised dually on representation and degradation of ghetto communities not write itself out of existence? How can such a genre find release from its anarchic motivations and present a more self-sustaining and life-extending story?

Interestingly, in his open farewell letter to the genre "An Urban 'Street Lit' Retirement," Tyree discloses that he actually intended to title the novel *The Writer*, not *The Last Street Novel*, but was informed that his chosen title was simply not edgy enough. Unable even to title his own books, the best-selling novelist seems much like his fictional creation, Shareef Crawford, in this instance. Perhaps *The Last Street Novel*, title and all, is less an assertion of Tyree's control over the street lit genre than a statement on the writer's bondage to controlling corporate and audience demands. The writer has literally lost the power to name. He is, then, no longer father to his own work but more the necessary adjunct in a complex process of creation. Bent to the whims of forces stronger and more rapacious than he, the writer is wrenched from his historical role and his moral centrality within the logic of the text and placed on the plantation with all the other workers who contribute to the crop.

The crop is a continuous narrative of urban decay and black despair. At the amoral center of the work is money itself, its flows, and its gain and loss. Circling round this center are the things that people will do for money, their romances, and their crimes. Attached to these romances and crimes and controlled by their desperate desire for romance, crime, and fortune is the audience. And the writer is here, too, coequal with the audience and at the mercy of romance, crime, money, and its controllers. The writer is now a controlled force in the logic of the street lit text.

It is telling that Shareef Crawford never comes to grips with the changes that his childhood friends and the neighborhood of his formative years have undergone. Equally telling is Jurrell's early admonition to Crawford that "a lot of things are changed in Harlem now. . . . It's about moving on up. And if you're not moving on up, then you're moving on out of Harlem" (144). Just as Crawford has developed into a successful romancer, Trap has turned from a friend into a vicious street criminal; similar to this class cleavage between Crawford and his friends is the fact that Harlem has changed from a declining ghetto into a place that while still characterized by blight is also full of problematic prosperity. Gentrification is repurposing Harlem, altering formerly dangerous and decrepit urban space in economically dynamic ways that draw in wealthier residents and compel the dispersal of poorer residents.

Unlike Crawford, Jurrell is at essence a capitalist, not a romantic, and has chosen Harlem as his base of operation not because it still contains some of New York's most degraded neighborhoods but because it presents fresh opportunities for capital acquisition and investment. Among his principal investments is his publishing business, focusing on street lit novels. Jurrell's literary enterprise is indicative of and in fact mirrors the changed reality of Harlem itself and urban cores across the country: the works he covertly sponsors at once create economic opportunity and cater to Harlem's underserved reader markets and yet also stratify black readership along economic lines. It is the capitalist understanding of the dynamics of gentrification in his hometown, and the writer's comparative cluelessness, that allows Jurrell to take advantage of Crawford in order to exploit the book market.

There are immense profits to be made from narrativizing and gentrifying the black poor and the poor in general. But exploitation of the vulnerable, though naturalized out of visibility by conservative rhetoric about free markets, profit imperatives, and self-reliance, is ultimately cowardice in the face of an elemental human reality. It simply "refounds" all power relations and reinforces all manner of hierarchy and division. It displaces poverty out of fear of the fact that poverty is more enduring than any enterprise or capital dream. Expelled out of now gleaming urban cores by university expansion, stadium design, or what have you, poverty merely relocates to ex-urban ghettos.

One irony of *The Last Street Novel* is that the book's narrative close signals not an end for street lit, as its title promises, but endless reproduction of the genre's most base aspects, all sourced from a wealthy black man's pen. Shareef Crawford can't stop, won't stop. The more surpassing irony is that, despite its castigation of street lit, the novel nevertheless is street lit, the very title, however unwanted, speaking to that reality. As such, it speaks to the genre's great potential for investigation of black male subjectivity and the social pressures placed on black masculinity. This street lit text also stands as likely the most technically innovative novel in what is characteristically a subgenre reliant on determinist and realist narrative structures. This formal point alone hints at the evolving complexities of this emergent popular form.

WORKS CITED

Harper, Phillip Brian. *Are We Not Men? Masculine Anxiety and the Problem of African-American Identity.* New York: Oxford University Press, 1996.

Tyree, Omar. *The Last Street Novel.* New York: Simon and Schuster, 2008.

———. "An Urban 'Street Lit' Retirement." Daily Voice, 19 June 2008. http://dailyvoice .com/.

On Street Lit

Ethan Iverson Interviews Gerald Early

Ethan Iverson

EI: You've recently edited four exciting anthologies of the best of current African American writing: one each for fiction and nonfiction in 2009 and 2010. On the fiction side there are two pieces about jazz in each book: "Body and Soul" by Wesley Brown is in *Best African American Fiction 2010*; an excerpt from *Harlem Summer* by Walter Dean Myers is in *Best African American Fiction 2009*; and both volumes conclude with excerpts of L. F. Haines's *Up for It: A Tale of the Underground*. Is there new interest in writing about jazz by African Americans? My impression is that if you had tried to make these anthologies, say, twenty years ago, you might not have found as many jazz-related pieces.

GE: Well, you may be right about that. These anthologies wouldn't have been possible twenty years ago in any case.

EI: What's changed?

GE: African Americans have become recognized as a particularly salient literary and intellectual audience over the last twenty years. Let me say that such an audience—African Americans constituting that kind of a public, an intellectual public or a literary public—has always existed! But it's reached a kind of critical mass point in recent years, and I think it's become recognized more generally by the white or mainstream institutions that such a black literary and intellectual audience exists. That's a big part of why these books were able to come out the way they did.

EI: I was struck by your online essay about the rise of "urban fiction," the genre fiction aimed for the African American market that sells so well, which I guess is controversial in content——

GE: Yes, it is.

EI: But I read nonliterary detective stories myself for pleasure. I believe in escapism and in the honorable tradition of genre fiction. And I like what you said, that on the way to literature, "urban fiction" is really a fabulous thing.

GE: Right. Yeah, there's quite a bit of controversy about that by some African Americans. Juan Williams, the noted commentator on NPR and Fox News, wrote an op-ed piece a couple of weeks ago where he condemned this type of writing, this black urban literature. And he quoted me! He took the quote out of context to make it seem like I was supporting him, you know. He just took a little snippet: "And professor Gerald Early said . . ." I thought that was pretty funny, since I was in fact suggesting just the opposite: it's actually a good thing that this literature exists. It's fine, it's wonderful, it's why we represent some of it in these books! Over time, the African American audience has gotten to be more sophisticated about the things it wants. That audience has also become more differentiated and more nuanced. It's a complex, complicated, and more sophisticated audience than people give it credit for.

Enigmas

Sterling Warner

Like an ice palace during
A free skate,
Everyone's on edge
Chipping away
While rappers twizzle
Laying out on the gold chains
Pontificating values of the hood,
Showcasing precious metals.

So when's the last time you been back to
Sleepless streets, alleys that never yawn,
Strategic thoroughfares that initiate
Nike photo-op footwork?
Pacing forms pop jump after jump
Create slinky shadows behind
Warped plywood plank backboards
Braided wire hanger hoops where
Rim shots morph each fragile circle until
Nothing drops through——
Only imaginations slam, dunk, spin in
Another universe without traveling.

Remember Friday afternoons?
High school kids choking on silver whistles
Bullies tossing tied tennis shoes over
Low-hanging power lines, sometimes
Walking home barefoot, victimized by
A familiar hustle, their own hostile game?
Escape artists, misty-eyed dreamers
Like Sufis, shaman, fakirs, and aesthetics
Center their social paralysis and

Disenchantment, find solace in
Future tattoos, exotic piercings
Becoming thoughtful enigmas,
Legends in their own minds.

Colson Whitehead's *Zone One*

Postapocalyptic Zombies Take Over Manhattan in the Age of Nostalgia, Despair, and Consumption

Kimberly Fain

Colson Whitehead's *Zone One* capitalizes on his childhood memories of a ruined city (Sunderman). By reflecting on the economic downturn and reversal of fortunes of his 1970s birthplace, imagining a postapocalyptic, dreamless New York was a minute leap. Writing a horror novel allowed him the space to recover from the hostile landscape of his birth. *Zone One* is a tribute to how a culture reconstructs hope and rebuilds itself, in the wake of an accident or trauma, such as the unfathomable tragedy on 9/11. Whitehead eloquently transforms the Manhattan landscape, centering the horrific action around the well-known and symbolic streets of Broadway and Canal, separating the survivors from the monsters (Rudin). Romero's *Escape from New York* and *Omega Man* served as inspirations for Whitehead's science fiction/horror–driven tale (Sunderman). Human nature causes most people to blindly follow the crowd, submissively consuming pop culture without introspection, without purging its capitalistic effects. This docility shields the terror within American culture, American cities, and American people. For Whitehead, "Your friend, your family, you[r] neighbor, your teacher, the guy at the bodega down the street, can be revealed as the monster they've always been" (Fassler). By using the zombie metaphor for the frustrated consumer culture that seeks nourishment from materialism, the zombie represents the consumptive nature and violent transformation within everyone when their hunger for fulfillment is ignored and denied. Whitehead is not the first African American literary author to examine the urban monsters that live figuratively or literally in every city. Richard Wright's *Native Son* and Ann Petry's *Street* shine a light on the raw, demented, monstrosity of violence lurking behind every corner, within every house, and in every building. However, while Wright and Petry emphasize the marginalization of blacks in the urban landscape, Whitehead takes a decidedly postracial view. Postplague Manhattan is a place where class is evident, but race and culture are vaguely mentioned and hardly noticed by the city's inhabitants. When literary authors such as Colson Whitehead expand the genre of street lit with urban gothic novels such as *Zone One*, transformative depictions of dehumanization, corporate greed, and political capitalization of urban culture are unveiled. *Zone One* depicts socially relevant themes such as nostalgia, despair, and consumption through a zombie metaphor, layered within the subtext of allusions, flashbacks, irony, and symbolism, and giving way to uncensored honesty, in an African American authorial perspective, set within a city landscape.

LEGITIMIZATION OF STREET LIT: DEFINITION, CRITICISM, AND AUTHORS' PURPOSE

The surge in street lit may be traced to the popularity of Donald Goines and Iceberg Slim in the 1960s and 1970s. Both writers create a realistic depiction of inner-city life featuring drug dealers, pimps, and prostitutes, expressing their stories in their uncensored, graphic, African American vernacular (Brooks and Savage, 49). Yet, despite the popularity of Donald Goines and Iceberg Slim and various contemporary street lit authors, the genre remains marred with reluctance from major publishers. With the exception of Triple Crown Publications, Urban Books, and a few other independent publishers, street lit has not been a welcome presence in the industry.

Nevertheless, modern-day authors such as Teri Woods, Vikki Stringer, and K'wan Foye continue the tradition of hip-hop literature with their fast-paced novels, illustrating ghetto realism and themes exemplifying the pitfalls and glory of gangsta life (Brooks and Savage, 49). Street lit authors such as Teri Woods may argue that their creative expression seeks to connect and relate to a black audience, who lack characters in other genres reflecting their physicality and inner turmoil. Street lit provides insight into a demonized urban culture, whose humanity is realized by the passion of authors who write literature embodying the emotional, mental, and literal truth of the African American experience. In the award-winning book *The Readers' Advisory Guide to Street Literature*, Woods insists that street lit represents the marginalized voices of a people whose story was meant "to be forgotten, swept under a rug, put in a box—better yet a cell—never to have a voice, never to cry out, and never able to speak out against the injustice we" experience in urban America (xi). Ultimately, street lit "depicts tales about the daily lives of people living in lower income city neighborhoods. This characteristic spans historical timelines, varying cultural identifications, linguistic associations, and various format designations" (Morris, 2). Street lit is not bound by the confines of an era, racial stereotypes, language, or narrative style. Boxing street lit into a narrow narrative style is to deny oneself the creative escape into the urban American experience.

However, critics of street lit unleash many of the same criticisms faced by rap artists. Perturbed black consumers cite an absence in originality and the exploitation of young African American minds (Ellison). Charles D. Ellison argues that those criticisms are "swirls in an ugly soup of moral relativism and pop-cultural melee" (1). Ellison balks at the negative response to hip-hop literature because white novelists write gritty, real-life dramas, too. Chuck Palahnuk, author of *Fight Club,* and Stephen King both "venture down that path of poor-White-trashiness that's just as ghetto as" street lit narratives. Furthermore, the words "urban experience" are not always synonymous with the word "black." Urban is the expression of a city life. *The Wire* is no more urban than the depiction of hip, gentrifying white yuppies on hit television shows such as *Sex in the City* or *Friends*. Ellison is confounded by these societal distinctions and identifies such divisions in pop culture as classist and elitist. Black people's acceptance of these polarizing limitations is a manifestation of self-hatred, reminding the audience that "there are just as many ghettos in Europe, the Middle East, and Southeast Asia as there are in Philly, New York, or Oakland." For instance, English steel ghettos feature prominently in Charles Dickens's *Hard Times*. Ellison acknowledges that there are stereotypes and racism present in some street lit. However, there is a duty to share the American experience in its entirety. Readers may not agree with everything they see on the shelves, such as porn-teasing covers, giving the impression that salaciousness and street cred is more important than the literature itself. But Ellison celebrates the fact that literature has evolved and black folks are reading and writing in the twenty-first century. Generation Xers should simply open their minds and stop lamenting over the misty-eyed days of the literary remnants from the twentieth century.

RICHARD WRIGHT AND ANN PETRY: THE FOREFATHER AND FOREMOTHER OF STREET LIT

Many contemporary critics fail to acknowledge that Richard Wright was criticized for his realistic depiction of sexual and violent characters, groping for emotional and physical survival. "*Native Son,* Wright's 1940 best-selling novel about a young black man who kills a white woman by accident and then a black woman on purpose, made him immediately famous and remains a classic" (Cassuto, B12). After *Native Son* was published, audiences began to accept not only the lonely rural narratives of African American characters but also the urban experience. Literary critic Leonard Cassuto asserts that "Bigger is a memorable inarticulate creature of the segregated Chicago ghetto, boiling with unchanneled rage against the white people who restrict his movements, and with hopeless ambition to fly airplanes he can't even approach, let alone enter" (B13). With both *Native Son* and his memoir *Black Boy*, Wright highlighted the unjust and terrifying social, living, and working conditions on both sides of the Mason-Dixon Line (B12). Thus, Wright stands as the forefather of early twentieth-century urban fiction.

Despite the elements of realism and naturalism in *Native Son*, there is a vein of urban Gothicism that is relevant to the interpretation of *Zone One*. *Native Son* is intertextual, interweaving the Great Depression, capitalism, and the advent of mass culture, overlapping with allusions to Hawthorne, Dreiser, and Poe (Smethurst, 31). During the 1930s, when Wright was working on *Native Son*, the popularity of horror flicks emerged. These stories were often inspired by Bram Stoker's *Dracula*, Mary Shelley's *Frankenstein*, and Poe's "Black Cat" and "Murders in the Rue Morgue" (32). James Smethurst asserts that the first two portions of *Native Son* mimic a typical horror flick of the 1930s (32). After Bigger's murderous rampage, he is pursued through an urban gothic landscape, anxiously fleeing from thousands of police officers with flashlights. This section parallels "the villagers with torches who chase Frankenstein's monster through an expressionist landscape." The demarcation between the monster and the man who bore him is blurred in both *Frankenstein* and *Native Son*. Similarly, Bigger is the monster produced by the murderous mainstream culture who views his black skin as a deformity or stain in the American landscape.

Both Richard Wright and Ann Petry depict characters that are pursuing the mythic, utopian, American Dream (Clark, 495). In that process, dynamic characters are developed around the psychological and material gratification that is sought but denied when chasing the American Dream. Both of these novels are generally discussed as protest novels, which may be an archaic term for modern readers of urban literature. Nevertheless, they expose the topical and fantastical delusion, insisting that American racism has made achieving the dream a nightmare for black folks. In *The Street*, Petry's beautiful protagonist, Lutie Johnson, a single mother, is forced to work as a domestic in Harlem, because of her broken marriage (Trilling, 291). Despite Lutie's optimistic outlook, she is forced to live in a decrepit Harlem apartment building, which symbolizes the filth and wretchedness of black degradation on 116th Street. The smell of the rooms is "a mixture that contained the faint persistent odor of gas, of old walls, dusty plaster, and over it all the heavy, sour smell of garbage—a smell that seeped through the dumb-waiter shaft" (Petry, 16). Lutie's only issue, with regard to her race, is the institutionalized racism that prevents her from enjoying the cleanliness and financial liberty of the white family she works for (Trilling, 291). Diana Trilling, book critic for *Nation* magazine, wrote that for "Mrs. Petry, equality of opportunity means a free capitalist economy in which the Negro individual, no less than the white, can gain as much as he desires and is capable of gaining" (291). This issue of capitalism, equal access, and consumption of material goods is a pervasive theme in Wright's, Petry's, and Whitehead's texts.

Ironically, protest writers in early urban fiction did not attack the existence of the American Dream. Instead, early urban writers such as Wright and Petry sought to "protest whites' insistence on treating blacks as outsiders and interlopers." Undoubtedly, it is this constitutional amendment, stipulating the equality of all human beings, that incurs the protest, Where is my piece of the American pie? Although literary urban foreparent narratives, such as *Native Son* and *The Street*, contain the monstrous yet realistic violence, the brutality is written for a deeper purpose (Trilling, 291). Smethurst argues that W. E. B. Du Bois, author of *The Philadelphia Negro*, could be deemed gothic based on his use of the term "veil" (30). As writers such as Wright and Petry have alluded to before, the veil "hides the black world from the white world and vice versa—or perhaps more accurately that by which the white ruling class of America conceals the black subject as human, much like a concealed skeleton in a classic novel" (30). Readers are asked to acknowledge the racism, the sexism, the capitalism, and their symbiotic relationship to the veiled masquerade of the American Dream. Subsequently, the emotionally invested audience is barraged with a violent narrative, compelling them to resist the status quo and overturn the wrongs perpetrated by the powers that be. In so doing, equal access will be a cure to the plague of broken American Dreams, the endemic virus within modern-day Biggers and Luties, birthing inner-city lawlessness and criminals, who are a monster manifestation of society's own making.

ZONE ONE: LITERARY INTERSECTION OF HIP-HOP, POP CULTURE, AND POSTAPOCALYPTIC ZOMBIES

Colson Whitehead's *Zone One* should be defined as urban gothic literature, street lit "couture," or high-art literature in an urban setting. Expansion of the term "street lit" should include a literary author who creates an intersection between hip-hop, pop culture, and postapocalyptic zombies invading Manhattan. In the process of penning *Zone One*, Whitehead was obsessed with horror flicks such as *Night of the Living Dead, Dawn of the Dead*, and *Day of the Dead*, which was the first George Romero trilogy (Fassler, 1). Ghastly aesthetics consume the pages of the narrative. Delightful nauseam of cinematic proportions fills one's stomach as if watching a horror flick. Suspension builds as the protagonist reflects on his childhood prior to the zombie plague.

> With the sidewalks hidden from view, the boy conjured an uninhabited city, where no one lived behind those miles and miles of glass, no one caught up with loved ones in living rooms . . . and all the elevators hung like broken puppets at the end of long cables.
> The city as ghost ship on the last ocean at the rim of the world. It was a gorgeous and intricate delusion, Manhattan, and from crooked angles on overcast days you saw it disintegrate, were forced to consider this tenuous creature in its true nature. (Whitehead, 7)

Whitehead's complex language describes the city as a grandiose entity, weaving mystery and beguiling language into such gothic subject matter as the apocalypse. The term "ghost ship" alludes to the deaths from the plague rendering the City of Lights barren of life. Meanwhile, the words "last ocean" imply that Manhattan is the world's final destination and possibly the last hope for recapturing America's grandeur. Yet, phrases like "intricate delusion," "crooked angles," and "tenuous creature" have gothic implications that veil the true nature of New York City and its inhabitants. "Millions of people tended to this magnificent contraption, they lived and sweated and toiled in it, serving the mechanism of metropolis and making it bigger, better, story by glorious story and idea by unlikely idea" (5). Again, there is a sense that Manhattan is a larger-than-life character, even before the zombie apocalypse, more important than its survivors, corporate sponsors, or bureaucracy. However, beneath this grotesque beauty of the city is the darkness that lives inside each brooding structure—the skels and the stragglers—the urban gothic nightmare.

Urban Gothicism is a literary genre that is dominated by African American authors yet is not exclusive to one ethnicity. Urban decay and moral dilapidation is the essence of the inner city. These characters are struggling with issues of poverty, broken families, drug abuse, and crime, yet their plight is aggravated or enlightened by the issues of the supernatural. Characters confront the nature of man's cruelty while fighting nightmares, visions, omens, ghosts, and spiritual conversions. Inner-city genocide, homicide, and suicide are realistic yet detrimental evolutions of their pain. Their eventual rise may be wrought with regret, violence, or immorality, but the character will feel that he or she is justified. Sometimes they flee the metropolis or abandon the values of their heritage or class in hope of salvation in the mainstream culture, only to find a tainted American Dream that bleeds tragedy in both the city and the suburbs. Ultimately, the protagonists must return to the city, mostly ruined by the time of their discovery, oftentimes to the place of their birth. Emotional, mental, or physical transformation may only derive from reuniting with one's personal and cultural identity. Redemption may be discovered in the streets, with their family, the community, or in becoming one with their inner spirituality. If catharsis occurs, an element of peace may be attained for the protagonist.

Street lit couture is Whitehead's unique blend of hip-hop, pop culture, and classic literature. Whitehead's eloquent sentence structure stretches the common perception of street lit as lowbrow and common. Critic Glen Duncan states that "in the action sequences we get essayistic asides and languid distentions, stray insights, surprising correspondences, ambivalence, paradox" (2). *Zone One*'s sentence structure is varied and complex, utilizing various techniques such as historical allusions and collective disillusionment to describe the Manhattan descent into the zombie takeover. "Their mouths could no longer manage speech, yet they spoke nonetheless, saying what the city had always told its citizens, from the first settlers hundreds of years ago, to the shattered survivors of the garrison. What the plague had always told its hosts. . . . I am going to eat you up" (Whitehead, 304). Whitehead's literary interpretation of urban decay, moral dilapidation, and the grotesque nature of the American Dream turned sour is a transformative signifier, deserving a designation within street lit as urban gothic literature.

Pop culture references, classic literature, and horror movie tropes are fused into a city landscape swarming with zombies, who are a metaphor for the corruptive influences consuming the streets, uptown and downtown, and condemning residents to a mindless cycle of misfortune. Undoubtedly, Whitehead's experience growing up in Manhattan influenced his awareness of the types of characters who make street lit such a phenomenon. *Zone One* is a dark ode to the Big Apple, the living dead version of Whitehead's exquisite essay collection *The Colossus of New York* (Charles). Later in the narrative, he describes the starving monsters as angry and ruthless chaos made into flesh. Affirming the gothic beauty of New York and its troubled citizens is facilitated by the lyrical allusions familiar to most audiences (Keehn, 2). Whitehead's selection of epigraphs—quotations from Walter Benjamin's "Dream Kitsch," Ezra Pound's "Hugh Selwyn Mauberly," and Public Enemy's "Welcome to the Terrordome"—"suggests that [he was] tackling head-on the challenge of marrying intellectual and literary substance with pop culture" (Keehn, 2). Whitehead refers to this harmonious marriage, metaphorically, as a worldly junkyard, garnishing the parts that function, maneuvering the machine to work as the operator pleases. However, Whitehead does not regard his style with such serious intentions. Pound's epigraph is a lyric that can be sung in transit, while Public Enemy's epigraph to move as a community is a sensible recommendation. Both lyrics operate as a literary work that breathes beyond its conception by speaking to divergent generations and cultures, or functioning within various contexts. Thus, references to Public Enemy's lyrics and Ezra Pound's poetry in *Zone One* are transcendent in nature and linguistically revolutionary in its merging of hip-hop and pop culture into an urban gothic narrative.

POSTAPOCALYPTIC CORPORATE INFRASTRUCTURE AND RECONSTRUCTION

Mark Spitz, member of the Omega Unit, is an allusion to one of Whitehead's favorite movies—*Omega Man*. Their job is to reclaim the island for the chosen, the privileged amongst the survivors—the intellectuals who will reside in Buffalo. This three-person squad must clean up the meandering monsters in Zone One, after a massive military unit has eliminated most of the skels (d'Arbonne, 2). The Omega Unit lives life five minutes at a time, which is a reactionary mindset that takes the readers through three days: Friday, Saturday, and Sunday (Rudin, 1). Throughout the thrill, Mark is revealed to the reader in bite-size pieces, and as a direct result of his job, he is fighting legions of teeth and fingers. There is the modernistic element of stream of consciousness as Mark's mind travels from one flashback to the next, all the while annihilating zombies, as a sweeper (d'Arbonne, 2). Thankfully, Mark and his team are not the only barricades preventing a potential blood fest. The barrier is guarded by snipers, patrols, and "woven-plastic miracle fabric that is the final separation between undead teeth and fresh flesh" (Rudin, 1). Despite the trauma faced by survivors, they have succumbed to a recovery plan called the "American Phoenix Campaign" that has a slogan, anthems, buttons, and hats from the merchandising department (d'Arbonne, 2). Sadly, this marketing distraction fails to heal the survivors of postapocalyptic stress disorder (PASD), which is caused by the trauma of witnessing loved ones becoming carnivorous, flesh-eating monsters. There are two types of zombies: skels and stragglers (Rudin, 2). The skels are bloodthirsty and representative of the classic zombies of the average American's youth or from AMC's *Walking Dead*. Whitehead reinvents the zombie genre with the stragglers who are frozen in time. Instead of walking slowly in the streets, they are stuck wallowing in their "'subconscious' choosing, be it flying a kite, photocopying their buttocks, or reading a palm" (Rudin, 2). They are doomed to one act for eternity. They are like ghosts who fail to pass into the afterlife, operating in a permanent state of purgatory. Sadly, they represent 99 percent of the zombies. Meanwhile, the drooling skels, half-decomposed shells of a monster, represent the violent 1 percent of the zombies. Whitehead turns the zombie survivalist narrative on its head; he creates a story where the survivors are more horrific than the empathetic zombies. Mark and his team don't hesitate to play "solve the straggler," as they meditate on what brought the zombie there, sometimes drawing Hitler mustaches across their faces.

Drawing Hitler mustaches is a historical reference to race discrimination, genocidal behavior, and the monstrous attempts at human destruction. However, Whitehead does not explicitly make ethnicity or racial heritage an element of his zombie narrative. After all, Mark and his team are the good guys, the zombie exterminators. On the surface, zombies and the survivors epitomize the malevolence and benevolence of the human race (Sen, 3). Within that broader metaphor, there is a more specific interpretation. Zombies are effective allegories, but what demographic are they symbolizing? African Americans? Minorities? White-collar workers? Or delusional suburban families? Arijit Sen, a writer for the *Missouri Review*, suggests that zombies are an allegory for the race relations in America. Postplague, there are segregated living areas, and there is the constant concern over gentrification once Manhattan has been obliterated of skels and stragglers. Mark Spitz and his team must eradicate all the structures of nondangerous stragglers. After all, Whitehead's narrative creates the impression that the zombie epidemic must be wiped out as the country reconstructs itself. But the black protagonist sweeps and cleanses the buildings for whom? The underclass? Or the privileged class? Who is the enigma controlling the tentacles of recovery? The audience never lays eyes on the individuals that operate in the shadows of the Buffalo headquarters. These dark figures delegate orders in this postapocalyptic milieu to the laborers, who clear the spaces without question, feeling thankful to have survived the plague. Mark and his team's supplies are sponsored by the surviving corporations; therefore, the sweepers have rigid directives to create minimal structural damage (d'Arbonne, 2). Jess d'Arbonne, an expert zombiephile, writes in the *Examiner*, "The new government, based in Buffalo, is obsessed with PR and image, often forgetting what the men and woman working toward rebuilding are facing on a daily basis" (2). Gentrification is a necessary part of this postplague reconstruction motif, that the streets are ruled by a distinct, distant few. Manhattan is barren with the exception of the legions of the damned and the soldiers who dispose of them (Whitehead, 35). Even Mark and his team realize that. In this way, low-income urbanites' fate is synonymous with the skels. Anyone can and will be eradicated if they are deemed uncivilized, dangerous, or subhuman, like the monstrous zombies in Zone One. The rebuilding motif is personal, physical, and structural. Personal reinvention is the domain of the intellectuals, athletes, corporate sponsors, and shadowy figures in Buffalo bureaucracy. After the zombie virus erupts, the American Dream is now being resuscitated but only for the benefit of a privileged few.

POSTRACIAL MARK SPITZ AND THE RELEVANT THEMES OF NOSTALGIA, DESPAIR, AND CONSUMPTION

Mark Spitz, who is now a civilian soldier in the recolonization of Manhattan, meanders through the streets, where the plague ridden are sometimes indistinguishable from the survivors who are suffering from PASD (Chiarella, 2). Spitz's story alternates between nostalgic flashbacks of his childhood and the postapocalyptic Manhattan. Frequently, Mark Spitz's mind flashes back to his suburban childhood, which is a time of normalcy and warm memories of the city. But the monster transformation of all things rational and normal is essential to the zombie metaphor. In one scene, Whitehead treats his readers like sexual exhibitionists, peeping into the bedroom of Mark's parents. When he was six, waking up from a nightmare, he regretfully seeks solace in the arms of his parents (Whitehead, 87). Mark creeps into the master bedroom and discovers his mother "gobbling up his father" as his father snarled for him to leave. On the Last Night, before the zombies take over Manhattan, Mark returned as an adult from Atlantic City and "witnessed his mother's grisly ministrations to his father. She was hunched over him, gnawing away with ecstatic fervor on a flap of his intestine, which, in the crepuscular flicker of the television, adopted a phallic aspect" (88).

Whitehead webs a connection between the stragglers and the sweepers who kill them. He is concerning himself with the demons of people by describing the transformation that is both metaphorical and literal. Whitehead's personal evolution, as the writer of the nostalgic *Colossus of New York*, is "from beloved New York semi-flaneur to the blacksmith of a myth that outlasts a movie season" (Chiarella, 2). Whitehead depicts a nation fluttering their eyes, trying to determine who in the ruined city is there to destroy us. This distinction is difficult because, like the stragglers, those survivors suffering from PASD move in a catatonic state, reveling in the past and reminiscing on the good times, when everything seemed normal. Ironically, there is not only an emotional price for nostalgia but also a mortal price for those who succumb to the temptation of pondering the past (Whitehead, 87). One of the more striking moments in the narrative is when the marines lose their way in the monstrous spectacle. Drifting off into "over idealized chapters of their former lives," they are overcome by memories, making them vulnerable to the zombie feast.

Overlapping the theme of nostalgia is the interweaving sense of hopelessness that is supposedly caused by PASD. Replaying the past and living in the present consumed by yesteryear demonstrates a lack of faith in the future. Grand buildings will remain grotesquely beautiful despite their plague-ridden history. But who will live in these spectral-like altered spaces? After the sweeper's mission is completed, Whitehead analogizes the hopefulness of postplague occupancy by everyday survivors to the optimism of immigrants freshly arriving to the harbor (73). Yet, Whitehead swiftly gnaws at this American myth of dreams realized in the zombie city. Despite the tireless work of the military and the sweepers, Buffalo headquarters remained secretive about Manhattan's postplague residents. Mark, Gary, and Kaitlyn discuss the dismal opportunities in their future living arrangements. Gary says to the group that rich people, politicians, pro athletes, and chefs from cooking shows are the most likely occupants, while Kaitlyn remains hopeful that there will be a less plutocratic process, such as a lottery. Gary insists that the government has other plans like Staten Island. "But we wouldn't live on Staten Island if they were giving out vaccines and hand jobs right off the ferry" (89). Hope rises and falls, instilling a state of despair amongst the characters and audience, because nothing in society has changed.

Spitz is like an overseer, wage slave, working for the establishment, but he will never enjoy the spaces he sweeps. As a zombie sweeper, clearing the spaces for the rich, he works in a subservient role, for a minimal reward called everyday survival. In the words of Henry David Thoreau,

> The mass of men lead lives of quiet desperation. What is called resignation is confirmed desperation. From the desperate city you go into the desperate country, and have to console yourself with the bravery of minks and muskrats. A stereotyped but unconscious despair is concealed even under what are called the games and amusements of mankind. There is no play in them, for this comes after work. But it is a characteristic of wisdom not to do desperate things.

This state of despair causes men to seek solace outside the confines of the city. In this subconscious search for meaning, men conceal their despair in the games and choice of entertainment they seek. For Spitz, there is no form of escape except for the memories and the games he and his team play with the stragglers. Manhattan is the chosen place for reconstruction-style gentrification. Mark Spitz's job is to kill harmless stragglers for the benefit of the capitalistic structure. Unlike the street narratives of Wright and Petry, Spitz feels incorporated into this laborious process of rebuilding America. In a sense, he is at the bottom ladder of the American Dream. Although Whitehead hints to the fact that Spitz and his comrades may touch the ladder of opportunity, the powers that be will never let them climb into the buildings he sweeps for them. Thoreau advises against resorting to desperate acts while in a state of despair. Unlike his modern counterparts, the murderous Bigger and Lutie, Spitz is complacent in his exclusion from the trappings of success. After all, Spitz is a mediocre man with mediocre expectations of his future, even before Last Night. Spitz's "averageness makes him the perfect Everyman Survivor," but Whitehead quickly reminds us that "hope is a gateway drug, don't do it" lest you be consumed by nostalgia (Duncan, 2). Then, the despair comes with the eradication of normalcy or the realization that nothing ever was, or ever will be, normal in the city. Whitehead remarks, "Everybody's fucked up in a different way, just like before" (Anders, 2). Memories of the horrors drag people down. Society has not changed; thus, they behave desperately and erratically.

Sag Harbor, *John Henry Days*, and *The Intuitionist* are all novels by Whitehead that demonstrate a concentration on the issue of race (Charles, 2). Yet, in *Zone One* he neglects to make casual reference to Spitz's racial heritage until the forty-six-page finale. Does Mark's race add to his social angst? On the contrary, Mark seems to realize both sides of this issue. "There was a single Us now, reviling a single Them" (Whitehead, 288). If the world was attacked by a common enemy, do all Americans treat each other as one race—the human race? At first Whitehead wants his readers to believe that *e pluribus unum*, out of many one. But even Mark comes to the conclusion, "If they could bring back paperwork, Mark Spitz thought, they could certainly reanimate prejudice, parking tickets, and reruns" (288). Mark's racial heritage is revealed because a character assumes that he can't swim due to his race. Therefore, literary critic Sen believes that Whitehead wants society to think about race. Furthermore, Whitehead is asking the audience to examine the way in which society dehumanizes, devalues, and degrades those whom we perceive as our enemy (Sen, 6). When the clearing squad ceases shooting chaotic zombies to paint their faces and pose with them, there is a message about how Americans treat those who appear "faceless, blending into one, non-understandable, ciphers and mysteries that pose some sort of danger even though we're not sure what" inside and outside this country (Sen, 6). Dehumanization of the marginalized other facilitates the capacity to kill without a conscience.

Ron Charles views Mark as blank and colorless (2). Although Whitehead sought inspiration from *Night of the Living Dead*, which featured Duane Jones, an African American at the center of a white mob trying to devour him, this racial element is absent from *Zone One*. "Mark is also a young black man, but strangely that element of his identity is bleached away in this novel, as though colorblindness and zombie-ism came to America at the same moment" (2). Yet, Charles's faith is restored in the narrative when Whitehead's prose novel elevates to the status of T. S. Eliot, F. Scott Fitzgerald, and Cormac McCarthy, while maintaining the macabre elements of cinematic horror. Even without the racial implications, "No matter the hue of their skins, dark or light, no matter the names of their gods or the absences they countenanced, they had all strived, struggled, and loved in their small, human fashion. Now they were mostly mouths and fingers" (Whitehead, 303). Consciously, Mark suffers from PASD but experiences no despair with regard to race. He has witnessed the plague infect humans without concern for race, creed, or color. He misses those he loved. His family is now his team. Living in the city, from day to day, and surviving five minutes at a time, is a very urban concept. In the future, the zombie equalizer gives way to race but not to issues of class, which some may argue is the real culprit of urban blight. Whitehead further transforms the genre of street lit by making his postapocalyptic narrative in a postracial America, simultaneously speaking against contemporary discrimination in the twenty-first century.

Even in Whitehead's postracial America, every social ill that plagued society prior to the apocalypse, such as class distinctions, the government bureaucracy, and corporate interest, still consume the city landscape. Whitehead deepens the zombie metaphor to represent this exchange. Within the context of the gothic genre expectation, the readers are expected to suspend their incredulity in the living dead and supernatural (Deaton, 95). Cultural references to the supernatural indicate a society on the edge of transformation. Zombies symbolize the hugest threat to humanity, other than humanity's threat to itself. This interaction between the human and the undead is always writhing with violence, usurpation, and consumption. In *Zone One*, the zombies are a reflection of our society holding a mirror to our history, our consciousness, providing a certain sense of critical insight that may only be perceived from a pop culture experience. The zombies' act of tearing and eating flesh is an act of literal and figurative consumption. In the figurative sense, there is a message about consumption as a consumer. The consumer is in a constant state of seeking an object to create a sense of individuality. However, this object fails to satisfy because it is a model of an idealized image that is mass produced (Deaton, 99). Whitehead plays on this symbiotic relationship between the capitalist and the consumer. The zombie metaphor is one of consumption fueled by consumerism. Consumers have lost their souls because they are manipulated by images and norms of society, marketing to individuals suggesting to them what they should buy. The model is an illusion but an image people seek as proof of their own aspirations or accomplishments. This obsession with material goods in a capitalistic culture transfers into an objectification of the individual. People transform into empty vessels, nothing more than the objects they seek and keep. In this instance, pop culture predisposes people to the zombie virus that causes desperate stragglers to nostalgically return to their wage slave jobs, white-collar offices, and malls—the place of their favorite sites.

Colson Whitehead has the vantage point of not living in a segregated America like Wright and Petry. Thus, he has the opportunity to fictionalize a world in *Zone One* where he may reject the contemporary issue of racism in postapocalyptic society. Color is ambiguous in the future. Everyday survivors are unified by a common state of disenfranchisement. Oppressed not because of the differences in their skin tone, the survivors are instead deprived by their daily need to survive the last remaining skels and stragglers. Whitehead's warnings about American materialism speak to all ethnic heritages of all class levels: people who place value on pop culture figures, themselves, or their social status and ability to amass goods that symbolize or embody wealth are like empty vessels. Thereby, they create a state of false self-worth and a means to judge and subjugate people who do not engage in the rat race of consumerism or fail to obtain the semblance of economic mobilization. In the end, the bureaucracy and capitalists will reign supreme in the postapocalyptic new world. Benefactors of privilege are granted the option to subjugate wage slaves and other survivors, segregating them with a patriotic marketing campaign aimed at gentrification of property as opposed to reconstruction of a populace's inner selves. Whitehead recognizes that American materialism afflicts both blacks and whites; therefore, in the future it is not hard to imagine that for a decimated society that has suffered so much, race will be the last factor on their minds. Although monsters are the marginalized other that society fears, metaphorically and literally, they are really all of us and we are them. They are the grotesque monster that dwells, in the city and beyond, waiting for a moment of consumptive despair to burst forth within us. Nevertheless, plague-free spaces, in Manhattan, that facilitate a sustainable future for the entire human race matter far more than the shade of black skin adorning the mediocre yet heroic face of Mark Spitz.

WORKS CITED

Anders, Charlie Jane. "Colson Whitehead's *Zone One* Shatters Your Post-apocalyptic Fantasies." Io9.com, 29 December 2011. http://io9.com/.

Brooks, Wanda, and Lorraine Savage. "Critique and Controversies of Street Literature: A Formidable Literary Genre." *ALAN Review* (Winter 2009): 48–55.

Cassuto, Leonard. "Richard Wright and the Agony over 'Integration.'" *Chronicle of Higher Education* 54, no. 6 (2008): B12–B13. http://search.ebscohost.com/.

Charles, Ron. "'Zone One,' by Colson Whitehead: Zombies Abound." *Washington Post*, 19 October 2011. www.washingtonpost.com/.

Chiarella, Tom. "How It Ends." *Esquire*, 19 September 2011. www.esquire.com/.

Clark, Keith. "A Distaff Dream Deferred? Ann Petry and the Art of Subversion." *African American Review* 26, no. 3 (Autumn 1992): 495–505. www.jstor.org/.

d'Arbonne, Jess. "Zombie Book Review: 'Zone One' by Colson Whitehead." *Examiner*, 16 January 2012. www.examiner.com/.

Deaton, Clifford D. "Seeing the Specter: A Gothic Metaphor of Subjectivity, Popular Culture, and Consumerism." *Gnovis Journal* 8, no. 2 (Spring 2008): 95–108. http://gnovisjournal.org/.

Duncan, Glenn. "A Plague of Urban Undead in Lower Manhattan." *New York Times*, 28 October 2011. www.nytimes.com/.

Ellison, Charles D. "Define 'Urban Lit' . . . ." *Huffington Post*, 23 June 2009. www.huffingtonpost.com/.

Fassler, Joe. "Colson Whitehead on Zombies, 'Zone One,' and His Love of the VCR." *Atlantic*, 18 October 2011. www.theatlantic.com/.

Keehn, Jeremy. "*Zone One*: Six Questions for Colson Whitehead." *Stream* (blog), *Harpers Magazine*, 17 October 2011. http://harpers.org/.

Morris, Vanessa Irvin. *The Readers' Advisory Guide to Street Literature*. Chicago: American Library Association, 2011.

NPR Books. "When Zombies Attack Lower Manhattan." Review of *Zone One*, by Colson Whitehead, 20 July 2012. www.npr.org/.

Petry, Ann. *The Street*. New York: Mariner Books, 1946.

Rose, Cedric. "Colson Whitehead in the Zombie Zone." *Cincinnati* 45, no. 7 (April 2012): 28–29. http://connection.ebscohost.com/.

Rudin, Michael. "The Forbidden Thought." Review of *Zone One*, by Colson Whitehead. Fiction Writers Review, 14 February 2012. http://fictionwritersreview.com/.

Sen, Arijit. "Zombie Nation." *Missouri Review*, 5 April 2012. www.missourireview.com/.

Smethurst, James. "Invented by Horror: The Gothic and African American Literary Ideology in *Native Son*." *African American Review* 35, no. 1 (2001): 29–40.

Sunderman, Eric. "Q and A: Colson Whitehead Talks Gritty New York, *Zone One* Zombies, and Frank Ocean's Sexuality." *Village Voice*, 11 July 2012. www.villagevoice.com/.

Thoreau, Henry David. "Walden, and On the Duty of Civil Disobedience." Project Gutenberg e-book of "Walden, and On the Duty of Civil Disobedience," 29 July 2012. www.gutenberg.org/.

Trilling, Diana. "Class and Color." *Nation* 162, no. 10 (9 March 1946): 290–91. www.ebscohost.com/.

Whitehead, Colson. *Zone One*. New York: Anchor Books, 2011.

Woods, Teri. Foreword. In *The Readers' Advisory Guide to Street Literature*, by Vanessa Irvin Morris. Chicago: American Library Association, 2011.

Wright, Richard. *Native Son*. 1940. New York: Harper Perennial Modern Classics, 2005.

Zinoman, Jason. "The Critique of Pure Horror." *New York Times*, 16 July 2011. www.nytimes.com/.

A Point West of Mount San Bernardino

Juan Delgado

For Father Bob

I

By the road she hovers in heat waves,
propped up on a cinderblock wall,
revived by mixed house paints,
fending for herself like wild mint.

She is behind your shoulder,
a blind spot, your city's poverty.
A figure waits under a freeway ramp,
gesturing as if she knows you.

The fences and lots have the same dogs,
peering through the chain links, curious.

While at the hospital, you see kids play another
game of tag outside the emergency room doors
and know how fingerprints squander their ridges
and how digital minutes dry up under a glare.

II

A stump is all that is left of a surveyor's point,
a ponderosa pine in the foothills that started
the city's perfect grid.

The sidewalks of Baseline
need more than a grocery bag's empty belly,

plastic, a ripped-up flame standing and calling
out to an old preacher like yourself.

By the cameras
mounted on the streetlights, you wonder
if they recorded the street sinking in the eyes
of the woman who died on a bus bench.

You pause in front of a freshly painted sign
that says, "Wrong Way," and see a sign within
a sign, a resistance to the newest strip mall,
the black lettering unevenly spaced and painted,
a homespun warning to keep moving on.

Stories We Might as Well Tell

A Conversation with Lynel Gardner

Keenan Norris

Lynel Gardner is a performance artist, novelist, and playwright. His work with the Hittite Empire Performance Art Group started in 1989. They toured the country and the UK doing work based on black male silence. An all-male performance art group, they focused on issues of the day: the "wilding incident," the Central Park rape case in New York, and the LA riots. He has written a play called *Stories I Never Told My Father* about growing up with a pimp for a father, how he survived, and how he found God in the process of trying to find his father before he died. He has written a book, *BEAST: The Destruction of Charles "Sonny" Liston*, based on the life of his grandfather, heavyweight boxing champion Sonny Liston, dispelling many of the popular misconceptions about Liston. He also has a company called Theater as Prevention where, depending on the demographic he's working with and its needs, he develops a play around those needs and brings the play to the stage. I interviewed Lynel in November, 2012.

KN: So my first question is, how would you grade the amount of reading that young black people do, say ages fifteen to twenty-five, and then twenty-five to forty?

LG: Amount of reading, for ages fifteen to twenty-five, maybe a six or seven; for adults, maybe a seven. Because of technology, reading has gone down because we have the Internet now. I think technology and the push for reading and education has gone down a lot, too.

KN: Yeah, and I guess that leads into my next question, which is a little bit trickier: how would you rate the quality of the reading that we as black people are doing?

LG: I still think that youth are looking for something that they can identify with when it comes to reading. A lot of the youth are saying that they're reading dead authors, and they're looking for stories that they can identify with, and I think a lot of the enthusiasm of reading has gone down. Still, I think European and American authors and poets and a lot of those books that they get at school and in library don't really tell their stories, and I think that is a major reason for why they don't read. Their stories are either ghettoized or a lot of the novels are based on inner-city romance. I guess they're trying to market the whole hip-hop, gangster music genre [as literature]. I think this ghettoizes our story. The quality's really bad because they're just reading gangster love stories. It's not really helping the youth.

KN: That segues perfectly into a discussion of street lit. Those are some of the big problems with street lit, but what might be the potential of street lit? And should we have a broader definition of what street lit is? Should we as writers be pushing for books to be included, for young black people, more books and a wider range to be included as "street lit" that's relevant to their lives?

LG: I think it's really important that we show the diversity of the black diaspora, that we don't all think alike. That's the whole problem with rap right now, it's all one dimensional. They have the idea that we all think alike, we all like pimp juice. But my whole thing is that we really need to show our diversity and that, as a community, we have different ways of thinking. I just want to show the whole palette of who we are, and it is also important that we bring writers of other populations, European, Latino, Asian, because when I was a kid I lived in the inner city yet I could escape through Jules Verne. I could escape the hood through different authors that weren't of my race or my population and then find ways to tell those stories in my own way as an African American. So I think it's really important that we bridge those gaps and borders between other writers of different cultures and populations, because we are more than just African Americans, we have American Indian in our blood, we have Latin and we have European in our blood. We're not just, you know, a homogenous population. So I think it's really important that yes, we continue to expand the horizons of the literature, because we're more than just African American people. We've shared our cultures with every race on the planet so we definitely have to identify those parts of us that are part white, part Latino, American Indian, and bring those stories to the forefront.

KN: Thank you for that answer. I think that is very important to acknowledge. Are you frustrated when you go into a bookstore and you see the African American book section, first of all dominated by a certain type of literature, but secondly, just that it's segmented off from everything else?

LG: Yeah, I've confronted Borders. I've confronted all these big bookstores. They don't really get it. They don't understand what they're doing, and I think that's a problem when these big conglomerate bookstores don't understand that they're projecting segregation, that they're segregating the races based on the fact of their ethnicity. The whole thing is we still haven't dealt with the fact that it's not about race; race is a human invention. We're a population that happens to share a certain culture, and we call it the black experience, but we really have to be careful, like I said, that we don't get caught up in race. And the fact that they're continually segregating the races even when it comes to where they put us in a bookstore; again, it's the same problem that the authors had in the '60s, having to be considered black authors and not authors, ghettoizing our work and not being accepted until we reach a certain amount of acclaim. I guess what I'm saying is that sometimes we feel like we have to write like a white person speaks in order not to have our work ghettoized. That's still a major problem, and I've found that to be a problem with writing this book [about Sonny Liston]. Do I have to justify, support my argument with the work of other white authors or sociologists who agree with my way of thinking? And yeah, I think I was forced to do that so that I could support my argument. I'm playing a game basically. Yes, I think it is a major problem that has yet to be addressed, and our voices are not being heard. When I went into Borders and told them about this problem, they just brushed me off like they didn't even care. They don't even identify that as an issue. So yes, it's a major problem. I think that we as writers need to really make this an issue, a political issue.

KN: You talked a lot about a kind of social segregation. This reminds me of another social situation that is highly segregated and that's within prison. You have whites, blacks, Latinos, and Asians in there. You know, it may not be segregated on the outside, but you go in and by force and in order not to become a target, you are compelled to take a racial side. Part of the reason that I'm interested in street lit is that more than any other genre of literature, it's dealing with one of the principal crises in America, mass incarceration. What could be the potential of an art form that seriously speaks to and markets itself to the incarcerated, the underserved, to those populations?

LG: I go into the prison, and I do work in the prison, juvenile hall, and such and I think what's important is to realize that, again, they're still connected to the outside world; they're still running the gang from inside. . . . They prepare the prisoners to go to jail, and they prepare the prisoners to come out of jail. But what I told San Bruno Jail is that you guys don't realize that this is ongoing and the relationship does not end with the family when a prisoner goes to jail; it doesn't begin again when the prisoner comes out of jail. This relationship is ongoing. What I tended to do, what I'm trying to do, is to let the police agencies know that they also are participating in that relationship between the families, the inmates, going in, back and forth, in jail and out of jail. Also parole, all these relationships, the family, the parole officers, the police officers, the wardens, all have an ongoing relationship with the inmates and their families, and the artist has to participate in that process, the artist has to, if he wants to make a difference, whether it be by performing or whether it be by bringing books that help prisoners relate the inside world with the outside world. That's the only way; we have to make a sacrifice as artists to continually maintain a relationship between that population and those around that population, if we're going to start turning the tide, getting them to turn and go in the other direction. Right now prevention is key, because locking people up is no longer cost effective. It's proven they don't have enough money to arrest everyone, and the tide is turning right now, and artists can really make a huge difference if that is important to them. So the thing is, we have to decide as artists and as citizens who want to take responsibility for other citizens within the community. We have to draw the line between commercial success and the success of making a change in our community. There has to be priority on saving our youth and using art as a means to do that, and that is a decision that the artist has to make. Like I said with my play, I went in there and did the play about fathers and sons, and a bunch of inmates came up to me and said, "Well, I haven't seen my son in twenty years." "I haven't seen my son in ten years." "My son doesn't care about me." But I told them, I said, "Look I'm forty-eight years old, I'm forty-eight years old, and I still need to maintain a relationship with my father." So I told them that the bond between father and son is something that can never be broken. You can wait for it your whole life. And just by doing my play, those guys after the show got on the phone and called their children for the first time in ten or even twenty years in some cases. So, those things would not have been possible if I had not made a commitment to my mission, which is to save my people, save people that are suffering, using my art as a vehicle to save as many people as possible. Unfortunately, African Americans are dying faster than most, so I'm going to put priority on them first, but at the same time, it's all related across races.

KN: That's powerful, and it speaks to where our intent ultimately lies. It struck me, and this is the last question I'll ask, but it strikes me that you talked about the kind of conflict between, or the decision between, commercial success and then on the other end, this social concept of intervention, but it strikes me that there's a whole 'nother issue that goes on. There's the art for art's sake crowd. This idea that your art is this pristine object up on a hill and the artists cannot afford to be too fully immersed in immediate social problems or risk diluting their art. What do you think of that, to that criticism of socially conscious art?

LG: Now, diluting their art as in the commercial viability of their art?

KN: Not the commercial viability, more like the artistic viability.

LG: I mean, there is such a thing as bad art to me. There's a lot of performance art that can be considered really bad art and, but because it's performance art, it's kind of like, oh, it's a process art, so it's excused as, oh, she's going through that process, therefore it's about the process, of her getting from A to B to C; she may not get to Z, but it's the process of her getting there. So is art in the eye of the beholder? I don't know. Maybe it is. . . . I think that's a good question. Who defines what art is? Look, I was standing on the street corner one day, and I watched this kid who wasn't old enough to drive a car. He made his bike into a car; he basically put house speakers on a trailer hitch and turned his bike into a low-rider bike and bumped his music as if he was driving a low rider. I said, "Damn, that's fucking art right there." That's fucking art, man. To take that and turn it into what he dreamed of it being. That's art, so I don't think we can define what art is. Working here at my house, there's Latino contractors who take scraps because they don't have anything else to work with and they'll make a wall out of it. You'll see these guys who have been contracting now for many years, who've lived in America many years, using machines now, and they've lost the ability to create with just their hands, and just with scraps, so they sit around and look at these guys that come from Mexico with awe because they're doing with scraps what they've been doing for years with machines now. So I don't think anyone can define what art is. I think it's up to the artist. The artist has to define it and has to ask him- or herself, "Am I doing the art that I feel is important? Am I expressing and manifesting art that is true to my purpose in life or true to what I envision as my mission?" I think it's up to the artist and the artist has to decide if he's living up to that or not. If I'm going to be a commercial artist, am I fulfilling that role? If I'm going to be a social justice artist, am I fulfilling that role? If I'm just going to be an artist that's not going to accept money, am I fulfilling that role? It's literally up to the artist to decide. I spent four years in LA. I didn't get paid a dime for my art, and I finally said, "Why am I doing this?" I said, "Oh, I love it. I love performance. I've been doing it since I was five years old." That's why I'm starving myself to death, and then the money came later, but if I would have only done it for the money, I would've been out of there in a year because I wouldn't have made anything, so that's how I define art for myself. I have to love it; I have to have a passion for it; I have to make a difference in the world or I'm not going to do it.

KN: Yeah, that's a great answer to the question and a good place to conclude. Is there anything else you'd like to add?

LG: I wish that African American artists would stop competing with one another. They taught us to compete with one another, and I think it's really important, especially when it comes to getting on that level where we're so successful that they're asking us, "Well, what does the black community think about . . ." We have to be careful that we don't speak on behalf of the African American people. We have to make sure that we don't allow the media to portray us as a monolith, making one person a spokesman and representing us as one dimensional. Unfortunately, we've now become elitist. I think it's really important that we're always bringing everyone with us along the way. I think it's really important that in our striving for success we don't push each other down.

Bibliography

Abbott, Megan E. *The Street Was Mine: White Masculinity in Hardboiled Fiction and Film Noir*. New York: Palgrave Macmillan, 2002.

Alexander, Amy. "Terry McMillan vs. Ghetto Lit." *Nation*, 29 October 2007. www.thenation.com/.

Anders, Charlie Jane. "Colson Whitehead's *Zone One* Shatters Your Post-apocalyptic Fantasies." Io9.com, 29 December 2011 http://io9.com/.

Andryeyev, Bonnie Rhee. "Hearts of Darkness: Race and Urban Epistemology in American Noir." PhD diss., University of California, Santa Cruz, 2012.

Arnold, Eric K. "Demythologizing Oakland's Pimp Culture (Analysis)." Oakland Local, 4 January 2013. http://oaklandlocal.com/.

Avila, Eric. *Popular Culture in the Age of White Flight: Fear and Fantasy in Suburban Los Angeles*. Berkeley: University of California Press, 2004.

Barbosa, Marcio, and Esmeralda Ribeiro. *Bailes: Soul, samba-rock, hip hop e identidade em São Paulo*. São Paulo, Brazil: Quilombhoje, 2007.

Barnes & Noble. "Meet the Writers: Nikki Giovanni." Accessed 20 May 2013. www.barnesandnoble.com/.

Beck, Robert. *Pimp: The Story of My Life*. Los Angeles: Holloway House, 1967.

Bennett, Bryant. "Are Pimp Films Too Instructive?" *Time*, 13 March 2006. www.time.com/.

Birkerts, Sven. "The Surreal Thing." *New York Times*, 9 May 2004.

Braxton, Greg. "'Carmen' Gets Hip." *Los Angeles Times*, 6 May 2001.

Brooks, Wanda, and Lorraine Savage. "Critique and Controversies of Street Literature: A Formidable Literary Genre." *ALAN Review* (Winter 2009): 48–55.

Broyard, Bliss. "Pulp Princess." *Elle Magazine*, 17 June 2009.

Butler, Paul. *Let's Get Free: A Hip-hop Theory of Justice*. New York: New Press, 2009.

Bynoe, Yvonne. *Encyclopedia of Rap and Hip-hop Culture*. Westport, CT: Greenwood, 2006.

Canagarajah, A. Suresh. "The Place of World Englishes in Composition: Pluralization Continued." In *The Norton Book of Composition Studies*, edited by Susan Miller, 1617–42. New York: Norton, 2009.

Cardoso, Ricardo, and Ana Christina Ribiero. "Dança de Rua." Campinas, Brazil: Editora Átomo, 2011.

Carter, Shawn (Jay-Z). *The Dynasty: Roc La Familia*. Roc-a-Fella, 2000, compact disc.

Cash Money Content, "Iceberg Slim Ebook Collection Released Today." 4 December 2012, http://cashmoneycontent.com/.

Cassuto, Leonard. "Richard Wright and the Agony over 'Integration.'" *Chronicle of Higher Education* 54, no. 6 (2008): B12–B13. http://search.ebscohost.com/.

CBS San Francisco News. "Child Prostitution Growth in Alameda County Outpaces Police Efforts." August 2011. http://sanfrancisco.cbslocal.com/.

Chandler, Raymond. *The Simple Art of Murder*. New York: Vintage, 1988.

Chang, Jeff. Can't Stop Won't Stop: A History of the Hip-hop Generation. New York: St. Martin's Press, 2005.

Charles, Ron. "'*Zone One*,' by Colson Whitehead: Zombies Abound." *Washington Post*, 19 October 2011. www.washingtonpost.com/.

Chiarella, Tom. "How It Ends." *Esquire*, 19 September 2011. www.esquire.com/.

Chiles, Nick. "Their Eyes Were Reading Smut." *New York Times*, 4 January 2006. www.nytimes.com/.

Christopher, Nicholas. *Somewhere in the Night: Film Noir and the American City*. New York: Free Press, 1997.

Clark, Keith. "A Distaff Dream Deferred? Ann Petry and the Art of Subversion." *African American Review* 26, no. 3 (Autumn 1992): 495–505. www.jstor.org/.

Cleaver, Eldridge. "From Soul on Ice." In *The Portable Sixties Reader*, edited by Ann Charters, 478–83. New York: Penguin Putnam, 2003.

Coleman, Beth. "Pimp Notes on Autonomy." In *Everything but the Burden: What White People Are Taking from Black Culture*, edited by Greg Tate, 68–80. New York: Broadway Books, 2003.

———. "Pimp Notes on Autonomy." In *Everything but the Burden: What White People Are Taking from Black Culture*, edited by Greg Tate, 69–71. New York: Harlem Moon Books, 2004.

Collins, Patricia Hill. *Black Feminist Thought: Knowledge, Consciousness, and the Politics of Empowerment*. Boston: Unwin Hyman, 1990.

———. *Black Feminist Thought: Knowledge, Consciousness, and the Politics of Empowerment*. 2nd ed. New York: Routledge, 2000.

———. *Black Feminist Thought: Knowledge, Consciousness, and the Politics of Empowerment*. New York: Routledge Classics, 2008.

———. *Black Sexual Politics: African Americans, Gender, and the New Racism*. New York: Routledge, 2005.

d'Arbonne, Jess. "Zombie Book Review: '*Zone One*' by Colson Whitehead." *Examiner*, 16 January 2012. www.examiner.com/.

de Jesus Felix, João Batista. "Chic Show e Zimbabwe a construção da identidade nos bailes black paulistanos." PhD diss., University of São Paulo, Brazil, 2000.

———. "HIP HOP: Cultura e Política no Contexto Paulistano." PhD diss., University of São Paulo, Brazil, 2005.

Deaton, Clifford D. "Seeing the Specter: A Gothic Metaphor of Subjectivity, Popular Culture, and Consumerism." *Gnovis Journal* 8, no. 2 (Spring 2008): 95–108. http://gnovisjournal.org/.

Dent, Gina, ed. *Black Popular Culture*. Seattle: Bay Press, 1992.

Diawara, Manthia. "Noir by Noirs: Toward a New Realism in Black Cinema." In *Shades of Noir*, edited by Joan Copjec, 261–78. New York: Verso, 1993.

Diawara, Manthia, et al. "A Symposium on Popular Culture and Political Correctness." *Social Text* 36 (Autumn 1993): 1–39. www.jstor.org/.

Dreiser, Theodore. *Sister Carrie*. New York: Oxford University Press, 1900.

Duncan, Glenn. "A Plague of Urban Undead in Lower Manhattan." *New York Times*, 28 October 2011. www.nytimes.com/.

Early, Gerald. "What Is African-American Literature?" Distributed by the Embassy of the United States of America, Brussels, Belgium. 10 February 2009.

Edwards, John. "Black English as Ebonics." In *Language Diversity in the Classroom*, 170–85. Bristol, UK: Multilingual Matters, 2010.

Elbow, Peter. "What Is Speaking on the Page and How Does Freewriting Teach It?" In *Vernacular Eloquence: What Speech Can Bring to Writing*, 147–64. Oxford: Oxford University Press, 2011.

Elder, Sean. "*The Coldest Winter Ever*: Sister Souljah Gives Herself a Starring Role in Her First Novel." *Salon*, 12 April 1999. www.salon.com/.

Ellison, Charles D. "Define 'Urban Lit'. . . ." *Huffington Post*, 23 June 2009. www.huffingtonpost.com/.

Fassler, Joe. "Colson Whitehead on Zombies, 'Zone One,' and His Love of the VCR." *Atlantic*, 18 October 2011. www.theatlantic.com/.

Ferguson, Roderick. *Aberrations in Black: Toward a Queer of Color Critique*. Minneapolis: University of Minnesota Press, 2004.

Flory, Dan. *Philosophy, Black Film, Film Noir*. University Park: Pennsylvania State University Press, 2008.

Foucault, Michel. *Discipline and Punish: The Birth of the Prison*. New York: Random House, 2012. Kindle edition.

Gates, Henry Louis, Jr. *The Signifying Monkey: A Theory of Afro-American Literary Criticism*. New York: Oxford University Press, 1988.

Gates, Henry Louis, Jr., and Nellie Y. McKay, eds. *The Norton Anthology of African American Literature*. 2nd ed. New York: Norton, 2004.

Geremias, Luiz. "A Fúria Negra Ressuscita: as raízes subjetivas do HIP HOP brasileiro." PhD diss., Federal University of Rio de Janeiro, 2006.

Gholson, Alfred Bilbo. *The Pimp's Bible: The Sweet Science of Sin*. 2nd ed. Chicago: Research Associates School Times Publications, 2001.

Gibson, Simone Cade. "Critical Readings: African American Girls and Urban Fiction." *Journal of Adolescent and Adult Literacy* 53 (2010): 565–74.

———. " Curriculum and Instruction. " In *Critical Engagements: Adolescent African American Girls and Urban Fiction*, 23–24. PhD diss., University of Maryland, 2009 . Proquest (UMI 3359273).

Gilmore, Ruth Wilson. *Golden Gulag: Prisons, Surplus, Crisis and Opposition in Globalizing California*. Berkeley: University of California Press, 2007.

Gilroy, Paul. "The Black Atlantic Modernity and Double Consciousness." PhD diss., Universidade Cândido Mendes, Rio de Janeiro, 2001.

———. "Wearing Your Art on Your Sleeve." In *Small Acts: Thoughts on the Politics of Black Cultures*, 237–57. London: Serpent's Tail, 1993.

Goines, Donald. *Dopefiend: The Story of a Black Junkie*. Los Angeles: Holloway House, 1971.

———. *Whoreson*. Los Angeles: Holloway House, 1972.

Gonzalez, Lélia. "O movimento negro na última década." In *Lugar de negro*, edited by Lélia Gonzalez and Carlos Alfredo Hasenbalg. Rio de Janeiro: Marco Zero, 1982.

Goode, Greg. "From Dopefiend to Kenyatta's Last Hit: The Angry Black Crime Novels of Donald Goines." *MELUS* 11, no. 3 (Autumn 1984): 41–48.

Graaff, Kristina. "Reading Street Literature, Reading America's Prison System." PopMatters, 12 February 2010. www.popmatters.com/.

Grady, Barbara. "Dealers Turning to Sex Business." *Oakland Tribune*, 24 April 2008. www.insidebayarea.com/.

Green, Lisa, "A Descriptive Study of African American English: Research in Linguistics and Education." *International Journal of Qualitative Studies in Education* 15, no. 6 (2002): 43–57.

Guimarães, Alfredo. "A modernidade Negra." *Teoria and pesquisa* (São Carlos, Brazil), nos. 42–43 (2003): 41–62.

———. "Notas sobre raça, cultura e identidade negra na Imprensa Negra de São Paulo e Rio de Janeiro, 1925–1950." *Afro-Ásia*, nos. 29–30 (2003): 247–70.

Hall, Stuart. "What Is This 'Black' in Black Popular Culture?" In *Black Popular Culture*, edited by Gina Dent, 21–33. Seattle: Bay Press, 1992.

———."What Is This 'Black' in Black Popular Culture?" In *Stuart Hall: Critical Dialogues in Cultural Studies (Comedia)*, edited by Kuan-Hsing Chen, 465–75. London: Taylor and Francis, 2007. Kindle edition.

Hall, Susan T., and Bob Adelman. *Gentlemen of Leisure: A Year in the Life of a Pimp*. New York: PowerHouse Books, 2006.

Hammett, Dashiell. *Red Harvest*. New York: Knopf, 1929.

Harper, Phillip Brian. *Are We Not Men? Masculine Anxiety and the Problem of African-American Identity*. New York: Oxford University Press, 1996.

Harris, Trudier. *Fiction and Folklore: The Novels of Toni Morrison*. Knoxville: University of Tennessee Press, 1991.

Haut, Woody. *Neon Noir: Contemporary American Crime Fiction*. London: Serpent's Tail, 1999.

Honig, Megan. *Urban Grit: A Guide to Street Lit*. Genreflecting Advisory Series. Santa Barbara, CA: Libraries Unlimited, 2010.

Hughes-Hassell, Sandra, and Pradnya Rodge. "The Leisure Reading Habits of Urban Adolescents." *Journal of Adolescent and Adult Literacy* 51, no. 1 (September 2007): 22–33.

Hurston, Zora Neale. *Their Eyes Were Watching God*. 1937. New York: Harper Collins, 2006.

Jackson, Bruce. *Get Your Ass in the Water and Swim Like Me: African American Narrative Poetry from the Oral Tradition*. New York: Routledge, 2004.

JanMohamed, Abdul. *The Death-Bound-Subject: Richard Wright's Archeology of Death*. Durham, NC: Duke University Press, 2005.

Jasper, Kenji. *Dark*. New York: Broadway Books, 2001.

———. *Seeking Salamanca Mitchell*. New York: Harlem Moon, 2004.

Jones, Leroi (Amiri Baraka). "The Myth of a 'Negro Literature.'" In *Within the Circle: An Anthology of African-American Literary Criticism: From the Harlem Renaissance to the Present*, edited by Angelyn Mitchell, 165–71. Durham, NC: Duke University Press. 1994.

Julien, Isaac. "Black Is, Black Ain't: Notes on De-essentializing Black Identities." In *Black Popular Culture*, edited by Gina Dent, 255–63. Seattle: Bay Press, 1992.

Kaplan, Karla, ed. *Zora Neale Hurston: A Life in Letters*. New York: Doubleday, 2002.

Keehn, Jeremy. "*Zone One*: Six Questions for Colson Whitehead." *Stream* (blog), *Harpers Magazine*, 17 October 2011. http://harpers.org/.

Kennedy, Liam. *Race and Urban Space in Contemporary American Culture*. Edinburgh: Edinburgh University Press, 2000.

Kirkus Reviews. Review of *Harlem Girl Lost*, by Treasure E. Blue. 1 August 2006. www.kirkusreviews.com/.

K'wan. *Gangsta*. New York: Triple Crown Publications, 2003.

Leland, John. *Hip: The History*. New York: HarperCollins, 2004.

Lewis-Kraus, Gideon. "The Last Book Party: Publishing Drinks to a Life after Death." *Harper's Magazine*, March 2009.

Locke, Alain. Review of *Their Eyes Were Watching God*. 1937. In *Zora Neale Hurston: Critical Perspectives Past and Present*, edited by Henry Louis Gates Jr. and Kwame Anthony Appiah, 16–23. New York: Amistad, 1993.

Lorde, Audre. *Sister Outsider: Essays and Speeches*. New York: Crossing Press, 1984.

Lott, Eric. "The Whiteness of Film Noir." *American Literary History* 9, no. 3 (1997): 542–56.

Lu, Min-Zhan. "Professing Multiculturalism: The Politics of Style in the Contact Zone." *College Composition and Communication* 45, no. 4 (December 1994): 442–58.

Macedo, Marcio. "Baladas black e rodas de samba da terra da garoa." In *Jovens na metrópole: etnografias de circuitos de lazer, encontro e sociabilidade*, edited by Jose Guilherme Cantor Magnani and Bruna Mantese de Souza. São Paulo, Brazil: Terceiro Nome, 2007.

———. "Warming the Black Soul through Vinyl Records: Media, Black Identity and Politics during the Brazilian Dictatorship." Lecture in Trabalho Final da Disciplina; Media and Social Theory. New School for Social Research, New York, Fall 2009.

Magro, Viviane Melo de Mendonça. "Adolescentes como autores de si próprios: cotidiano, educação e o hip hop." Campinas, Brazil: CEDES, 2002.

McCann, Sean. *Gumshoe America: Hard-Boiled Crime Fiction and the Rise and Fall of New Deal Liberalism*. Durham, NC: Duke University Press, 2000.

McCord, Mark. "The Next Hustle." *Wax Poetics*, no. 38 (December 2009). http://hiphopandpolitics.wordpress.com/.

McFadden, Bernice. "Black Writers in a Ghetto of the Publishing Industry's Making." *Washington Post*, 26 June 2010.

McMillan, Terry. *Getting to Happy*. New York: Viking, 2011.

Milner, Richard, and Christina Milner. *Black Players: The Secret World of Black Pimps*. Boston: Little, Brown, 1972.

Morgan, Jennifer. "Some Could Suckle over Their Shoulder: Male Travelers, Female Bodies, and the Gendering of Racial Ideology, 1500–1770." *William and Mary Quarterly*, 3rd ser., 54, no. 1 (1997): 167–92.

Morgan, Marcyliena. *The* Real Hiphop*: Battling for Knowledge, Power, and Respect in the LA Underground*. Durham, NC: Duke University Press, 2009.

Morgan, Marcyliena, and Dionne Bennett. "Hip-hop and the Global Imprint of a Black Cultural Form." Daedalus 140, no. 2 (2011): 176–96.

Morris, Vanessa Irvin. *The Readers' Advisory Guide to Street Literature*. Chicago: American Library Association, 2011.

Morris, Vanessa J., Sandra Hughes-Hassel, Denise E. Agosto, and Darren Cottman. "Street Lit Flying Off Teen Fiction Bookshelves in Philadelphia Libraries." *Young Adult Library Services* (Fall 2006): 16–23.

Morrison, Toni. *Sula*. New York: Vintage, 1973. Reprinted with a new foreword by the author. New York: Vintage International, 2004.

———. "Unspeakable Things Unspoken: The Afro-American Presence in American Literature." Lecture presented at the Tanner Lectures on Human Values, University of Michigan, Ann Arbor, 7 October 1988.

Muller, Eddie. Dark City: *The Lost World of Film Noir*. New York: St. Martin's Griffin, 1998.

Naremore, James. *More Than Night: Film Noir in Its Contexts*. 1998. Berkeley: University of California Press, 2008.

Nieto, Sonia. *Affirming Diversity: The Sociopolitical Context of Multicultural Education*. 4th ed. Boston: Allyn and Bacon, 2004.

NPR. "Trafficked Teen Girls Describe Life in 'the Game.'" *All Things Considered*, 6 December 2010. www.npr.org/.

NPR Books. "When Zombies Attack Lower Manhattan." Review of *Zone One*, by Colson Whitehead, 20 July 2012. www.npr.org/.

Oliver, Kelly, and Benigno Trigo. *Noir Anxiety*. Minneapolis: University of Minnesota Press, 2003.

Pardue, Derek. *Ideologies of Marginality in Brazilian Hip Hop*. New York: Palgrave Macmillan, 2008.

Patterson, Orlando. *Slavery and Social Death: A Comparative Study*. Boston: Harvard University Press, 1982.

Patton, Stacy. "Who Is Afraid of Black Sexuality?" *ChronicleofHigherEducation,ChronicleReview*, 3 December 2012. http://chronicle.com/.

Petry, Ann. *The Street*. New York: Mariner Books, 1946.

Phillips, Gary. "The Cool, the Square and the Tough: The Archetypes of Black Male Characters in Mystery and Crime Novels." *Black Scholar* 28, no. 1 (Spring 1998): 27–32.

Pimentel, Spency K. "O Livro vermelho do HIP HOP." PhD diss., University of São Paulo, Brazil, 1997.

Pimpin' Ken and Karen Hunter. *Pimpology: The 48 Laws of the Game*. New York: Simon Spotlight Entertainment, 2007.

Pinho, Osmundo de Araújo. "'Voz ativa': Rap—notas para leitura de um discurso contra-hegemônico." *Sociedade e cultura* 4, no. 2 (2001): 67–92.

Pough, Gwendolyn. *Check It While I Wreck It: Black Womanhood, Hip Hop Culture, and the Public Sphere*. Boston: Northeastern University Press, 2004.

Quinn, Eithne. "'Who's the Mack?': The Performativity and Politics of the Pimp Figure in Gangsta Rap." *Living in America: Recent and Contemporary Perspectives*, special issue of *Journal of American Studies* 34, no. 1 (April 2000): 115–36.

Rabinowitz, Paula. *Black and White and Noir: America's Pulp Modernism*. New York: Columbia University Press, 2002.

Rigney, Barbara Hill. *The Voices of Toni Morrison*. Columbus: Ohio State University Press, 1991.

Rose, Cedric. "Colson Whitehead in the Zombie Zone." *Cincinnati* 45, no. 7 (April 2012): 28–29. http://connection.ebscohost.com/.

Royal, Mickey. *The Pimp Game: Instructional Guide*. Los Angeles: Sharif, 1998.

Rudin, Michael. "The Forbidden Thought." Review of *Zone One*, by Colson Whitehead. Fiction Writers Review, 14 February 2012. http://fictionwritersreview.com/.

Santos, Gevanilda. "Relações Raciais e Desigualdade no Brasil." São Paulo, Brazil: Selo Negro, 2009.

Santos, Jaqueline Lima. "Negro, Jovem e Hip Hopper: História, Narrativa e Identidade em Sorocaba." PhD diss., Universidade Estadual Paulista (UNESP), Marília, Brazil, 2011.

Sapphire. *Push*. New York: Vintage, 1997.

Schrader, Paul. "Notes on Film Noir." 1972. In *Film Noir Reader*, edited by Alain Silver and James Ursini, 53–64. New York: Limelight Editions, 1996.

Sen, Arijit. "Zombie Nation." *Missouri Review*, 5 April 2012. www.missourireview.com/.

Slim, Iceberg (Robert Beck). *The Naked Soul of Iceberg Slim*. Los Angeles: Holloway House, 1986.

———. *Pimp: The Story of My Life*. Los Angeles: Holloway House, 1969, 2004.

Smethurst, James. "Invented by Horror: The Gothic and African American Literary Ideology in *Native Son*." *African American Review* 35, no. 1 (2001): 29–40.

Soitos, Stephen F. *The Blues Detective: A Study of African American Detective Fiction*. Amherst: University of Massachusetts Press, 1996.

Souljah, Sister. *The Coldest Winter Ever*. 1999. New York: Pocket Star Books, 2006.

Souza, Ana Lúcia Silva. "Letramentos de (Re)existências." São Paulo, Brazil: Parábola, 2011.

Spillers, Hortense J. "Mama's Baby, Papa's Maybe: An American Grammar Book." In *African American Literary Theory: A Reader*, edited by Winston Napier, 257–79. New York: New York University Press, 2000.

Sunderman, Eric. "Q and A: Colson Whitehead Talks Gritty New York, *Zone One* Zombies, and Frank Ocean's Sexuality." *Village Voice*, 11 July 2012. www.villagevoice.com/.

Suskind, Ron. *A Hope in the Unseen: An American Odyssey from the Inner City to the Ivy League*. New York: Broadway Books, 1998.

Tate, Greg, ed. *Everything but the Burden: What White People Are Taking from Black Culture*. New York: Broadway Books, 2003.

Thompson, Jon. *Fiction, Crime, and Empire: Clues to Modernity and Postmodernism*. Urbana: University of Illinois Press, 1993.

Thoreau, Henry David. "Walden, and On the Duty of Civil Disobedience." Project Gutenberg e-book of "Walden, and On the Duty of Civil Disobedience," 29 July 2012. www.gutenberg.org/.

Trilling, Diana. "Class and Color." *Nation* 162, no. 10 (9 March 1946): 290–91. www.ebscohost.com/.

Tyree, Omar. *The Last Street Novel*. New York: Simon and Schuster, 2008.

———. "An Urban 'Street Lit' Retirement." *Daily Voice*, 19 June 2008. http://dailyvoice.com/.

Universal Zulu Nation. "The Beliefs of the Universal Zulu Nation." Accessed 20 May 2013. www.zulunation.com/.

van Sickle, Milton. "Introduction." In *The Naked Soul of Iceberg Slim*, by Iceberg Slim. Los Angeles: Holloway House, 1986.

Vaquera-Vasquéz, Santiago. "Meshed America: Confessions of a Mercacirce." In *Code-Meshing as World English: Pedagogy, Policy, Performance*, edited by Vershawn Ashanti Young and Aja Y. Martinez, 89–97. Urbana, IL: National Council of Teachers of English, 2011.

Waiselfish, J. J. *Mapa da Violência 2012: A Cor dos Homicídios no Brasil*. Rio de Janeiro: CEBELA, FLACSO, 2012.

Walker, Alice. *In Search of Our Mothers' Gardens*. Orlando: Harcourt, 1983.

Walker, Rebecca. "Lusting for Freedom." In *Listen Up: Voices from the Next Feminist Generation*, edited by Barbara Findlen, 19–24. Seattle: Seal Press, 2001.

Weir-Soley, Donna Aza. *Eroticism, Spirituality and Resistance in Black Women's Writings*. Gainesville: University Press of Florida, 2009.

West, Cornel. *Race Matters*. Boston: Beacon, 1993.

Wheeler, Rebecca S. "Becoming Adept at Code-Switching." *Educational Leadership* 65, no. 7 (April 2008): 54–58.

Wheeler, Rebecca S., and Rachel Swords. *Code-Switching: Teaching Standard English in Urban Classrooms*. Urbana, IL: National Council of Teachers of English, 2006.

White, Miles. *From Jim Crow to Jay-Z: Race, Rap, and the Performance of Masculinity*. Urbana: University of Illinois Press, 2011.

Whitehead, Colson. *Zone One*. New York: Anchor Books, 2011.

Wilkerson, Isabel. *The Warmth of Other Suns: The Epic Story of America's Great Migration*. New York: Vintage, 2011.

Wilson, William Julius. *The Truly Disadvantaged: The Inner City, the Underclass, and Public Policy*. Chicago: University of Chicago Press, 1993.

Woods, Teri. Foreword. In *The Readers' Advisory Guide to Street Literature*, by Vanessa Irvin Morris. Chicago: American Library Association, 2011.

Wright, Richard. "Between Laughter and Tears." *New Masses*, 5 October 1937. Repr. in *Zora Neale Hurston: Critical Perspectives Past and Present*, edited by Henry Louis Gates Jr. and Kwame Anthony Appiah, 16–17. New York: Amistad Press, 1993.

———. *Native Son*. 1940. New York: Harper Perennial Modern Classics, 2005.

Young, Vershawn Ashanti. "Should Writers Use They Own English?" In *Writing Centers and the New Racism: A Call for Sustainable Dialogue and Change*, edited by Laura Greenfield and Karen Rowan, 61–72. Logan: Utah State University Press, 2011.

Young, Vershawn Ashanti, and Aja Y. Martinez, eds. *Code-Meshing as World English: Pedagogy, Policy, Performance*. Urbana, IL: National Council of Teachers of English, 2011.

Zinoman, Jason. "The Critique of Pure Horror." *New York Times*, 16 July 2011. www.nytimes.com/.

Index

About the Editor

Keenan Norris holds an MFA from Mills College and has completed PhD studies at the University of California, Riverside, as of spring 2013. His research areas include urban literature and the publishing industry. He teaches English and African American literature and promotes the AFFIRM program at Evergreen Valley College. His works, both fiction and nonfiction, have appeared in a wide range of literary journals including *Inlandia: A Literary Journey through California's Inland Empire*, *New California Writing 2013*, and *Post-Soul Satire*, as well as the University of California Press's magazine *BOOM: A Journal of California*. He is the editor of *Street Lit: Representing the Urban Landscape*. His novel *Brother and the Dancer* (2013) is the winner of the 2012 James D. Houston Award.

About the Contributors

Tristan Acker is in the MFA poetry program in his hometown at Cal State San Bernardino. He is trying to interpret and share the middle-class ethnic values and nascent counterculture that he observes so much of in his life here in the Inland Empire. He is the cowinner of the Wild Lemon Project's Sense of Place Poetry prize, and this year, his work will be featured in *Inlandia* journal.

Bonnie Rhee Andryeyev is currently a postdoctoral visiting scholar at the University of California, Berkeley, where she also received a bachelor's degree in English. She received her doctorate in literature at the University of California, Santa Cruz, in 2012. Her essay "Harlem Is Nowhere: Race and the Noir City in Chester Himes" will be published in the upcoming critical anthology *New Chester Himes Criticism*. Her primary research areas include twentieth-century American literature and culture, critical race theory, popular culture, and film studies. She has taught courses on American noir fiction and film, Korean American literature, and the pedagogy of literature.

David Bradley is the author of *The Chaneysville Incident* (winner of the PEN/Faulkner Award) and *South Street*. He has published literary (as opposed to scholarly) essays on Jean Toomer, Richard Wright, Herman Melville, William Melvin Kelley, and Alice Walker, and has published articles in *Esquire*, *Redbook*, the *New Yorker*, the *New York Times Magazine*, the *Philadelphia Inquirer Magazine*, the *Los Angeles Times*, the *Village Voice*, and other periodicals. His awards and honors also include a National Endowment for the Arts Literature Fellowship for creative nonfiction (1991), a Guggenheim Fellowship for fiction (1989), and an Academy Award from the American Academy and Institute of Arts and Letters (1982).

Celena Diana Bumpus, BA, AODA, is CEO of OceanMoonSpirit Designs and published author of *Confessions* (1998). She is a graduate of the University of California, Riverside, in psychology and sociology with emphasis in personality development, perception, social psychology, neuroscience, scientific research and methods, and substance abuse. She has been a bilingual Spanish counselor, case manager, and coordinator/program designer for programs servicing children, adults, couples, and families. She was also a court dependency unit investigative social worker for Riverside County Child Protective Services and workforce and career development director of Goodwill Southern California for the San Bernardino and Palm Desert, California, facilities.

Debra Busman is a fiction and creative nonfiction writer and has been an activist all her life, beginning in utero at marches and protests with her labor union mother. Raised in Los Angeles, she is currently codirector of the Creative Writing and Social Action Program at California State University, Monterey Bay, where she also coordinates the Division of Humanities and Communication's Service Learning Program. She is coeditor of the award-winning anthology *Fire and Ink: An Anthology of Social Action Writing* (2009). Her work has been published in the *L.A. Review*, *Women's Studies Quarterly*, *Combined Destinies: Whites Sharing Grief about Racism*, and *Social Justice Journal: Pedagogies for Social Change*. Busman received her MFA from Mills College. Her "like a woman" series of short stories received an Astrea Foundation Award for fiction.

Nikia Chaney is a founding editor of *shufPoetry*, an online journal for experimental poetry, and a poetry editor for *Inlandia: A Literary Journey*, a journal for regional literature. She has been published or has works forthcoming in the *Iowa Review*, *Saranac Review*, *491*, *Pearl*, *Portland Review*, and the *New York Quarterly*. Chaney's poetry has been chosen by Nikki Giovanni as the winner of the 2012 OSA Enizagam Poetry Award. Chaney has been the recipient of grants from Cave Canem and the Barbara Demings Memorial Fund, and her book *thump* was a finalist for the Marsh Hawk Press Poetry Prize. Chaney holds two MFAs, one from Antioch University, Los Angeles, and one from California State University, San Bernardino. She was chosen to read for Literary Uprising at Antioch University, and she competed in the CSU Oral Research Competition in 2012 for her linguistic research. She has two chapbooks forthcoming, *ladies please* and *Sis Fuss*. She teaches English at San Bernardino Valley College.

Juan Delgado is the author of four books of poetry, including *Green Web* and *A Rush of Hands*. His book *El Campo* is a collaboration with renowned artist Simón Silva, and his forthcoming *Vital Signs* is a collaboration with photographer Tom McGovern featuring evocative scenes of San Bernardino and the Inland Empire. Delgado is the director of the MFA program. He holds an MFA from the University of California at Irvine, where he was a Regent's fellow.

Gerald Early is the Merle Kling Professor of Modern Letters and the director of the Center for the Humanities at Washington University in St. Louis, where he joined the faculty in 1982. He is the author of several books, including *The Culture of Bruising: Essays on Prizefighting, Literature, and Modern American Culture* (1994), which won the 1994 National Book Critics Circle Award for criticism. He is also editor of numerous volumes, including *This Is Where I Came In: Black America in the 1960s* (2003); *The Sammy J. Davis Reader* (2001); *Miles Davis and American Culture* (2001); *The Muhammad Ali Reader* (1998); and *Body Language: Writers on Sport* (1998). The most recent books he edited include *Best African American Fiction* (2009) and *Best African American Essays* (2009). He has served as a consultant on Ken Burns's documentary films on baseball, jazz, Jack Johnson, and World War II, all of which aired on PBS. He was elected a fellow of the American Academy of Arts and Sciences in 1997 and serves as a member of the Academy's Council.

Kimberly Fain, JD, is an adjunct professor at Texas Southern University (TSU). She has written various articles or essays for both legal and literary publishers on luminaries such as Ray Bradbury, Spike Lee, Edgar Allan Poe, Colson Whitehead, and Richard Wright. Due to her background in literature and research as a legal intern for federal judges and a Texas state senator, Fain has written on the sociopolitical intersection of race, gender, and class in both classic literature and pop culture. She earned a doctor of jurisprudence degree and a master of arts degree in English from TSU and a bachelor of arts degree in English from Texas A&M University at College Station. Fain is a licensed attorney who won the Rice University Center for the Study of Women's Gender and Sexuality Scholarly Award in 2012 and was awarded two teaching and writing fellowships from the Houston Teachers Institute at the University of Houston's Honors College. In 2012, the *Buffalo Journal of Gender, Law, & Social Policy* published her coauthored law article "Socio-Economic Status and Legal Factors Affecting African American Fathers." In 2013, she served as a proofreader for *Professional Conduct and the Law*, a book focused on legal ethics. Fain is a book reviewer, the associate editor of *World Literary Review*, and a freelance editor for various legal, literature, and religious scholars.

Lynel Gardner is a performance artist, novelist, and playwright. He has written a play called *Stories I Never Told My Father* about growing up with a pimp for a father, how he survived, and how he found God in the process of trying to find his father before he died. He has written a book, *BEAST: The Destruction of Charles "Sonny" Liston*, based on the life of his grandfather, heavyweight boxing champion Sonny Liston, dispelling many of the popular misconceptions about Liston.

Ethan Iverson is a pianist, composer, and critic best known for his work in the postmodern jazz trio The Bad Plus with bassist Reid Anderson and drummer Dave King. Iverson writes about jazz and other subjects at length at his blog *Do the Math*.

Kemeshia Randle, a Mississippi native, holds an MA from the University of Mississippi. She is currently a doctoral candidate in literature at the University of Alabama. Her research examines black female stereotypes and compares the depiction of black female sexualities in canonized works to those in popular fiction works. Randle is a graduate instructor at the University of Alabama and an adjunct instructor at Kaplan University Online.

Jaqueline Lima Santos earned a BA in social sciences by the Pontifícia Universidade Católica (PUC) of Campinas and a master's degree of social science in anthropology at Universidade Estadual Paulista (UNESP). She is a PhD student in social anthropology at Universidade Estadual de Campinas (UNICAMP) in Brazil. She completed a fellowship at the W. E. B. Du Bois Institute (Harvard University) as a Hip-hop Archive fellow and currently is a nonresident fellow at the Du Bois Institute. Her subjects of interest and research are hip-hop culture, the black movement, black women, and identity and memory in the African diaspora. She is a member of the Black People Center for Research and Extension (NUPE) and the Anthropological Focus Group. She was awarded the Kabengele Munanga prize for best scientific work by the Africa Forum in 2007 with her research "The Meaning of Blackness in Hip Hop: From Maroons to Periphery," and second classification in an article contest for "The Fight against Racism for Women in Latin America and the Caribbean" with the essay "Lelia Gonzalez: Black Women and Intellectual" in 2010.

Ana Lúcia Silva Souza holds a PhD in applied linguistic from UNICAMP (State University of Campinas), in Brazil. Her subjects of interest and research are literacy, African diaspora culture, hip-hop culture, identity, and education. Currently she is a professor at UFBA (Federal University of Bahia, Salvador) and has been a member of the research groups Rasuras: Studies on Reading and Writing Practices, and Language and Literature: Racial

Relations, Socio-cultural Diversity, and Interculturality in Portuguese-Speaking Countries.

Cherie Ann Turpin completed her PhD in English at the University of Connecticut in 2005. Turpin is an associate professor in the Department of English at the University of the District of Columbia. Turpin's research areas include literature of the African diaspora, gender studies, American literature, pop culture, and film studies. She recently published *How Three Black Women Writers Combined Spiritual and Sensual Love: Rhetorically Transcending the Boundaries of Language* (2010), as well as publishing articles in *Feminist Teacher, Bodily Inscriptions: Interdisciplinary Excursions into Embodiment*, and *Diaspora: Journal of the Annual Afro-Hispanic Literature and Culture Conference*. Her recent poetry appeared in the fall 2010 edition of *Reverie: Midwest African American Literature*.

Omar Tyree is a *New York Times* best-selling author, an NAACP Image Award winner, a Phillis Wheatley Literary Prize recipient and an HBCU Legends Award winner. As the true trailblazer of contemporary urban fiction and a living legend, he has published twenty-one books and counting, with more than two million copies sold worldwide, which has generated more than thirty million dollars. His new creative projects will feature an "Ebook Nation" of never-before-published titles and ideas, including poetry, nonfiction debate, original screenplays, and the much-anticipated "Traveler" series of international adventure. Tyree continues to advocate for early education through his Urban Literacy Project (ULP) and is an informed, passionate, and tireless speaker on various community-related and intellectual topics.

Sterling Warner, award-winning author and poet, has for the past twenty-nine years taught English and creative writing at Evergreen Valley College, where he has also served as director of the Creative Writing Program, organizer of the Author's Series, and chief editor of the *Leaf by Leaf* literary magazine. Warner's fiction, nonfiction, and poetry include *Thresholds* (1997), *Projections: Brief Readings on American Culture* (2nd ed. 2003), *Without Wheels: Poems* (2005), *World Literature and Introduction to Theatre* (5th ed. 2008), *ShadowCat: Poems* (2008), *Memeto Mori: A Chapbook* (2010), *Edges: Poems by Sterling Warner* (2012), and *Visions Across the Americas* (8th ed. 2013). His works also have appeared in many magazines and journals, including *In the Grove, The Chaffey Review, Faculty Matters, inside english, Leaf by Leaf, The Messenger, Metamorphoses, TETYC, The Monterey Poetry Review*, and the *National TYCA Poetry Month Archive*.

Alexandria White is an adjunct professor of English composition, literature, and black studies at San Jose State University, Evergreen Valley College, and Foothill College. She studied creative writing at San Francisco State University, which included a year abroad in the United Kingdom. She later attended the University of California, Santa Cruz, and earned an MA in literature. Her creative writing has been featured in the online African American literary journal *ChickenBones: An African-American Literary Journal*. Her nonfiction piece "The Only Black Ones" is published in a collection of personal essays called *America Is: Personal Essays for Social Justice*.

Arisa White is a Cave Canem fellow, an MFA graduate from the University of Massachusetts, Amherst, and author of the poetry collections *Hurrah's Nest* and *A Penny Saved*. Her debut collection *Hurrah's Nest* was nominated for an NAACP Image Award and was selected as a finalist for the California Book Award. She is coeditor for *Her Kind*, the online literary community of VIDA: Women in Literary Arts, and the editorial manager for *Dance Studio Life* magazine. White has received residencies, fellowships, or scholarships from Port Townsend Writers' Conference, Rose O'Neill Literary House, Squaw Valley Community of Writers, Hedgebrook, Atlantic Center for the Arts, Prague Summer Program, Fine Arts Work Center, and Bread Loaf Writers' Conference. Nominated for a Pushcart Prize in 2005, her poetry has been widely published and is featured on the recording *Word* with the Jessica Jones Quartet. White is the winner of the 2012 San Francisco Book Festival Award in Poetry.

Khalid Akil White is an ethnic studies professor and the Umoja program coordinator at San Jose City College, where he joined the faculty in 2008. In the 2010–2011 academic year, White was voted male faculty member of the year at San Jose City College. He is currently a doctoral candidate in education at the University of California, Davis, where his focus centers on African American male students and their academic engagement in the California community college system.

Dennis L. Winston received his bachelor of arts degree in English and his master of arts degree in English and African American literature from North Carolina A&T State University in 2002 and 2004, respectively. In 2012, he was the first African American student to earn a PhD in English from Texas A&M University. He is also a poet. His poems "Estill's Daughter," "Solset," and "Pirates" are published in the 2009 special issue of *Callaloo*, celebrating Texas writers. He is currently a professor of English at Howard University in Washington, D.C.